IMPROVING STUDENTS'
LEARNING OUTCOMES

Editors
Claus Nygaard
Clive Holtham
Nigel Courtney

IMPROVING STUDENTS' LEARNING OUTCOMES

Copenhagen Business School Press

Improving Students' Learning Outcomes

© Copenhagen Business School Press, 2009
Printed in Denmark by Narayana Press, Gyllling
Cover design by Klahr | Graphic Design

1st edition 2009

ISBN 978-87-630-0232-5

Distribution:

Scandinavia
DBK, Mimersvej 4
DK-4600 Køge, Denmark
Tel +45 3269 7788
Fax +45 3269 7789

North America
International Specialized Book Services
920 NE 58th Street, Suite 300
Portland, OR 97213-3786
Tel +1 800 944 6190
Fax +1 503 280 8832
Email: orders@isbs.com

Rest of the World
Marston Book Services, P.O. Box 269
Abingdon, Oxfordshire, OX14 4YN, UK
Tel +44 (0) 1235 465500
Fax +44 (0) 1235 465655
Email: client.orders@marston.co.uk

Table of Contents

Improving Students' Learning Outcomes
- A Ruminative Foreword, Prompted by this Title

John Cowan

An educational colleague of mine liked to quote the wise words of her grandmother, who often pointed out to her that: "If you don't know where you're going, any bus will do." The moral of that advice – educationally - is that learners arc unlikely to make real progress towards achieving outcomes which they will value, if they do not have their intended outcomes in mind, while they are learning. Ever since Mager in the middle of last century stressed the importance of what he then called "learning objectives", the desirability of all concerned being clear about the desired outcomes of any learning activity should have been appreciated in education. And so the purpose and emphasis embodied in the editors' carefully chosen title for this anthology is pertinent, timely and potentially useful. For each of the four words in the title offers a pointed promise about what we readers should find in the pages and inputs which follow. In considering that challenge myself, though, I'm aware that I must write cautiously. For this is the first time I have been asked to tackle such an introduction. And I am mindful of the advice that a foreword should be like an item of high couture in a Parisian fashion show. It should cover the subject effectively, while being brief enough to provoke interest. I shall do my best in regard to both requirements.

Let's begin immediately, then, with that first word – "Improving". Even as I draft this foreword, I am anticipating my next activity with my post-graduate students of Human Resources Management. They are charged, *inter alia,* to plan for their personal, professional and academic development. They must choose and specify worthwhile aims from outwith the declared curriculum; then they have to specify in SMART goals what they want to achieve; and next they should plan to bring about that development in a self-directed manner, accumulating, as they progress, data which they will use to monitor and evidence their progress. None of that will be an easy task for them - or for me, as their facilitative tutor. And every year the task becomes more difficult. My students want to improve themselves by selecting and achieving worthwhile learning outcomes as their goals. As their tutor, I want to improve the end result for them, by facilitating self-directed development of the highest possible standard, helping them to be the best that they can be - without brain surgery or working much harder. But every year this does become more demanding.

In my admittedly long lifetime in academia, desirable learning outcomes in higher education have changed almost unrecognisably. The world into which I emerged as a graduate expected me to have stored in my memory, and to be able to recall and apply with understanding, much pertinent professional knowledge. Nowadays, that's neither necessary nor valued any more. Graduates, like today's school children, can all use search engines for recall, and can obtain from the internet clear explanations, at the time they need them, of that which they want to understand. And they can then, with little effort, employ commonly available software to apply basics, and much beyond basics as well. Today's graduate is expected, much more than was the case 50 years ago, to engage in sophisticated analysis and problem-solving, to think creatively, to make professional judgements objectively and systematically, and to have a high level of ability in regard to the interpersonal skills which were only developed serendipitously in the past. Such learning outcomes arc nowadays relevant, valid and important – and ever more demanding, educationally, as each passing year calls for further sophistication in response to the relentless progress of technology. It is increasingly difficult for teachers or learners to plan programmes of development, and especially of self-development, to achieve such outcomes to the standards that we, and society, would wish. Yet improvement in our target demands is constantly expected of us, more and more so with every passing and changing year. It will be of great interest and usefulness to readers to learn what contributors to this volume have to offer us in terms of imaginatively effective pedagogies and wide-ranging embracing of possibilities, in response to this important double-barrelled challenge. For they and we must improve the outcomes we have in mind, and accommodate aspirations of learners and of the pedagogy which grow ever more demanding.

That, of course, then takes me on to the other aspect of the improving which teachers and institutions are expected to pursue – namely to having more success with more students, in terms of the learning outcomes which each cohort can hope to carry out into the world of employment. This interpretation of "improving" focuses my mind immediately on the changing circumstances within which I have to teach. Not only is the world expecting different and progressive outcomes; but that demand faces me, and you, I suspect, within a context where our nations seek to radically increase participation in higher education. The result of that growth in numbers is that our intake includes a higher proportion of applicants of lower ability, and so presents us with classes in which variation of ability is more and more striking. In my country, the added impact of internationalisation has in addition resulted in intake cohorts whose prior experience, expectations, priorities, attitudes and abilities, vary more markedly than we have ever before experienced. For serving teachers like me, to improve in this ever-changing context often means that we must first strive zealously simply to maintain standards in the face of increasing demands for improvement, and ever changing circumstances – and usually with lessening resources. Yet the world, and our paymasters, still expect us to show tangible improvement in our institutional outcomes.

There is a subtle challenge here, for those who aspire to improvement. It concerns standards. The shrewd English playwright, Alan Bennett, had one of his characters quiz an aged headmaster, in a play called *Forty Years On:* "Have you ever thought, Headmaster, that your standards might perhaps be a little out of date?" To which the headmaster replied "Of course they're out of date. That is what makes them standards." Consequently, for you and I who read this volume, part of our challenge is thus to push forward beyond the established and out-of-date standards of our world, and make and pursue our own new developing aims and standards. How will you and I do that in the immediate future? It's another important question, and we will both look to contributors in this volume to help us to answer it.

The second word in our title is "Students'". That's perhaps a fairly obvious inclusion. However I do sincerely hope that the editors and their contributors really mean "***students'*** learning outcomes". I often quote the simple story told by James Thurber. It was set in a primary school class where the pupils had been reading a book about penguins, after which each had had to write an essay on that subject. One small girl wrote a short, one-sentence, essay: "This book told me more about penguins than I wanted to know."

In over four decades of my involvement in higher education, it has often seemed to me that too often teaching activity, and assumed learning activity, focus on what the *teachers* have decided should be the learning outcomes, rather than as what the learners want to know, *and know that they need to know.* Like the little girl, students may well be introduced to subject matter whose point eludes them, or which does not respond to their immediate interests and concerns. I recall evaluating a remedial first year university class in mathematics, where open-ended feedback had been requested from the learners after a carefully planned workshop activity. One student wrote with feeling: "Now I (still) know *how* to integrate by parts; but I don't know *when* to integrate that way." *His* desired outcome, and his teachers' priorities, had unfortunately not quite coincided.

In discussing student-determined learning outcomes, I find myself quoting my experience in a recent module where my students set out to develop, through self-directed learning, the abilities they would need for subsequent undergraduate project work in social studies. They carried out self-appraisals, identified their priorities, and made plans accordingly. Most of their desired outcomes were predictable, although they might subsequently feature in individual plans to a greater or lesser extent. One woman, however, stressed an aim which stood out for me as somewhat special. She had reflected in her learning log that she had a female brain, with a greater number of connections between the two hemispheres, which gave her a greater potential than have males for multi-tasking. However she was aware that the effectiveness of that multi-tasking needed to be enhanced. "It's like my juggling. Sometimes I juggle too many things at once, and drop some of them. Sometimes I don't juggle with sufficient items to be effective and efficient. I want to improve my multi-tasking." She put that item on her individual agenda of abilities to be developed. She determined to work purposefully towards that learning outcome (amongst others), and in due course she demonstrated to her own satisfaction (and to mine) that she had improved her mastery of this particular ability – to good effect. I hope that example, which I have found rather inspiring, illustrates why I value putting considerable stress on the outcomes of learning programmes being, or at least including, the students' choices. I trust that the contributors to this volume, and readers, will feel the same way, and will focus our attention accordingly.

Next in our title we come to "Learning". That immediately prompts me to wonder if we teachers can usually be aware of what learning, and impact, our activities have had on our learners' development. For I am not sure how well we as a profession identify and judge and respond to the impacts of our "teaching" in terms of the students' learning outcomes which promise to endure and to have potential. At present, much depends on opinion; educational judgments and evaluations are still distinctly subjective. Students may tell us, sincerely, how well they *think* they are learning, or have learnt. These claims can be tested in respect of their retention of simple, factual inputs. Students can be invited to opine in focus groups about deeper learning. But we have few examples in practical terms of evaluative approaches which help us determine, in terms of hard data, the nature of students' immediate learning experiences, or of their immediate and retained learning and development, and the associated affective outcomes, especially following discussions, workshops and seminars.

Over 30 years ago, I was experimenting with a new (at the time) technology-based approach to student learning. When my students emerged from the carrels where they had been studying, I asked their opinions. "That's a great development!" they enthused. "Give us more of that; we learn so much more effectively." I asked if they would mind taking a 90/90 test of their simple recall of some of the simpler content of the sequences. Readily they agreed to assist, expecting that nine out of ten of them would score at least nine correct answers out of the ten questions posed. A few minutes later they would return the answer sheets, normally with crestfallen faces. "I know I should have been able to answer; the questions were fair and straightforward; the answers were in the material, and we used it only half an hour ago. But I've forgotten many of them already." Sincere *opinions* about the enduring or even immediate learning which occurs within learning activities may not be confirmed by hard data. Professionally, we need to move on to purposeful and sound action-researching of the learning and achieved personal and professional development which our programmes engender.

That point, of course in turn takes me smoothly on to the last word in our title, which is "Outcomes", and to teachers' and students' identification of them, together with their judgement of their value. An American cynic once commented that the making of educational judgements by teachers and students reminded him of how they used to weigh hogs at markets in Texas. They set up a big beam, and tied the hog on one end. Then they found a boulder to tie on the other end, and shifted the beam until the boulder and the hog balanced. They measured the position of the boulder, to include that accordingly in their equations. They then calculated the weight of the hog - having guessed the weight of the boulder. Many of today's educational evaluations of the enduring outcomes of learning still seem to me to be a deceptive mixture of seemingly precise measurements, sophisticated calculations, and great reliance on the opinions at the heart of it all, which are almost guesswork. Let's hope our contributors can help us to improve the ways in which we determine the value for our students of the long term outcomes of our innovations.

These, then, have been the thoughts on which that title prompted me to ruminate, in a rambling manner. Many years ago, in their published profiles of their teachers, my students described me as "Famous for his digressions". Mindful of that valid judgement, I can see as I re-read that I should return from my ramblings to my remit, and to an item on which I should have expanded before I moved on to these four title words. I should of course have dwelt on the venerable grandmother's advice, about knowing where we are going before we set out, and as we journey. For that implies that we should *all* know where we are going. So, before I finish, I should remind us all that, before we give consideration to this business of improvements in students' learning outcomes, we should re-assert our commitment to declaring and using transparent, well-articulated intended learning outcomes of whose meaning we have all confirmed that there is a shared understanding, as well as acceptance.

Many years ago I led a Sunday School in my local church. One of the teachers was an earnest young girl, who told her class one day that they were going to study the prophets. Wishing, with a sound pedagogical (yet problematically oral) approach, to confirm that this outcome was understood, she asked if anyone could tell her what a prophet was. One small boy eagerly volunteered that a profit (*sic*) was when you bought something and sold it for more than you had paid for it. The teacher smiled kindly, valued the answer because it related to her employment in a bank, and amplified the intended outcome. "Yes, but today, we're going to be studying *Biblical* prophets. What's a Biblical prophet?*" The same small boy responded with equal enthusiasm and conviction: "It's when you buy a *Bible* and sell it for more than you paid for it." The point I want to make here about our title and purpose, then, is that it is always important to ensure that all concerned know what are the intended outcomes and desired standards, and should attach the same meaning to their descriptions of them.

In my work as an external examiner in a variety of settings, I check students' and teachers impressions of the desirable qualities, for example, of sound project work. I usually find marked discrepancies of which the teachers are unaware, and to which both sides can usefully give urgent attention, in both their interests. I hope our writers can help us with this matter of ensuring a shared and commonly understood understanding of the desired outcomes of student learning.

But I feel another digression coming on, I'm afraid. I close my remarks with the apocryphal tale of the young American backwoodsman who won a magazine competition which took him to New York for a wonderful week's holiday. He wrote each night to his family, describing the immensity and bustling vigour of the great city, but especially the wonder of the luxurious five-star accommodation in which he was located. He described the carpets into which his feet sunk, the range of sumptuous leather armchairs and settees in his enormous sitting room, the generous mini-bar, the massive bed in his bedroom – but especially the enormous bathroom. He described that it seemed to have two toilets, every other facility he could wish and many of which he had never imagined. And the bath! It was enormous, had gold taps, and all sorts of other refinements. He declared enthusiastically: "I just can't wait until it's bath night on Saturday!"

Like that young man, I just cannot wait... In *my* case, and in this context, I just cannot wait until I can read how the contributors to this volume, expertly steered by the editors, will take you and me forward to engage with the rewarding challenges promised in these four words of that demanding title, and the wise words of an old grandmother.

John Cowan
Emeritus Professor of Learning Development, the UK Open University
Edinburgh: June, 2009

CHAPTER 1

Learning Outcomes – Politics, Religion or Improvement?

Claus Nygaard, Clive Holtham & Nigel Courtney

Setting

In this anthology we focus on ways in which students' learning outcomes can be improved. Using a downright popular phrase we are particularly interested in how to generate as much activity as possible between the ears of our students. We aim to fascinate both students and teachers to engage in experiments that will help students learn as much as possible during their years of study.

In the sixteen chapters that follow we present a range of empirical cases where the curriculum has been developed in such ways that its mix of Learning, Teaching, and Assessment-methods (LTA-methods) has improved students' learning outcomes. The cases offer valuable insights into everyday practices of students, teachers, and administrators, and put forward a wide range of theoretical arguments for why and how students' learning outcomes (SLOs) have been improved.

This book sets out to deliver clarification, insight, and inspiration. To us as editors (and to the group of international researchers who have written the chapters) there is no doubt that an increased focus on students' learning outcomes, and an alignment of LTA-methods in curricula in order to improve students' learning outcomes, are an important and valuable part of quality enhancement of Higher Education (HE). We dare to go so far as to state that a shift in paradigm from supply-driven to outcome-based HE is a prerequisite for the survival of HE institutions (HEIs) as we know them today.

Before we turn to the empirical cases and their underlying theoretical philosophies, we shall dig into some of the overall aspects of the concept of learning outcomes in order to position the book in the theoretical landscape. We shall also address some of the more critical aspects of learning outcomes. First we look at some possible explanations as to why at all we have experienced an increased focus on learning outcomes in today's HE-sector.

Why learning outcomes?

What are learning outcomes, and why deal with the concept? As a term, 'learning outcome' covers the desired outcomes that students expect from participating in any particular program of higher education. It also covers the expectations of professional bodies and employers. There are multiple reasons for defining a learning outcome of a study program: 1) it shows to students what competencies they are expected to develop during their studies; 2) it shows to future employers what they can expect when they employ a graduate; 3) it shows to teachers what competence development they have to facilitate in their curriculum; 4) it shows to faculties on which dimensions they can measure student achievements in their study programs; 5) it shows to accreditation institutions the focus of the HEI; 6) it shows to politicians the focus of the HE-sector in general.

At a political level a demand has emerged for measurement of quality, and to change HE from being supply driven ("delivering" what the faculty believes will be best for the graduates) to being demand driven ("delivering" what the job market/society and to some extent the graduates themselves find to be most relevant). In the European region, the Bologna-process is a prime example of a political macro-level initiative, which has required that HEIs develop curricula centered on learning outcomes. The ten action lines of the Bologna Accord require a harmonization of HE based on learning outcomes, qualification frameworks, ECTS, and increased modularization.

The institutional perspective

National competence strategies have also built on qualification frameworks and pushed for an increased focus on learning outcomes and many HEIs have become much more seriously involved in quality enhancement than. In fact, many are in the process of changing from an input-based to an output-based model of HE (Rassow, 1998). The key question is no longer if students are given the right knowledge, but rather if students are provided with possibilities to develop the 'right' competencies. This means right in the sense that they are both relevant for the job market (Harvey & Green, 1994; Falconer & Pettigrew, 2003) and transformative (Harvey, *et al.,* 1992; Harvey & Knight, 1996). And it is the HEIs which have to justify that this is the case. For politicians this change in paradigm is seen as a way to further develop the quality of HE. Some HEIs have experienced this increased regulation as overregulation and some have seen it as an attack on their freedom to develop educational programs of the highest possible academic standards. In our view, the truth lies somewhere in between the two extremes. We have no doubt that an increased focus on learning outcomes on the political level benefits HEIs, primarily because it provokes them to reflect on the value of their educational programs for students and society. Such reflective processes are generally valuable.

Recently, an increasing number of HEIs have placed a stronger emphasis on learning outcomes. This is driven by obvious political reasons but also because the development of study programs can be more focused when one of the key questions addresses what the students have to learn and how that learning can be used on the job market. This enables an HEI to differentiate its study programs from those of others and allows the overall portfolio of programs to be compared and assessed. A positive consequence of focus on learning outcomes may also be that it naturally calls for an increased focus on the underlying pedagogical approach and the philosophy of learning.

Another side-effect of this is that it becomes somewhat easier for HEIs to market their study programs, hence brand the institution, when they can link to an underlying pedagogical approach. Harvard is well known for its case methodology. Maastricht University is well known for its focus on problem-based learning (PBL). Roskilde University is well known for its focus on problem-oriented project-work. These pedagogical methodologies specifically aim to enable students to develop their analytical skills and reflective competencies. Indeed, our own research at business and education schools in nine universities across Europe and in Australia revealed that the primary focus of each was on a particular pedagogical orientation. Their discrete approaches ranged from discipline-based, case-based, problem-based, inquiry-based to practice-based (Holtham & Courtney, 2008).

In essence, they could readily pinpoint their focus on a spectrum spanning from theory to practice. Working with curriculum development at an institutional level is not necessarily easier when there is a focus on learning outcomes, but it should help address the needs of students and society. Again we will argue that such reflective processes are generally valuable.

The instructional perspective
When it comes to the instructional level (concerning the relations between individual teachers and their students), we have also seen an in-

crease in the focus on learning outcomes. There seems to be a growing understanding among teachers that the competencies required by students, and by their future employers, have changed significantly over the last decades. New technologies and new organization principles now enable alternatives to didactic lecturing to be developed.

In the past, the university teacher was seen as an expert delivering deep knowledge within a particular scientific domain, whereas today the university teacher is more often seen as an expert who facilitates the competence development of students. These days knowledge is less often seen as a commodity transmitted from teacher to student and, instead, as something developed by students in relation and interplay with fellow students, teachers and other stakeholders relevant to the learning situation (Nygaard & Andersen, 2005; Nygaard & Holtham, 2008). For individual teachers engaged in enhancement of their teaching quality, an increasingly key concern seems to be the alignment of LTA-methods in order to improve students' learning outcomes at this instructional level. How this is done in practice is a big issue – and it is exactly this issue we deal with in the chapters of this anthology. At this level too, we will argue that such reflective processes are generally valuable. So, in an institutional context, organizational-level approaches to the improvement of learning outcomes can be quite different from those at the level of the individual teacher.

As we have argued above, there are several factors on different levels that govern and inspire for an increased focus on learning outcomes. Below we will discuss the theoretical positioning of learning outcomes in order to further outline the approach of the book.

Learning outcomes – a theoretical positioning

Within the field of HE it is possible to locate two broad streams of research that both focus on outcomes. One stream deals with students' learning outcomes. These have been defined as cognitive outcomes such as knowledge, skills, competencies, personal attributes and abilities, and affective outcomes such as personal goals, values, attitudes, identity, world views, and behaviours. The other stream deals with student outcomes – the aggregate institutional outcomes such as graduation rates, retention rates, transfer rates, and employment rates.

'Student learning outcomes' (SLO) and 'student outcomes' (SO) are not to be confused. Research on SLO and SO calls for different kinds of research methods. Studying the cognitive outcomes of HE typically requires qualitative methods, whereas the study of aggregate institutional outcomes typically requires quantitative methods. SLO-research is often represented by single-case studies with the aim of understanding the cognitive aspects of learning, whereas SO-research often is comparative with the aim of benchmarking the institutional outcome between different HEIs or HE-sectors. The difference in research methods and data does not mean that the streams of research cannot be integrated or combined. There are fruitful studies that for example link together students' learning outcomes with their employability rate.

In this anthology our main focus is on the improvement of SLO. We are particularly interested in the effect of practices at the individual, instructional level. Therefore, we look at ways in which students, teachers, and administrators can make use of different LTA-methods in order to increase SLO and how these are influenced by pedagogical and didactical practices surrounding the learning processes of students. It is our aim to provide concrete ideas to ways in which the curriculum can be changed to increase SLO.

When one looks at the theories surrounding research on SLO it is clear the view of the learner has evolved. This view builds on current learning theories such as contextual learning theory and situational learning theory, which abandon the view that students learn when teachers transmit knowledge to them. Instead, learning is seen as a personal process affected by the embeddedness of the learner in social collectivities (Nygaard *et al.,* 2008). In practice it means that learning is both individual and social, and that the identity of students and their thoughts about the relevance of their study program affects the way in which they learn.

Several studies of students' approach to learning and their learning outcome highlight these connections. Trigwell & Prosser (1991) show that students' perceptions of their learning context influences their approaches to learning. Entwistle & Ramsden (1983) and Meyer *et al.* (1990) show that these factors influence their approaches to study. Marton & Säljö (1984) show that approaches to study will affect their learning outcome. They argue that students may take a deep approach to study, which helps them to achieve high quality learning outcomes, or they may take a surface approach to study, which leads to low quality learning outcomes. Trigwell & Prosser (1991) add that heavy workload and less freedom in learning relates to a reproducing orientation (surface approach), whereas good teaching, clear goals, and independence in learning relates to a meaning orientation (deep approach). Thomas & Bain (1984) show that the type of assessment affects students' approaches to study. Gulikers *et al.* (2006) show that the authenticity of study program, tasks and assignments are likely to improve students' learning outcomes, as they can easier relate to and understand the subject studied when it is exemplified with real life experiences. Crawford (2001) supports that view by upholding the importance of contextual teaching. This is supported by Mauffette-Leenders *et al.* (1997) and Erskine *et al.* (1998) who argue in favour of case based learning; Fogarty (1998) and Dean *et al.* (2002) with PBL (problem based learning); DeFillipi (2001) with project-based learning; as well as Olsen & Pedersen (2003) with Research-based learning. The common factor of all these studies is that their detailed recommendations all address aspects that affect students' learning outcomes.

Within these theoretical domains learning is seen as a process of knowledge construction rather than a simple recording of information (Nygaard & Andersen, 2005). Learning is experience based and as such it is dependent on existing knowledge because students use their knowledge to construct new knowledge (von Glaserfeld, 1995; Nygaard & Holtham, 2008).

To summarise these studies, learning activities can be either passive or active; learning outcomes can be either deep or surface. The underlying argument is that active learning activities will have a tendency to lead to deep learning, whereas passive learning activities will have a tendency to lead to surface learning. Table 1 sums up these arguments about learning activities and learning outcomes.

	Passive learning activities	Active learning activities
Type of student learning activity	Teachers take responsibility for students' learning process. Students are receivers of information. Knowledge is seen as a commodity transmitted from teacher to students. Students are usually challenged with discipline-based assignments, which have to be solved in one right way using a predefined selection of research methods and theories.	Students take responsibility for their own learning process. Students have autonomy to direct their own learning activities. Students are active constructors of knowledge. Students are usually challenged with problem based work (be it PBL; project based; case based; research based) which has to be "solved" using self selected repertoires of research methods and theories.
	Surface learning	Deep learning
Type of student learning outcomes	New knowledge is created through memorization of facts and practice. Lack of context inhibits transferability but surface learning can be a pre-requisite (eg in medical diagnosis) for deep learning. Similar to assimilation.	New knowledge is created by actively linking existing knowledge and experience with new information and practice. Students are able to further contextualize or synthesize the knowledge. Similar to accommodation.

Table 1: Learning activities and learning outcomes

If the main focus of HE is not on what teachers' teach but rather on what students' learn, HEIs face a range of challenges. This focus must affect the interaction between teachers and students because it will vary all the way down from an institutional level to the activities going on in the classroom. In the following section we will look at some of the typical challenges surrounding the task of improving students' learning outcomes.

Challenges when working to increase SLO

Working with curriculum development and/or pedagogical practices to increase students' learning outcomes can be challenging. Two of the most obvious challenges are concerned with the individual teacher's view on learning and on the ownership of the learning process.

Learning? What learning?

When working to improve students' learning outcomes the central challenge is learning itself. Without a clear perception of learning it is difficult to work with improvement and assessment of students' learning outcomes. In theory and practice, learning and associated outcomes has been characterized in a number of different ways. Diverse disciplines such as psychology and education draw on different perceptions of learning, mostly categorised as behaviourism (Thorndike, 1966; Skinner, 1974), cognitivism (Piaget, 1953; Rogers, 1969; Kolb, 1984) or constructivism (Freire, 1985; Usher & Solomon, 1999). Instead of repeating this "traditional" outline of learning theories, we take a more pragmatic approach and link perceptions of learning to curriculum and assessment of learning outcomes. That leads us to present two different views on learning: a prescriptive and a descriptive.

In perhaps the broadest of all senses, learning is often associated with obtaining knowledge about something or mastering a certain skill, such as speaking a foreign language, using a computer program or driving a car. When they come to the university many students tend to think of learning in this way. They seek to learn something concrete that can be used in their future life as professionals. They are anxious to learn the "right" knowledge and skills. When learning is perceived as knowledge or skills, it is often closely linked to curricular content, such as certain theories, methods or similar subject matters. In this view, learning outcomes become an almost linear and ideal product of higher education. Students come to university to obtain knowledge and skills, the university defines the curriculum, and the university teachers examine students to assess their knowledge and skills before they

graduate. What learning is and what has to be learned are clearly identified in the curriculum (and/or the syllabus) and it is perceived as
something that can be managed in a prescriptive way. In this scenario,
the focus of the curriculum is on ensuring that the right knowledge is
transferred to the students and that they receive enough training to develop the prescribed skills. In the context of this prescriptive approach,
curriculum theory can be labelled as a "content stream" where the
main functions of teachers are to *design, develop, implement and
evaluate* students' learning activities (Nygaard & Holtham, 2008; Nygaard & Bramming, 2008) and the responsibility clearly lies with the
teacher.

What if learning is not deliberate and cannot be prescribed? In its
simplest form learning is also about changing ones understanding of
things, concepts, subjects, etc. This is not necessarily in opposition to
the view of learning presented above. Obtaining knowledge or mastering a certain skill may well lead to changes in understanding. However, this is not automatically the case. Students may enter university
and learn a certain skill without gaining new understanding or without
changing their perceptions of the world around them. They may be in-
strumentally trained in accounting principles, without understanding
the deeper art of accounting as a judgment-based profession, working
in a climate of risk and uncertainty. They may learn how to conduct a
statistical test on a certain population of data, without being able to
transfer their statistical knowledge and skills to a broader setting.
Work done within music (Reid, 1997, 2000, 2001), design (Reid &
Davies, 2003), law (Reid *et al.*, 2006), mathematics (Reid *et al.*, 2003,
2005; Petocz & Reid, 2006) and statistics (Petocz & Reid, 2001; Reid
& Petocz, 2002) shows how a progressive view of professional formation may lead students to change their focus from techniques, rules and
skills to life, self and meaning. This may well be a product of higher
education where it is acknowledged that students need more than disciplinary knowledge and skills to act as professionals. They need what
has also been characterised as transformative skills (Harvey, *et al.,*
1992; Harvey & Knight, 1996).

So if higher education is about developing new personal understandings and perceptions, and in that way develop students to see not only
the world around them but also themselves in a different way, it requires of the curriculum that it explicitly includes activities for such
personal development. In this view, learning outcomes becomes a
more non-linear product of higher education. Students come to university to develop as reflective persons, the curriculum is defined as a col-

laborative effort between the university and the student, students self-assess their own personal development, and university teachers assess students' knowledge and skills and personal development projects before they graduate.

In the context of this descriptive approach, curriculum theory can be labelled as a "process stream". This differs from the prescriptive approach in that here the main functions of teachers are to *facilitate, co-ordinate, supervise, and evaluate* students' learning activities (Nygaard & Holtham, 2008; Nygaard & Bramming, 2008). Here the responsibility for learning is shared between the student as an active and responsible learner and the teacher as an active facilitator.

Table 2 sums up these two characteristics of learning and shows their relation to curriculum and assessment of learning outcomes.

Issue for the individual teacher	Prescriptive approach to learning (aka the 'content stream')	Descriptive approach to learning (aka the 'process stream')
Conceptualisation of learning	To learn is to acquire new knowledge and skills.	To learn is to develop new understandings and perceptions.
Role of higher education	To transfer new knowledge and skills to students.	To facilitate students' development of knowledge, skills and new personal understandings and perceptions.
Focus of curriculum	To ensure that students get the right knowledge and skills.	To enable students to develop as reflective persons.
Role of the teacher	Design, develop, implement, and evaluate.	Facilitate, coordinate, supervise, evaluate.
Assessment of students' learning outcomes	Assessment of students' knowledge and skills in relation to a fixed curriculum and/or syllabus (eg via reflective portfolios)	Assessment of students' knowledge, skills, personal understandings and perceptions with the outset in a scientific domain but with clear links also to a future professional application.

Table 2: Distinctions between prescriptive and descriptive approaches

Although this bipolar view presents a simplified caricature of student learning, curriculum and assessment, we find that it helps highlight important challenges facing us when we work to improve SLO.

Who owns the learning process?
Another important challenge concerns the ownership of the learning process. It is closely related to the conceptualisations of learning above. When we develop curriculum in higher education, do we see the student as an individual learner with an individual need for learning, or do we see the student as one of a cohort to be educated to achieve the same set of learning goals? Is it the student or the univer-

sity that owns the learning process? We present two views: the university-driven model and the student-driven model.

In the university-driven model, faculty formulates learning goals on behalf of all students. It is taken for granted that faculty knows best and can decide what students have to learn. This approach is used regardless of gender, age, nationality, past experiences and future career challenges of students. This "one size fits all" approach is often rooted in disciplinary learning goals and is useful to universities for a number of practical reasons. In terms of delivery it is not necessary to distinguish between different students; generic learning materials can be presented to all students; the responsibility for learning is left with the students (for convenience we can distinguish between good students and bad students in regards to how they perform); generic learning material can be widely used and distributed. This approach may also be characterised as mass education or commoditized education. Despite its practical advantages, it may contain some disadvantages for the students. For examples: being one of many in a commoditized curriculum may be alienating for the student if it is difficult to sense the meaning of the content and/or teaching and learning approach (*"everybody else seem to relate, what is wrong with me?"*); it may be demotivating for the student to have to fulfil learning goals that are defined by others (*"why do I have to learn this?"*); it may be difficult for the student to relate the course of study to own personal and professional development (*"this has not much to do with the job/career I am dreaming about"*). Within a standardised curriculum the assessment of students' learning outcomes are the same. All students are expected to learn the same knowledge and skills, and can thus be assessed in the same way.

The student-driven model is different. Here students are perceived as individual learners engaged in processes of personal development. The curriculum becomes a learning-centred action plan, tailored to the needs of each individual student. Tailoring to each student may appear to have many practical disadvantages. However complicated this approach may sound, it need not imply that there are thousands of curricula and course descriptions at a university to suit each individual student. What it does imply is that the curriculum is open for instances of student ownership so that both the ways in which individual students learn and the more detailed learning goals of each student are accommodated by the curriculum.

Changing the curriculum from a university-driven, content-based approach to a student-driven, learning-based approach involves an increased focus on the pedagogical issues affecting students' learning. One solution could be to move from teacher-driven and theory-based education to a student-driven and problem-based education (Chehore & Scholtz, 2008; Nygaard *et al.*, 2008; Meier & Nygaard, 2008). Here the curriculum would require students to identify problems, be they theoretical or empirical, in relation to their content of study to and address these via individual work or group work. However, the student-driven model also has some practical disadvantages. For examples: it requires more work from faculty and administration to develop a descriptive approach to teaching and learning because it requires new roles to stakeholders and thus often implies cultural changes within the universities; in addition, when the personal learning process is centred, more continuous follow-up and personal feedback to students from faculty and administration is required.

Focusing on individualised student learning may also have some disadvantages to students: it becomes transparent to teachers and fellow students (social peers) if the individual student does not perform well; it requires continuous work from students to engage and reflect about their own learning process; some students will be reluctant to take responsibility for their own learning process if they are not trained to do so. Despite these possible disadvantages our own practice, mirrored with research on student learning, leaves us no doubt that students increase their learning outcomes in the student-driven model.

Having said this, we also sense that we are witnessing a paradox within higher education today. An increasing body of research and practice points towards a student-driven model for learning. Yet external standards for accreditation, certification and modularisation are pushing HE inexorably towards increased centralisation and commoditization. This paradox is not something for which we can provide an answer in this anthology but we find it to be an important issue if the political requirements put on higher education institutions are really to help us improve students' learning outcomes.

A change in focus

As can be sensed from the discussion above, there is no single route or easy solution to improving students' learning outcomes. Work may be done on the instructional level, the programme level and/or the institutional level. Work may be rooted in different perceptions of learning, curriculum, learning outcomes and assessment methods. Work may be guided by a university-driven or a student-driven model. Although we would argue that there are approaches that make more sense than others, no single approach can be argued to be the only correct approach. In their own ways, the chapters in this anthology show the various advantages of multiple approaches to improve students' learning outcomes. Common to all chapters is that they demonstrate awareness of the need to change the ways in which higher education is developed and managed. To sum up, the improvement of students' learning outcomes demands that we acknowledge that:

1. students are active participants who own and define their individual learning processes.
2. learning is contextualized, situated and linked to students' past experiences and future expectations.
3. both teaching-centric and learning-centric activities are essential and complementary.
4. institutional practices may have to change from ways in which we govern and administrate, to ways in which we evaluate study programmes.
5. All stakeholders – students, teachers, and administrators – may need to develop and adopt new roles in study programs
6. assessment should focus on learning outcomes more than on students' satisfaction.

Navigating the contributions in this anthology

Our reflections on institutional and instructional perspectives have suggested two spectra: one enabling pedagogical focus to be plotted on a continuum from theory to practice, the other characterizing the fact that actions to improve learning outcomes will differ at the individual, departmental and organizational level. Juxtaposition of the two spectra offers the opportunity to map the chapters in this book – and the authors' key messages – in order to assist you, the reader, to find the material of closest relevance to your current interests or needs. Figure 1 shows this mapping and highlights the emergence of three clusters: "Theoretical perspectives", "Integration of theory and practice", and "Practice at the individual level" which we trust will also help you to navigate our anthology.

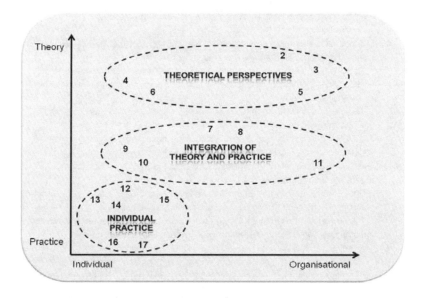

Figure 1: The chapter map and clusters

Key to the chapters' titles and the authors' key messages:

Ch#	Title, author and key messages
1	Learning outcomes – politics, religion or improvement? By Claus Nygaard, Clive Holtham & Nigel Courtney
	Cluster A: "Theory at all levels"
2	Improving students' learning outcomes: what about doctoral learning outcomes? By Leizel Frick. • Doctoral learning outcomes are not easily defined because doctoral study is individualised, discipline-based and constructivist in nature. • Doctoral students need to develop both ontologically, epistemologically and methodologically if they are to reach the outcomes associated with 'doctorateness'.

3   A personalised approach to improving students' learning outcomes.
    By Andrea Raiker.
    • E-portfolios automatically personalise learning, whether that learning is
      individually or collaboratively constructed, as they are student-owned.
    • Personalised learning gives control of learning to the student.

4   Develop, Use, Extend: promoting deep learning through pedagogical progression.
    By Juliet Hinrichsen.
    • Teachers need tools which help them map, or align, learning outcomes with
      teaching methods.
    • 'DUE' introduces a methodology for designing developmentally aligned learning
      activities to support deep learning.

5   Developing a coordinated strategy to both encourage innovation and improve
    student learning outcomes.
    By Paul Bartholomew, Stuart Brand & Luke Millard.
    • Recognise those staff who have taken transformative action.
    • For real impact on student learning outcomes a coordinated strategy is needed.

6   Can students' conceptions of learning improve their learning outcomes?
    By Despina Varnava-Marouchou.
    • Students conceptions of learning can influence their learning outcomes.
    • The implications of students' conceptions of learning may contribute to teacher
      training programmes and curriculum designs.

Cluster B: "Integrating theory and practice"

7   Enhancing mathematics across the disciplines through an institutional initiative
    By Dorothy Wallace.
    • It is possible to identify learning goals that span a variety of content areas,
      implement a strategy for achieving those and measure the results.
    • Long term institutional change requires a special set of strategies and
      knowledge in order to succeed.

8   Putting Humpty Dumpty together again: learning as integrated performance in
    context.
    By Anne Jordan and Orison Carlile.
    • Although useful, discrete learning outcome statements are problematic; they
      need to be complemented by disciplinary values embodied in the teacher.
    • Teaching needs to support disciplinary understanding and integrated student
      performance in context.

9   Analogical learning in Higher Education.
    By John Branch, Huai-Mei Chiang & Ivan Goenawan.
    • Take stock of the theoretical and empirical research on analogy in learning.
    • Review analogical curricular models and study methods which can be put into
      practice by instructors in higher education.

10 Reflective teaching: a tool to improve students' learning.
    By Saretha Brüssow & Annette Wilkinson.
    • Engage student and facilitator buy-in for successful assessment alignment.
    • Select appropriate methods and tools for assessment in a new learning
      environment.

11 A new focus on assessment of student learning outcomes
    By Hesta Friedrich-Nel .
    • Select methods and tools for assessment alignment.
    • Engage student and academic buy-in to get successful assessment alignment.

Cluster C: "Practice at the individual level"
12 Improving students' learning outcomes via teamwork and portfolios. By Antigoni Papadimitriou. • Teamwork as a teaching technique improves Student Learning Outcomes. • The use of portfolios as assessment methods motivates student participation.
13 Using Assessment Centre approaches to improve student learning. By Arti Kumar. • Assessment centres make key competencies visible and comprehensible as effective behaviours that can then be observed and assessed against specific criteria. • Assessment centre approaches open up new ways of conceptualising and aligning learning outcomes with experiential activities, peer observation, developmental feedback and self-assessment.
14 Learning with masters – using art in a research methodology class. By Widya Suryadini. • Teaching students to appreciate fine art will prepare them to grasp new intellectual concepts. • It requires perseverance to develop and embed an innovative teaching approach.
15 Learning outside the classroom: environments for experiential enrichment. By Sue Waite, Roger Cutting, Robert Cook, John Burnett & Miles Opie. • Effective teaching and learning can take place outside of conventional study environments. • Effective teaching and learning will flourish in an unstructured, spontaneous environment.
16 Enhancing the affective learning outcomes of trainees in teacher education: an immersive learning approach. By Nor Aziah Alias and Nor Aiza Alias . • Technology can be used effectively in improving trainee teachers' affective learning outcomes. • The affective learning outcomes must be considered in learning design alongside cognitive outcomes and psychomotor skills.
17 The effectiveness of curriculum maps for alignment in Higher Education. By Isabel Huet, José Manuel Oliveira, Nilza Costa & João Estima de Oliveira. • Curriculum maps help faculty to align learning outcomes, teaching and learning strategies, assessment and students' workload. • The design of curricula must be based on constructive alignment

About the authors

Claus Nygaard is Professor in Management Education and Director of Research at CBS Learning Lab, Copenhagen Business School, Denmark. He can be contacted at this e-mail: cn.ll@cbs.dk

Clive Holtham is Professor of Information Management and Director of the Learning Laboratory at Cass Business School, City University London, UK. He can be contacted at this e-mail: c.w.holtham@city.ac.uk

Nigel Courtney is Honorary Senior Visiting Fellow at Cass Business School, City University London, UK, where he gained his PhD. He can be contacted at this e-mail: nigel@city.ac.uk

CHAPTER 2

Improving Students' Learning Outcomes: What about Doctoral Learning Outcomes?

Liezel Frick

Introduction

An anthology of improving students' learning outcomes in higher education should recognise the full scope of the higher education experience – including both undergraduate and postgraduate perspectives. This chapter therefore investigates how doctoral education is conceptualised within higher education, and how such conceptualisations influence the learning outcomes doctoral students achieve. The contribution of this perspective lies in providing a theoretical discussion on students' learning outcomes in a distinct area of higher education – that of doctoral education. The chapter proposes a formative process throughout the doctoral learning journey with an alignment between the conceptualisation of how students view themselves in relation to research (in essence a process of becoming a scholar, also known as ontology), how students relate to different forms of knowledge (also referred to as epistemology), and knowing how to obtain and create such knowledge (methodology).

Students' learning outcomes are influenced and sometimes determined by learning environments (Deem & Brehony, 2000). Walker *et al.* (2008) refers to the value of the intellectual community as part of the learning environment. Such a community influences how students engage with ideas, the value placed on teaching, how students learn to relate to senior colleagues, if failure is seen as part of learning (or something that should be avoided at all costs), if and how collaborative endeavours are structured, the way in which independence and creativity are fostered, and how community members stay connected to the advances in the discipline. Harris (2005) describes scholarly identity as a product of an individual's values and beliefs, as well as institutional culture and positioning of the particular discipline. Scholarly identity therefore seems to imply more than a thorough grasp of methodological issues, but also a sense of self therein (ontology) and positioning within the knowledge used and created (epistemology). If students entering higher education are encultured into a discipline-based and teaching (rather than learning)-centred curriculum, what are the consequences for their further studies – especially at the doctoral level?

Doctoral studies form an important part of the preparation for academic and/or professional practice – depending on the focus of the particular doctoral programme. Doctoral studies, by implication, build on previous learning and continue to prepare the student to become an expert scholar in a particular area. Barnacle (2005) describes this process as moving from being a scholarship student to becoming a responsible scholar. A responsible scholar has a commitment to lifelong learning and forms part of a scholarly community. The initiation into this community of practice primarily takes place through doctoral studies.

However, the literature indicates a strong focus on discipline-based research outcomes (Lovitts, 2007; Walker *et al.,* 2008). Such outcomes seem to relate more to methodological issues than to students' understanding of their contribution to their own development as experts in a discipline (ontology) and the greater body of knowledge (epistemology). An argument could be made that the pinnacle of postgraduate studies – a doctoral degree – does not adequately prepare future experts for practice if doctoral programmes follow such a singular focus. The central questions addressed in the chapter are therefore:

- What constitutes a doctoral degree?
- What learning outcomes are envisioned within doctoral education?
- How can these learning outcomes be conceptualised within doctoral education?
- What are the implications of these learning outcomes for the curriculum in doctoral programmes?

The framework for this anthology provides a useful point of departure from which to explore these questions. This chapter starts by exploring how a doctorate is conceptualised, followed by a discussion on the translation of such a conceptualisation into student learning outcomes. The concept of a curriculum creates a space for theoretical debate on how the curriculum relates to students' learning outcomes in doctoral education.

The use of a discourse on doctoral education in the anthology is twofold. Firstly, an investigation into the nature of doctoral education may facilitate debate on how students are prepared at a high academic level for success not only in the programme itself, but also thereafter. Secondly, an investigation on what a doctorate itself entails may be helpful to align doctoral programmes to the intended learning outcomes. In this chapter, I will argue that the learning outcomes of doctoral education need to be framed within ontological, epistemological and methodological considerations.

The doctorate: process or product?

A doctorate, or degree of doctor of philosophy (PhD), is the highest degree awarded by a university faculty. The origins of the term can be traced back to the ancient Greek words *philos,* referring to a form of love, and *sophia,* meaning wisdom. Therefore, philosophy implies the love of wisdom, and a philosopher can therefore be described as a lover of wisdom. Barnacle (2005) describes the essence of a doctorate as a perpetual desire and search for wisdom. The term *wisdom* in itself entails more than mere knowledge; it refers to a comprehensive understanding of knowledge, sound judgement, and insight. A doctor of philosophy is therefore more than a mechanic of knowledge, but can judge knowledge and can advise with insight.

Barnacle (2005) adds another interesting dimension to what constitutes a doctorate – that of becoming (or *un*becoming – unlearning that which could inhibit doctoral becoming – as described by Colley & James, in Archer, 2008). Becoming implies movement over time, progression, and transformation. Batchelor & Di Napoli (2006:14) note that transformation takes place at both an ontological and epistemological level: "your voice for being and becoming, as a person, as well as your voice for knowing". The process of becoming can take on various forms, such as a professional doctorate (which can be described as a doctorate aimed at practising professionals and one that contains coursework components) or a more traditional PhD (which refers to a mostly research-based programme) (Lester, 2004; Neumann, 2005; Park, 2007). The central question, irrespective of the programme format, remains the same: what is the postgraduate student becoming through the doctoral experience? These arguments seem to imply a strong ontological undertone, but the following discussion on definitions of the doctoral degree will highlight that ontological becoming is only one facet of doctorateness.

Various definitions of a doctoral degree provide an indication of the purposes of a doctorate. The British view on a traditional PhD focuses on the development of professional researchers (Bourner *et al.,* 2001)

35

who, through the creation and interpretation of knowledge within a discipline, will eventually be able to conceptualise, design and implement projects (United Kingdom Quality Assurance Agency for Higher Education, 2001). The United Kingdom Research Council's (2001) Joint Statement of Skills Training Requirements of Research Postgraduates (2001) is used by most institutions across the United Kingdom to inform their notions of what a doctorate entails and refers to the multiplicity of learning outcomes expected of doctoral candidates. Park (2007:33) summarises the most common types of doctoral awards in the United Kingdom, which reflects such a broad range of programmes that the difficulty in defining the doctorate and its outcomes is understandable. The Australasian Qualifications Framework Advisory Board (1998:53) also emphasises the undertaking of an original research project that results in a significant contribution to knowledge and/or the application thereof within a specific discipline. Lovitts (2005:138, referring to the Association of American Universities 1998 definition) describes the PhD as "… a research degree, one that signifies that the recipient has acquired the capacity to make independent contributions to knowledge through original research and scholarship". This definition corresponds with that of the United States of America Council of Graduate Schools (1977, as quoted in Lovitts, 2008:296), which refers to the main purpose of a PhD as a preparation for "a lifetime of intellectual inquiry that manifests itself in creative scholarship and research", with its completion marking "the transition from student to independent scholar" (United States of America Council of Graduate Schools, 1995:9). The New Zealand Qualifications Authority (2001) refers to the development of both skills and knowledge necessary for an original contribution to knowledge through research or scholarship – as judged by independent experts employing international standards.

The importance of independent and original research in doctoral studies is evident in all these definitions. There seems to be a worldwide trend for doctoral studies to be aimed at the development of the candidate as a researcher. Examples from Europe (Enders, 2005; Enders & De Weert, 2004; Schreiterer, 2008), Britain (Enders, 2005; Henkel, 2005; Leonard *et al.*, 2005; McAlpine & Norton, 2006), the USA (Enders, 2005; Lovitts, 2005; Manathunga *et al.*, 2006), Canada (McAlpine & Norton, 2006), and Australia (Alpert & Kamins, 2004; Barron & Zeegers, 2006; Lizzio & Wilson, 2004; Kemp, 1999; Manathunga *et al.*, 2006) emphasise the doctoral student as researcher, even though various authors critique this limited notion of "doctorateness" (Campbell *et al.*, 2005; Dall'Alba & Barnacle, 2007). The transferability of the doctoral experience to eventual academic or professional practice comes into question.

The emphasis on comparable qualifications, academic mobility and employability espoused in international agreements, such as the Sorbonne Joint Declaration (1998), the Bologna Declaration (1999) and the Berlin Communiqué (2003) provides pressure to trade in knowledge as a commodity, where universities take on an entrepreneurial role in commercialising research findings through partnerships with industry. Doctoral candidates become key contributors in creating prosperity through innovation, and consequently a doctoral degree becomes a product rather than a process (Barnacle, 2005). However, it is arguable whether this focused approach to doctoral development adequately prepares the student for becoming a responsible and versatile "scholar".

McClintock (2007) argues that education systems generally have failed higher degree students, as such students are not adequately prepared to take care of their responsibilities independently. Dall'Alba & Barnacle (2007) add that higher education programmes have favoured epistemological concerns rather than ontological development. This emphasis has led to the transfer and attainment of knowledge and skills (generic or discipline-specific) to the detriment of student knowing, acting and being. If meaning is created through experience (Lin & Cranton, 2005:453) and doctoral candidates are only given limited opportunities to experience a certain kind of learning, such candidates will be ill-prepared to practise in other settings (Le Grange *et al.*, 2006). Paul & Marfo (2001) add that doctoral students often decide on methodological preferences before they have conceptualised their research questions properly, with little understanding of the underlying philosophical assumptions of the chosen methodology. On the surface, it may seem that doctoral students are performing well and meeting the requirements of the programme. However, the compliant student has not necessarily found his/her own scholarly voice, identity, or confidence – a vital step in becoming a responsible scholar (Lovitts, 2005). According to Freire (1970, as quoted in Lin & Cranton, 2005:458), a responsible scholar "has the courage and confidence to take risks, to make mistakes, to invent and reinvent knowledge, and to pursue critical and lifelong inquiries in the world, with the world, and with each other". The same argument could be made for the doctoral graduate moving into the world of work outside academe, as these traits could equally apply to a responsible worker. However, what constitutes a

doctoral degree presently seems to focus on a product (a methodologically sound dissertation), rather than the process of becoming a responsible scholar (encompassing the dimensions of ontology and epistemology).

What does this outline tell us about possible outcomes expected of
doctoral students?

Doctoral outcomes: learning as a complex phenomenon

Alpert & Kamins (2004), Kember & Leung (2005) and Leonard *et al.*
(2005) argue that the development expected to take place in a doctoral
programme entails more than acquiring the knowledge base of a specific discipline; it also encompasses skills that should enable the student to think and act beyond the knowledge boundaries of the discipline. Barnacle (2005) argues that an instrumental approach to knowledge in doctoral education removes the student from the knowledge
and the knowing, which is contrary to integrative models of learning
(as proposed by Barnett, 1997, 2000 and Schön, 1983). Such an approach inhibits the transformative power of knowledge, as Barnacle
(2005:187) describes: *"...we need to situate Doctoral candidates for
the knowledge economy but in such a way that we also engage fully
with the potential of Doctoral becoming. An account of Doctoral becoming that treats the learning outcomes purely as a commodity is im-
poverished, and misses the real import of the learning experience: that
it is transformative."*

Becoming part of and being eloquent in an epistemic community
demands the acquisition of both formal (knowing *that*) and informal
(knowing *how*) knowledge (Lovitts, 2005). Lin & Cranton (2005:449)
summarise shortfalls in doctoral education as: *"...being educated is associated with knowing lots of things rather than knowing how to think
about those things."* The question arises whether current doctoral programmes enable students to develop the latter outcome expected of a
responsible scholar.

Archer (2008:386), building on the work of Bourdieu, describes
higher education as "a contested territory that entails constant struggles
over the symbols and boundaries of authenticity". Within such an ever-
changing environment, the ontological meaning associated with 'being' and the meaning of what constitutes academic work continue to be
challenged. Oppressive ideologies and organisational structures may
inhibit creativity and doctoral becoming. Becoming an authentic
scholar means playing by the current rules of the game – as such, universities have become "sites of contested identity" (Archer, 2008:390).

Clegg (2008:223) rightfully asks: "...*is it possible to find the intellectual space to develop an authentic social engagement with students, and to act as midwife to students' creativity?*"

Archer (2008) and Batchelor & Di Napoli (2006) emphasise that the process of becoming is not clear-cut, even, linear or mechanical (but neither is the research process itself). Becoming sometimes leads to conflict, feelings of inauthenticity, marginalisation and exclusion. The work of Lovitts (2008) adds to our understanding of doctoral students' experience of ontological insecurity as a necessary part of the process of becoming. Batchelor's personal reflection (in Bachelor & Napoli, 2006:13) characterises doctoral becoming as a (research) journey into the unknown, and research as "a voyage of vulnerability". Lovitts (2008) argues that frustration and uncertainty are inevitable elements in the development of original research. Students who are able to cope with uncertainty are therefore more likely to succeed.

McAlpine & Norton (2006) provide an integrative framework to explain the wider social, economic and cultural influences on doctoral students' experiences. However, the framework does not address students' learning outcomes. Lovitts (2005) provides a more comprehensive model of factors influencing doctoral completion. Such frameworks and models are useful in providing an understanding of doctoral becoming, but fail to pinpoint the learning outcomes doctoral students are expected to achieve. The work of these authors shed light on how vaguely defined doctoral outcomes are in practice. Clegg (2008) and McAlpine & Norton (2006) attribute these nebulous notions of what doctoral education entails to the nested contexts in which the processes associated with doctoral becoming are often invisible. Furthermore traditional admission requirements do not provide evidence of the learning outcomes that will be expected of doctoral students. Ill-prepared students and/or supervisors, as well as doctoral programmes that do not always support doctoral becoming, afford us a glimpse of the complex interplay of factors in doctoral becoming (Lovitts, 2005).

Envisioned doctoral outcome	Prevalent authors	Implications for outcome dimensions
Independent/ autonomous and original research	Lovitts, 2005, 2008; Schreiterer, 2008	Methodology seems to be the most important issue, although students also need a sound epistemic knowledge of the field of study in order to make an original contribution. The inherent messiness and non-linearity of the research process demands that doctoral students are able to cope with uncertainty and change. Doctoral students need to be able to tolerate discomfort in the learning situation. Ontological becoming is therefore also an important in reaching independence and becoming experts.
Integration into an intellectual community of scholars	Deem & Brehony, 2000; Lovitts, 2005	Epistemic knowledge will be important for interaction within an intellectual community, but students also need to be aware of the latest methodological issues and need to ontologically position themselves in relation to the community and its knowledge.
Insight into current and authoritative existing research related to the study topic	Lovitts, 2005, 2008	Epistemological and methodological learning are obviously important in achieving this outcome, but students still need to position themselves as researchers (ontology) in relation to the existing research. Rapid knowledge change and develop-ment, as well as the decreasing monopoly higher education has on knowledge emphasise the need for information literacy beyond simplistic epistemic and methodological knowledge of the discipline.
Insight into the approaches by which the topic can be investigated	Paul & Marfo, 2001	Methodology and epistemology are important concerns in determining the most suitable investigative approach, and self-knowledge will enable the student to capitalise on their strengths as researchers in making these choices.
Production of a scholarly thesis or dissertation	Campbell et al., 2005 Lovitts, 2008 Park, 2007	The production of the end-product (dissertation) demands that students have sound knowledge of both the epistemic and methodological bases of their fields of study, but they still need to ontologically position themselves as researchers within this work.
Oral communica-tion through pub-lic defence of the research and/or presentation of conference papers	De Rosa, 2008 Maheu, 2008 Lovitts, 2008 Park, 2007	The defence and communication of the end-product demands that students have sound epistemic and methodological grounding and their ontological positioning will be important to convince the wider audience of the merit of the work.
Broader dissemination of the results through publication	Archer, 2008 Lee & Kamler, 2008 Kamler, 2008 Maher et al., 2008 Park, 2007 Schreiterer, 2008	Publication, as in an oral defence, demands sound epistemic and methodological grounding and their ontological positioning will still be important to convince the wider audience of the merit of the work and deal with the peer review process.
Ability to work in teams	Campbell et al., 2005 Lovitts, 2008 Maheu, 2008	A secure sense of being a researcher within the world of science will be important for students' ability to work in teams with self-confidence, but they also need to bring epistemic and methodological knowledge to the team to add value.

Envisioned doctoral outcome	Prevalent authors	Implications for outcome dimensions
Teaching within the field of study	Campbell et al., 2005 Maheu, 2008 Miclea, 2008	A secure sense of being a researcher within the world of science will be important for doctoral students/graduates to teach with self-assurance, in order to convey their epistemic and methodological knowledge to other students.
Ability to supervise postgraduate students	Deem & Brehony, 2000 Lee, 2008 Miclea, 2008 Park, 2007	If doctoral candidates continuously develop an ontological stance, they may be more able to supervise other students with wisdom and insight. They may also be more prepared to deal with the uncertainty and messiness associated with research (which is often not a neat, linear process). They will not be able to supervise without the necessary epistemological and methodological foundation.
Attaining funding for research	Archer, 2008 Park, 2007	Funding proposals demand an epistemological grounding in the focus area, as well as methodological rigour. Selling an idea to funding agencies requires ontological skills.
Eventual employability in academe or elsewhere	Deem & Brehony, 2000 Campbell et al., 2005 Kumar, 2007 Maheu, 2008 Park, 2007 Schreiterer, 2008	Doctoral graduates can prove their epistemic and methodological background through the end-products of their research, but prospective employers are often interested in the more generic (and less tacit) skills a future employee can bring into the organisation. Ontological development is therefore also important. An integration of the different dimensions of doctoral outcomes by students themselves (through tools such as PDPs) may enable students to understand their own unique set of skills, knowledge and attitudes, which they can then translate into self-promotion.

Table 1: An overview of doctoral outcomes and their relation to ontology, epistemology and methodology

Such factors include different forms of intelligence, based on Sternberg's (1997) theory of intelligence as analytical, creative or practical; knowledge; thinking styles, based on Sternberg's (1997) creative/legislative, executive and judicial styles; personality; and both intrinsic and extrinsic motivation (Beaty *et al.*, 2005; Biggs, 1987). Whilst methodologies tend to be discipline-specific and are perpetuated within the cultures of disciplines (McAlpine & Norton, 2006), the above-mentioned factors arguably stretch beyond the methodological to how students position themselves in the learning context both ontologically and epistemologically.

Literature provides some clues to the learning outcomes expected of doctoral candidates. Table 1 provides an overview of learning outcomes associated with doctoral education. Various authors allude to a broader conception of doctoral learning outcomes, and therefore an indication of the relationship between the three dimensions these outcomes may address (ontology, epistemology and methodology) is included. Embedded within these outcomes envisioned of doctoral education are the notions of creativity, innovation, collaboration, problem solving, ethical conduct, interpersonal communication, interdisciplinary understanding, and entrepreneurial initiative (Campbell *et al.,* 2005; De Rosa, 2008; Lovitts, 2005). These notions correspond to Killen's (2003:10) description of quality learning as "understanding (rather than memorisation), creativity (rather than reproduction), diversity (rather than conformity), initiative (rather than compliance) and challenge (rather than blind acceptance)." The identified outcomes also suggest a complex interplay between the notions of ontology, epistemology and methodology. Do doctoral candidates receive adequate preparation to attain these outcomes and become responsible scholars – in academe or other places of work? If such a wide array of outcomes is to be reached in order to achieve a doctorate, we may need to take a critical look at the doctoral curriculum.

Curriculum in doctoral education

Despite the apparent complexity of doctoral outcomes, institutional conceptions of doctoral education are commonly built on the assumption that the apprenticeship model is followed (Barron & Zeegers, 2006; McCormack, 2004; Phelps *et al.*, 2006), also referred to as the scientist-practitioner model (Nixon, in Lizzio & Wilson, 2004). The model focuses on applying science and scientific findings to practice through acculturation into the discipline by following a master (the supervisor), but it disregards the affective, intuitive and ethical elements integral to professional competence (Max-Neef, 2005). Lizzio & Wilson (2004:470) emphasise the affective and experiential nature of learning that informs practice and which leads to "adaptive flexibility". Traditional educational processes may add little value to the development of students' applied meta-cognitive ability – that is, awareness and control over implementing their knowledge in a practical and unpredictable professional setting. Enders & De Weert (2004) argue that these changes have an influence on research training. Doctoral candidates still need competence in research design and techniques, but the outcomes they need to achieve reach far beyond the methodological.

Levin (2000) argues that curricular re-interpretations need to take note of the student voice and constructivist ideas about learning. Constructivism pre-supposes that students are active constructors of knowledge rather than passive recipients. As such, constructivism puts pre-determined and clearly specified learning outcomes into question as constructivist learning environments foster active student involvement, take into account students' prior learning, allow students to experience the interplay between knowledge, problem solving and application, and also make provision for students to monitor their own performance. Constructivism is a key element in many educational reforms, but it does not seem to feature prominently in discussions on the doctoral curriculum. This may be due to a lack of consensus on what constitutes doctorateness (Swain, 2007), again pointing out the difficulty in defining doctoral outcomes across the broad spectrum of systemic, country-specific, disciplinary and timing variables associated with the doctorate.

Developing a scholarly identity has become increasingly difficult in an environment that makes multiple demands on the doctoral student (Harris, 2005). Tensions may result from the difference between student needs and institutional and supervisor demands. Brew (2003:13) describes the elements of this tension as *"...the potentially transformative power of research through engaging with ideas over time versus the pressure to swiftly conclude projects"*. The apprenticeship model presumes a one-size-fits-all linear approach to research, which disregards the intricacies of the transformation that takes place in postgraduate learning (McCormack, 2004). The influence of external stakeholders, such as employers of the doctoral graduates, is gaining impetus. Graduates often experience a reality shock when they enter the workforce (Lizzio & Wilson, 2004). Their assumptions about work are often challenged and proven inaccurate. Part-time employed doctoral students may experience different challenges, such as balancing and aligning work and study interests. Doctoral education seems to vary considerably among systems, countries, disciplines (for example natural and social sciences), and timing (part-time versus full-time study). A one-size-fits-all approach to doctoral education may therefore not be suitable (Lovitts, 2007). The current challenge to postgraduate education is ensuring that the curriculum is not sacrificed due to market-related forces that demand output and massification of higher education (Barron & Zeegers, 2006; Clegg, 2008). Increasingly blurred boundaries within the academic environment and between the academic environment and other fields of professional practice are noticeable. The increasing diversity in institutional and inter-institutional structures warrants a constant re-interpretation of what contribution a doctorate makes to the becoming doctoral candidate.

Enders & De Weert (2004) argue that a uniform curriculum for doctoral education may not be the ideal, as national contexts and disciplinary cultures warrant a variety of programme structures. However, higher education institutions need to consider how best to address the variety of roles and relationships expected of the doctoral graduate (in this regard see Jordan & Carlile (in this volume) on learning as integrated performance in context). Kumar (2007) proposes the use of personal development plans (PDPs) to align the different dimensions of doctoral outcomes (ontology, epistemology and methodology) through developing students' reflective abilities. In this way doctoral students can identify, articulate and record their own learning and development as a process of achievement and outcomes reached, which they can then promote to potential employers. Students may need support and structure to develop their reflective abilities in this regard (also see Raiker (in this volume) on improving students' learning outcomes through a personalised approach).

Alpert & Kamins (2004) argue that coursework included in a doctoral programme broadens and deepens the student's knowledge of research in general and develops the subtle skills of judging the quality of research (note Huet *et al.* (in this volume) on curriculum maps and Hinrichsen (in this volume) on instructional design when considering coursework in the doctoral curriculum). There are, however, various counter-arguments to a more structured approach to doctoral education, which serve as an indication of the contested nature of doctoral education. McAlpine & Norton (2006), Enders (2005), and Enders & De Weert (2004) provide evidence that a significant portion of doctoral graduates do not enter academic practice, but progress to industry or other research organisations. To this, Alpert & Kamins (2004) add that coursework components in doctoral programmes can be perceived as dogmatic, which is counterproductive to original thought and contribution imperative to this level of education. McAlpine & Norton (2006) and Leonard *et al.* (2005) also found that doctoral studies consisting of only a research project tended to have a shorter completion time than doctoral programmes that incorporated compulsory coursework and non-research-related skills development. The current emphasis on throughput rates will strengthen the argument for an approach that facilitates the shortest possible completion time. Manathunga *et al.* (2006) state that students may find the demands of coursework and a research project overwhelming and may struggle to negotiate divergent views and expectations of supervisors.

Therefore, doctoral development cannot be seen in isolation from the wider academic environment. Christiansen & Slammert (2006), Jawitz (2007), Johnson (2006) and Sorcinelli (2002) advocate collegiality as a medium of development. Johnson (2006:60) describes collegiality as *"...the special practices of a community of scholars or academics, since it refers to their professional autonomy, their quest for knowledge and their recognition of working together, whether formally or informally, in striving towards their scholarly accomplishments"*. Collins (2000), as quoted in Christiansen & Slammert (2006:17) refers to this type of collegiality as *"interaction rituals"*, where scholars obtain both emotional energy and cultural capital to further their scholarly development. Arguably, intellectually engaging communities provide more opportunities for doctoral development than incentives or financial support.

Wenger's (1998) notion of communities of practice makes an important contribution to understanding such forms of interaction, and include the elements of *meaning* (how individuals and/or groups communicate on understanding the world and what is considered as meaningful), *practice* (the sharing of historical and social resources, frameworks and perspectives), *community* (specific social configurations that influence what is seen as worthwhile actions and within which competence is defined and recognised), and *identity* (how learning leads to change and creates personal histories of becoming in the context of a particular community). Communities of practice can serve as a place of belonging and a sounding-board for doctoral students (Christiansen & Slammert, 2006; Johnson, 2006; Maher *et al.*, 2008; Sorcinelli, 2002), but Batchelor & Di Napoli (2006) emphasise that such support should not be based on a student deficit model and should therefore preferably be non-compulsory. Jawitz (2007) warns that doctoral communities of practice are still fragmented. Such fragmented communities often determine the doctoral student's career trajectory. The trend set during doctoral education therefore easily becomes legitimised in eventual professional practice through acculturation into a distinct academic tribe (McAlpine & Norton, 2006).

Enders & De Weert (2004:135) attest to the importance of disciplinary environment (the tribe, as initially described by Becher & Trowler, 2001) as a so-called *"invisible community"*. However, the shift in emphasis in recent times from Mode 1 (basic) to Mode 2 (applied) knowledge (Enders, 2005; Enders & De Weert, 2004; Gibbons, 1998) and public demands for higher education accountability (Barron & Zeegers, 2006) encourages increased connection to the world outside the traditional disciplinary community. Henkel (2004:179) summarises the need for a more integrated view thus: *"In this way they may be more prepared to confront the political changes in the world of research, a task for which they will need skills not just of presentation but of argument that can incorporate the perspectives of multiple worlds."*

Andresen's (2000) distinction between scholarship at the micro (disciplinary) and macro (trans-disciplinary) levels and Henkel's (2004) conceptualisation of academic identity adds to our understanding of doctoral development. Henkel (2005) emphasises the importance of communities of practice in establishing scholarly identity. The individual's identity is established at the micro level (discipline) through a self-regulating community of peers – the foundation of this identity being traditional doctoral education. The public identity (at the macro level), which extends beyond discipline-based research, is built on this initial foundation. The community into which the doctoral candidate is initiated remains important, as it forms the values and epistemic basis on which interaction with the wider scholarly community is built – even if the disciplinary self-regulated influence has faded somewhat in recent times due to larger social, economic and environmental factors impacting on higher education (Henkel, 2004).

Enders & De Weert (2004) argue that the influence of the singular discipline and the doctoral thesis as an original contribution in the particular field needs to adjust to a more transdisciplinary approach positioned within a wider community of practice. The production of knowledge (and by implication the doctoral curriculum) may take on a different and varied form in comparison to previously accepted proof of doctoral competence (Enders, 2005). In doctoral education, trans-disciplinarity implies that *"...students are being exposed to a greater variety of values, choices and working environments and expected to develop a wider range of skills and knowledge"* (Henkel, 2004:176).

The concept of transdisciplinarity can be related to what Lee *et al.* (2000) refer to as a "hybrid curriculum", where the three intersecting spheres of university, profession and workplace infuse doctoral education. Transdisciplinarity provides room for innovative and integrated scholarly development in doctoral education.

The conceptualisation of the doctorate, the learning outcomes envisioned for doctoral candidates and the consideration of doctoral curricula indicate that doctoral becoming centres on three main developmental areas: ontology, epistemology and methodology. If doctoral candidates are to reach the envisioned outcomes, the doctoral curriculum needs to support the development of such candidates in all these areas. Doctoral students need to position themselves ontologically as scholars, negotiate their understanding of and contribution to the discipline (episteme), and navigate the myriad of methodological issues surrounding all research endeavours amidst this dynamic environment. The academic environment can ill afford doctoral becoming through a curricular system focused on linear, reductionistic modes of knowledge acquisition. The doctoral student who is able to reach learning outcomes that transcend disciplinary boundaries may be the responsible scholar of the future.

Conclusion

A discourse on learning outcomes of doctoral education may lead to more questions than answers. Before learning outcomes of doctoral students can be improved, we need to establish an understanding of what a doctorate is. The two conceptualisations of doctoral education what constitutes a doctoral degree presently seems to focus on a product (a methodologically sound dissertation), or the process of becoming a responsible scholar (encompassing the dimensions of ontology and epistemology). Park (2007) notes that the variance in what constitutes a doctorate, may lead to a superficial dichotomy between process and product outcomes, where a balanced combination suited to a particular context might be a more sensible conclusion. The influence (sometimes deterministic influence) of the model of supervision, the context, the expectations of academic departments and disciplines, as well as the work environment may obscure the idea of what a doctorate is (or can be) and the expected associated learning outcomes.

The positioning of doctoral outcomes needs to take into account the progression from undergraduate to postgraduate and in particular doctoral levels of education. The question arises whether academics always understand the differences between levels, and whether these differences can be properly articulated (see for instance the long and intense debates on level descriptors). Doctoral outcomes are not easily defined, but this is to be expected considering that doctoral becoming encompasses ontological, epistemological and methodological development within a typically individualistic, project-based and constructivist learning environment.

If doctoral outcomes are so difficult to pinpoint, an ideal doctoral curriculum will remain elusive because there will always be a differences in emphasis and variance in interpreting and dealing with the learning phenomenon – especially in academic circles and policy. A higher degree of unintended learning outcomes that are not easily measurable in doctoral education may lead to a higher degree of uncertainty regarding the outcomes. By introducing ontology, epistemology and methodology as dimensions of doctoral learning outcomes, a

47

clearer distinction in learning outcome requirements for doctoral students is possible. Hence, it will be possible to develop doctoral curricula that actively address the improvement of doctoral students' learning outcomes.

The curriculum in doctoral education can be viewed as a path of learning. The influence of the stakeholders who determine the doctoral curriculum – such as students, supervisors, disciplines, professions, epistemological concerns, and contract research requirements (Park, 2007) – remains open to debate and warrant future research. In addition, issues of power, as theorised by authors such as Foucault (1972) and Bourdieu (1991) and wider curriculum theory through the lenses of authors such as Scott (2008) need to form part of these discourses, but fall outside the scope of this chapter.

About the author

Liezel Frick is a lecturer at the Centre for Higher and Adult Education, Faculty of Education, Stellenbosch University, South Africa. She can be contacted at this e-mail: blf@sun.ac.za

CHAPTER 3

A Personalised Approach to Improving Students' Learning Outcomes

Andrea Raiker

Introduction

As an educator, I am committed to supporting my students' learning in the best possible way. I am aware that improving students' learning outcomes is currently attracting increased attention. Roles and responsibilities in students' personal, home, academic and work lives are being revised because of changing perspectives on how students learn and, consequently, on how I teach. Research and my own practice have shown that improvement means more than teaching my students to attain higher degree classifications. It embraces all areas of student life, demanding a holistic approach to their university education. This chapter explores how the literature and my own work support personalisation of the curriculum because personalisation allows students to learn better. My various roles in being an educator have allowed me to do this. I have found that personalisation can be achieved through personal development planning (PDP) with students interacting with both academics and peers. Interaction can take place face-to-face or online, for example through the use of e-portfolios. PDP and better learning can be supported through the use of e-portfolios. They enable students to reflect upon and to plan their personal, educational and career development, individually and through relations with others.

The starting point for this discussion on personalization is, paradoxically, traditional university courses in the United Kingdom (UK). In such courses learning outcomes are carefully worded academic statements to which assessment criteria can be directly related. For example, a learning outcome from a Year 1 module on a UK undergraduate degree in Education Studies is: *"By the end of this unit students should be able to analyse the role, purpose and function of education at macro level in today's society with reference to at least two cultural and theoretical teaching and learning perspectives*". The associated assessment criterion is: "*To achieve the learning outcome you must demonstrate the ability to analyse and discuss educational theories and educational policy at macro level, and their outcomes in terms of different levels of success in various communities*". At the end of their degree course students are awarded classifications of first, upper or lower second, third or unclassified, demonstrating concurrence with similar but suitably leveled assessments against academic learning outcomes. To accord with tradition, 'improving students' learning outcomes' would mean developing students' academic abilities so that a greater number could enter the job market having attained the benchmark of a minimum lower second classification. This view is based on an assumption that a function of education is to categorise students to fill jobs that are 'out there' and always will be. A second assumption is that education can sort students according to degrees of intelligence. Another assumption is that there will be graduate jobs for the governments' target of 50% of school leavers entering higher education.

The university curriculum in the UK has traditionally been *discipline* orientated with academics the gatekeepers to subject knowledge, methods of delivery and assessment. This instrumental behaviourist (Jarvis *et al.*, 1998) approach may have led in the past to didactic teaching methods with students being dependent on academics. One configuration of Atherton's (2005c) threefold sculpt of teacher-subject-learner reflects this. The threefold sculpt is an arrangement of learner, teacher and subject that denotes priority. An order of teacher-subject-learner would represent a pedagogy where academics have prime importance because they are the repository of all useful knowledge in curriculum areas. It is the academic's interpretation and delivery of that knowledge that enables students to assimilate what is deemed useful and to represent it in a form to meet learning outcomes through assessment. In this scenario students have little or no autonomy. It was assumed that responsibility for learning lies in them absorbing and retaining what they are told.

However students entering universities already have a complex amalgam of situated academic, personal/social and work experiences, designated by Bourdieu (1989) as *habitus*, an internal structure being the totality and embodiment of an individual's thoughts and experience organized into perceptions of correctness of practices of which learning is one. *Habitus* is unique to the individual. *Habitus* can be related to Heidegger's (1962) *dasein* which translates as being-in-the- world. 'Being' reflects the individual's continual and inexorable state of change. This change can either confirm or develop an individual's authenticity or sense of self, or lead to unauthenticity whereby the individual absorbs others' conceptions that are incompatible with *dasein*.

This suggests that all aspects of students' lives affect their learning. However, the use of the term 'practice' as applied in university education hints at behaviourism and that learning is linear, a simple relationship between cause and effect. Wertsch (1998), building his theory of mediation on the work of Vygotsky (1986), clearly demonstrates that learning is 'fuzzy'. It requires intermediaries of analogy and resource reflecting the individual's experience, faith, trust, goal orientedness, memory, imagination, intentions, and perceptions. The importance of analogy is explored in depth with reference to theoretical and empirical perspectives in Branch *et al.*'s chapter (this volume).

Another perspective that argues against a linear model of learning is given by Meyer & Land (2005) in their threshold concept theory (TCT). Their perception of a threshold concept grew out of an insight that there were some aspects of learning that form portals, the passage through which provides access to landscapes of understanding critical for students' progress. The effect of these aspects is so profound that they can transform students' perceptions of their courses, their disciplines or even their world views. Meyer & Land (2005) argue that these learning landscapes are bounded but capable of expansion at any point or points on that boundary at any time depending on the stimulus.

It is clear from the perspectives outlined above that the perceptions of individuals' abilities to learn cannot be bound by parameters imposed by academics. Furthermore they suggest that the phrase 'improving learning outcomes' should include acknowledgement that the pace and pathways of students' learning are personal. Currently, curricula on the whole follow a 'one size fits all' model of subject knowledge selected by academics and transmitted as lectures, seminars or workshops and supported to a greater or lesser extent by a system of tutorials (Cranmer, 2006). In contrast, a personalised approach would take account of diversity in students' preferences in pace and pathways with the objective of improving their learning outcomes.

Personalised learning is defined as a partnership between student, tutor and other support professionals that connects pedagogy, curriculum and learning support with responsibilities, needs and aspirations, to enable the personal and academic development of students (Atlay *et al.*, 2008). Appropriate learning outcomes would therefore acknowledge module and course objectives for students to understand themselves -

who they are and who they want to be - by exploring their learning approaches and improving their success as students. It could also mean that students become involved in setting their own learning outcomes. Varnava-Marouchou (this volume) explores this process in depth in her chapter.

However, such a personalized approach cannot be considered in a vacuum. Students learn socio-cognitively (Vygotsky, 1986). This is encouraged through group work. Also the spaces in which learning takes place have to be considered in terms of location and resource. This will include electronic resource, particularly e-portfolios which are seen as vehicles for PDP. This chapter describes the e-portfolio concept and discusses the issues in realising a personalized approach to improving students' learning outcome. It will begin with consideration of personalisation and PDP.

Personalisation and PDP

The traditional university course delivered by prescribed, transmissive delivery modes and assessed by examination encourages reliance and routine. However perspectives on how students learn are changing. Furthermore, Kumar (2008) suggests that such an approach has never been appropriate for students to respond creatively, confidently and with autonomy to the demands, risks and opportunities presented by their personal, social and working lives. So the curriculum in higher education institutions needs to respond to a vision of graduates having the skills, self-confidence and self-regulatory abilities to manage their own development both within and beyond academia. The educator engaged with such a curriculum would assume the role of facilitator of process, not producer of product.

In terms of Atherton's (2005c) model of the threefold sculpt the positions of teacher-subject-learner would change to learner-subject-teacher. In this configuration, learner and subject are in close proximity, but the learner has dominance because s/he is constructing the subject. As Atherton observes, 'truth' is no longer regarded as being objective and non-negotiable. It has become subjective and open to debate. In this scenario, the teacher acts as facilitator and is available when needed. In this configuration the learner/teacher distinction could disappear with the learner becoming teacher as s/he develops insights in the area being studied which may or may not be the subject, for example, to develop understanding of self-efficacy.

In this scenario, learning has become personalised. However, the learning outcomes to which this personalized learning is directed must now be defined. There has to be a process whereby students' personalised learning is made explicit to both students and tutors. Students need to know how much they have learnt in relation to learning outcomes, what they still need to know, where this might be found, and what difficulties there might be. Tutors need to know how their students are progressing in relation to learning outcomes so that they can support them in appropriate ways. Personal development planning (PDP) is such a process.

The Higher Education Academy (2009:1) defines PDP as being: *"...a structured and supported process undertaken by an individual to reflect upon their own learning, performance and or achievement and to plan for their personal, educational and career development"*. This equates with Bruner's (1996) concept of 'scaffolding', being the process whereby learners acquire the skills and knowledge necessary to traverse the Zone of Proximal Development (ZPD). According to Vygotsky (1978:86), the ZPD is: *"...the distance between the actual developmental level as determined by independent problem solving and the level of potential development as determined through problem solving under adult guidance, or in collaboration with more capable peers"*. The person providing the scaffold gradually cedes control and support as the learner gains mastery and displays autonomy and responsibility for constructing his/her own learning and even their own learning outcomes (Mezirow, 1997).

I became interested in the concept of scaffolds and their role in personalized learning when writing a two year Foundation Degree (FdA) for teaching assistants (TAs). The objectives of the degree were not only to increase the subject knowledge and related teaching skills of TAs whose primary function was to support classroom learning. An additional objective, arguably more important, was to give the students the confidence and reflective skills to carry out simple classroom action research. This included giving the students the necessary experience of simple methodologies and the educational theory on which these were based. The students would then be prepared on completion of their FdAs to enroll on a third year 'top-up' course leading to a BA Honours degree. Such an approach demands reflection on the part of the tutor. Brüssow & Wilkinson (in this volume) explore the potential value of reflective teaching in understanding students' learning.

The FdA was aimed at widening participation in higher education to first generation, mature students. Thirty-five students were admitted on the basis of classroom experience as well as, occasionally in place of, academic qualifications given at the end of the secondary phase. Some of the students found the transition to university life problematic; others had personal, social and/or work-based issues that impacted on their academic work. All needed support beyond that required by most students entering the university directly from secondary school. These students had to have their learning personalised by myself and other tutors on the course so that they could benefit from the learning opportunities we presented to them. At first we attempted to address their issues in face-to-face tutorials. It soon became obvious that the short time we could offer them was not sufficient to identify their learning needs amongst the complexities of their situations, in other words, their *habiti*. I decided that the way forward was to enable students to identify for themselves their learning needs, and group students with similar needs together. Grouping would provide an environment where students would be encouraged to support each other.

The resource used for identification of learning needs was the Effective Lifelong Learning Inventory (ELLI) (Crick, 2006). ELLI is an online questionnaire, the answers to which produce a spider diagram, or profile, representing scores on seven dimensions that appear to underpin learning. These dimensions are: changing and learning; resilience; learning relationships; creativity; critical curiosity; strategic awareness; and meaning-making. Figure 1 gives an example of an ELLI profile (Crick, 2007).

Each ELLI dimension has a short but precise definition. These definitions were discussed with the students before they were asked to complete a blank profile before accessing the questionnaire which produced a scored profile. This made explicit assumptions and perceptions that were or were not confirmed by the scored profile. These were used as bases for discussion between tutor/students and student/students in tutorials and during a course session. The feedback of the process was in the main positive. For example one student commented that "*Things emerged that you knew you had to work on*". However there were reservations: "*It will only be accurate at the beginning because there will changing and learning due to you being on the course*".

Subsequently tasks were devised in the dimensions of critical curiosity and developing resilience, the two areas most students felt were areas requiring development. In addition students were asked to plan what they wanted to do to address their other concerns, be they social, academic or work-based. These plans formed the bases for tutorial discussion.

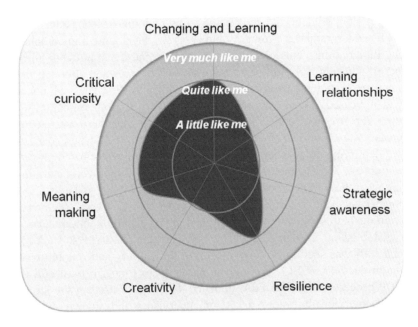

Figure 1: An example of an ELLI profile

Reflection on the course evaluations of the first cohort completing their Honours degree prompted the realization that the students had been scaffolded by PDP processes with the objective of improving their learning outcomes. In terms of scaffolding, the process had been transferred from myself and my colleagues to an online resource and the students themselves. At the time of writing, two cohorts totaling 56 students have progressed from their FdAs to the Honours degree, with seven students achieving First Class classifications and two continuing to study at Masters level. There are many factors behind the students' mastery of their discipline. Their end-of-course evaluations indicated that the personalized approach was contributory to their ability to work autonomously and to self-regulate. As Brüssow & Wilkinson argue (this volume) encouraging students to become active participants in the learning process has positive results.

   The size of the FdA cohorts was small. I decided to embark on a larger research project to identify opportunities for introducing PDP processes supporting the development of autonomy and self-regulation. The objective of this development was to improve student learning outcomes in terms of mastery of their discipline. This research at the University of Bedfordshire in the UK is investigating, over a two year period, student and staff perceptions of initial teacher education (ITE) undergraduates' strengths and areas for development in completing dissertations. This cohort was selected because a significant number of students were not performing as well as expected although the number of students receiving grades equating to First Class Honours had increased. Three research questions emerged from reflection on this. The first was concerned with discovering why there was an increase at each end of the classification spectrum; the second focused on identifying areas where PDP processes might usefully be employed to improve achievement at the lower end; the third involved determining what these PDP processes might be. The ontological and epistemological perspective through which the research was viewed stemmed from the philosophical position outlined in this chapter's introduction.

Establishing a shared language between the researchers, students and staff was seen to be fundamental to the validity and reliability of the project. The ELLI terms given above were found to be useful in PDP processes with the FdA students. These were used in the structured interview questions asked of supervisors and student groups. Qualitative data from these interviews and also tutorial records were subjected to discourse and content analysis respectively. The findings were triangulated with quantitative data gathered from student grades and tutorial attendance. From the outcomes of this, online PDP resources are being devised for student use in November 2009 when students begin their dissertations. The choice of developing online resources rather than those for face-to-face use was made on the assumption that the former would be more likely to encourage autonomous, learning and self-regulation. Qualitative data of supervisor and student perceptions of the PDP online support for dissertations, students' grades and tutorial records will be subjected to appropriate analysis. PDP resources found to be useful in providing access to landscapes of understanding critical for students' progress, using Meyer & Land's (2005) terminology, will then be extended for trial by other departments within the university.

Preliminary findings from the research have suggested that the more able students responded to and enjoyed the passing of control to them by the academics. By this is meant that they appreciated the supervisory process. Up to this point they had attended taught sessions where tutors had greater control of what was learnt and how. Supervisors reported that the more able students were critically curious. They had strategic awareness of their learning. In other words, they could evaluate the strengths and weaknesses in their work and determine how to address the latter. Able students demonstrated creativity in meaning making. They could reflect upon, synthesise and critically evaluate information from a variety of sources, producing insights that were supported by analyses of evidence. Supervisors were unanimous in their perceptions that all students completing their dissertations were resilient. However eight per cent of the 120 students in the cohort did not. Almost one in five did not know how to start their dissertations, despite being given a detailed handbook and lectures on the dissertation process. However, handbook and lectures are indicative of a 'one size fits all' model. Analysis of the qualitative data demonstrated that these students, and some of those who felt able to progress with their dissertations, had *personal* mental 'blocks' that were preventing them from proceeding autonomously. The states of anxiety, confusion and inaction reported by these students placed them in liminal space. This is a term coined by Meyer & Land (2005) to describe a mental state where students are trapped and unable to proceed with their learning. Blocks were principally concerned with inability to focus on a realistic research question, to organise the dissertation, a lack of understanding of the domain specific language and difficulties in adopting an academic writing style. It is suggested that these can be regarded as threshold concepts because, once they were surmounted, most students proceeded with their dissertations without requesting further support from academics. In other words, they had passed through Meyer & Land's (2005) portal and had accessed the dissertation landscape.

It is significant that both students and supervisors perceived that the quality of dissertation supervision was a factor in determining students' grades. Supervisors reported their regret that they were not given training in dissertation supervision. They learnt 'on the job' and were concerned about the quality of their feedback and their ability to grade accurately in comparison to others. However all six supervisors interviewed expressed the view that not all supervisors gave equal support to their students. In the handbook students were advised that they could have five one hour tutorials with their supervisors. Analysis of the tutorial records revealed 60% of the students had two tutorials or less with their supervisors. Content analysis of the tutorial records will give some indication on possible reasons for this.

Discourse analysis of the three student group interviews (17 students were involved) demonstrated that, although attaining a higher grade in their dissertations was a motivator, other drivers were evident. Examples are *"to see how all the bits fit together"*; *"to find out what I think"*; *"to know more about how theory and what I do in the class-*

room work together so that I can help more children learn better"; *"to impress with my depth of knowledge at interview"*. The indications so far are that students had personal viewpoints taking them beyond their courses to the world of work. Another indication from the student group interviews is that some students see little relevance in the dissertation. Their concerns are with performing well during their final school experience which is also graded. The dissertation process begins and ends after final school experience, both of which entail a great deal of preparation and thought. It may be that some students put their efforts into their final school experiences rather than their dissertations because the former appears more relevant to their chosen vocation and their first post. Further research is needed for clarification.

Although secondary analysis of the data is required, it appears that personalized learning could be supported by PDP processes in several areas. It is envisaged that the online resources developed according to the research's findings will be hosted on an e-portfolio platform, a key component of the University of Bedfordshire's blended learning approach to learning, teaching and assessment.

E-portfolios, habitus and the concept of field

E-portfolios (see Figure 2) are the vehicles for PDP processes with electronic content repositories (sometimes known as assets) and publishing functionality (through some form of gateway) to evidence development and learning for internal and external audiences. Individual assets or a selection of assets collected in an electronic portfolio (for example, the presentation space in Figure 2) can be published and disseminated for feedback. An e-portfolio enables a student to reflect on his/her knowledge and understanding, acquired both formally and informally, of personal, social, academic and work-based issues. Through e-portfolios, students can communicate with other learners and academics, and publish multi-media content according to individual learning preferences all within one site (Stephani *et al.*, 2007). This encourages students to consider all aspects of their personal, academic and work-based learning and make creative, evaluated links (Meyer & Land, 2005; JISC, 2008) which could be termed 'Eureka!' moments. Such work is interdependent in that it allows not only individual reflection and content accumulation but also cooperative and collaborative relationships to stimulate thought, analysis and critical evaluation in accordance with Vygotskian (1986) thought.

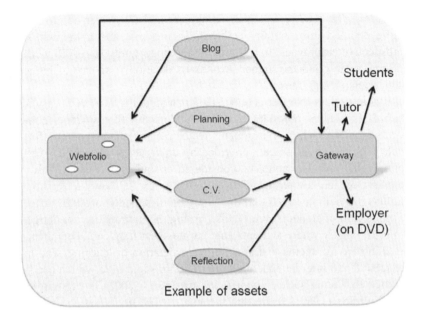

Figure 2: Communication links in a simple e-portfolio

E-portfolios are owned by the students. They choose what is recorded in their e-portfolios and what is published to others. In other words, the individuality of a student's construction of concepts, knowledge and understanding is acknowledged by significant control of that learning being given to them. What is more, the structure of an e-portfolio appears to reflect cognitive processes in that elements of learning are chosen, combined and communicated according to purpose.

Selections of assets can be collected in the presentation space and transferred to identified audiences, examples being other students, tutors and potential employers. An important role of the e-portfolio in accord with the employability and lifelong learning agenda is that selections collected in the presentation space could form the Higher Education Achievement Record (HEAR). This was created in response to the Burgess Group (2007) whose findings concluded that the current degree classification system was no longer it for purpose. A more personalised transcript with evidence of students' strengths and areas for development is required by employers and other authorities, in whose areas students would like to progress, for example, charity work and school governorship. It is anticipated that the HEAR will replace the higher education academic progress files now widely used in UK universities. The HEAR will give employers and the wider community more detailed information on the skills, progress and attainment of prospective employees. It will provide the opportunity to record work-place learning and the higher level skills developed as part of higher education programmes.

It is important that tutors understand that students have very varying *habiti*. It is also important that they understand that students come from equally varying environments which may or may not sit comfortable with the environments provided by universities. Bourdieu (1989) argues that *habitus* cannot be considered or understood isolated from context, which he terms 'field'. Research by Jankowska & Atlay (2008) has demonstrated that university environments, or *fields*, affect engagement of students' with their learning. So universities are obliged to create *fields* where students can learn as best they can. This means creating environments that enable personalization of learning. The interrelated and interdependent nature of *habitus* and *field,* which can be related to Kumar's *'self-opportunity dynamics'* (2008) is exemplified by Bourdieu (1989:43) through metaphor: *"The notion of habitus…is relational in that it designates a mediation between objective structures and practices……. Social reality exists, so to speak, twice, in things and in minds, in fields and in habitus, outside and inside agents. And when habitus encounters a social world of which it is the product, it finds itself as a 'fish in water', it does not feel the weight of the water and takes the world about itself for granted."*

So a university should provide environments that enable students to feel as 'fish in water'. An e-portfolio is an example of such an environment.

Group work and improving students' learning outcomes

The discussion so far proposes that the academic's knowledge of an individual learner's actual level of development is crucially important. Students will be able to learn more only if the tutor relates current learning to it, being constantly ahead and enabling the way forward. In the real world of large cohorts such an approach to individual learning dependent on one-to-one interactions would be difficult to achieve and maintain. A way forward is through the development of structured group work. Research by Jankowska & Atlay (2008) has suggested that the use of creative learning environments has enhanced student engagement at the University of Bedfordshire. They continue by proposing group work is enabled by these environments because they encourage socio-cognitive learning. Vygotsky (1986:57) has written of social cognitive processes: *"Every function in... cultural development appears twice: first, on the social level, and later, on the individual level; first, between people (interpsychological) and then inside the child (intrapsychological). This applies equally to voluntary attention, to logical memory, and to the formation of concepts. All the higher functions originate as actual relationships between individuals."*

It is suggested that group work has an important role to play in achieving improved learning outcomes and also in developing the collaborative skills required by society in general and employers in particular.

Group work can be defined as guided participation (Rogoff, 1990), the activity of individuals having defined aims acting in a particular environment. By organising a cohort into groups, an academic establishes communities of practice (Lemke, 1988) that can be encouraged to be self-supportive through interaction, either online through e-portfolio or face-to-face.

In 2004 I was involved with the design of an environment to support such communities of practice. It involved working with Library Services and the University architect to refurbish a kitchen/dining hall area into an e-learning environment. The original plans outlined a typical ICT suite arrangement with computers in rows. Such an arrangement tended to encourage individual study. I was a member of the planning team and introduced to the discussions my thoughts on Vygotskian principles of socio-cognitivism and my knowledge and understanding of current technologies and students' everyday use of them. In addition I stressed the need to enable students to combine the informal learning techniques used outside the University with formal academic support from librarians, academic tutors, audio-visual and information technology technicians, learning advice and electronic resources. The result was the Learning Hub, a dynamic learning environment where exchange of ideas is encouraged in a comfortable social setting. This has been created by installing good quality sofa and table arrangements for students who have their own laptops, and fixed PCs in hexagonal configurations. Close by is a coffee bar, and students can bring drinks and snacks from there into the Learning Hub. This environment positively encourages interaction and group learning.

The starting point of group interaction, within the Learning Hub or elsewhere, is that all group members know something about the purpose of the group (Seifert, 2002). Participation is sustained in relation to shared understanding, developed through the mediation of a common language and appropriate resources (Wertsch, 1991), of particular common practices of the *field*. In this discussion, *field* is suggested to be the academic and socio-economic learning outcomes of the module or course being studied. *Field* can also be a social learning environment like the Learning Hub. *Fields* are not necessarily exclusive, depending on their nature. As has been proposed in the discussion above, these learning outcomes have been 'improved' by opportunities given to individuals to demonstrate greater personal and academic achievement through a personalized learning approach. Some form of teaching will have been part of pre-group interaction, either face-to-face or through technological resource. However, teaching might not be part of the learning taking place in the group work. As Lave & Wenger (1991:157) observe: *"Learning [is] taken here to be the first and principally the identity-making life projects in communities of practice"*. So in group work, the power inherent in the academic can be handed over to the group so that individuals as participants can construct their learning, their 'identity-making life projects'. According to Kutnick *et al.* (2005), such participation raises achievement, an aspect of improving students' learning outcomes.

This is confirmed by interview data collected by the University's Library Services shortly after the Learning Hub opened in 2006. One student said: *"It's convenient and accessible. It's right near my lecture room and it's near the coffee bar. Perfect!"* Another emphasised how important it was to talk: *"It's very comfortable. I don't just use the computers, it's a good place to discuss work. I've been talking about a presentation I've been doing"*. Another liked the layout and saw its relevance to group work: *"It is so refreshing to see the computers in circles, to have open spaces, and to be able to see round the room, not a wall. I come here every morning to meet my friends and the group work is great. It's relaxing"*. Not all students had such positive views. This student makes it clear that there is still a place for traditional 'quiet' e-learning environments: *"I like it in here because it's usually quiet. I find I can reflect better. The Hub gets too noisy"*. This suggests that choices of various layouts and ambiances are appropriate in a personalised learning approach to improving students' learning outcomes.

These extracts confirm that a significant factor in group work is interaction through spoken language. Following Vygotsky, Bruner (1996:59) points to the *"...joint attention of common objects for the meeting of minds"* through language and the frequent revisiting of concepts via his metaphor of the spiral curriculum. Precision in spoken language is of particular importance because talk forms the principal bridge in students' engagement with their social, academic and work-based environments. It is essential that the quality of talk is commensurate with activities that are generating the learning. Quality can be enhanced by making explicit the structure of discourse through the establishment of rules (Mercer & Littleton, 2007). An example of an appropriate rule is that the views of all participants are sought and considered; another is that explicit agreement precedes discussions and actions. Thus participants first interact on the edge of the community and gradually acquire the understandings and values embodied in language that constitute the community. This can be achieved in face-to-face meetings or online through blog functionality on e-portfolio. In both environments the process reveals a tension between Bourdieu and Wenger. For Bourdieu the setting within which the community of practice operates is a generative infrastructure, whilst for Wenger it is "...*an emerging property of interacting practices.*" (Lave & Wenger, 1991:96). However, as the inseparability of individual and social is an essential part of both Bourdieu's and Lave & Wenger's rubrics, the former's structuring structure which is created by *habitus* is not so far removed from Lave & Wenger's position.

Conclusion

Theoretically and pragmatically, improving students' learning outcomes to meet personal, social, academic and work objectives should become priority for the higher education sector. It appears that a way forward is through a personalised learning approach, using e-portfolio as a vehicle for PDP, incorporating group work and encouraging focused talk. This process is crucial to give students control of their own learning. A university's role in providing the resources to realise that control within the parameters of appropriate learning outcomes, is crucial. As learning in all areas of life is embraced it can become more difficult to establish learning outcomes leading to evidence - currently degree classification - that have meaning for stakeholders, particularly employers. Learning outcomes linked to measurable assessment criteria leading to a degree classification of first, upper or lower second, third and unclassified is simple to transmit and digest. However, as argued above, stakeholders such as employers are already devising their own assessment criteria for employment to which a traditional degree classification is but a gateway. The current degree classification system appears to be no longer fit for purpose.

From a national perspective it is essential for new products and services to be generated and for a competitive edge to be developed during all economic conditions - and particularly during downturns. From an individual perspective young people must be given opportunities to enable adjustment to meet the challenge of a world where they are most unlikely to spend their working lives in a single job or occupation. Therefore graduates must be able to demonstrate, and provide evidence for, flexibility, adaptability, and autonomous and collaborative creativity. They will also be expected to create their own outcomes and devise strategies to achieve them. A university's contribution could be to generate improved graduate learning outcomes that provide more detailed information on the skills, progress and attainment for prospective employees. This will involve the development of opportunities for students to demonstrate autonomy, self-regulation, workplace learning and higher level skills developed as integral aspects of University courses. What is more, such learning outcomes must be capable of transmuting to be meaningful and purposeful throughout a lifetime of learning. This process could begin with students working with the academics and employers to produce course learning outcomes that not only showcase student potential in terms of academic achievement, employability skills and lifelong learning opportunities but can be directly evidenced in the HEAR.

About the author

Andrea Raiker is a Fellow of the Centre for Excellence in Teaching and Learning at the University of Bedfordshire in the United Kingdom. She can be contacted at this e-mail: andrea.raiker@beds.ac.uk

CHAPTER 4

Develop, Use, Extend: Promoting Deep Learning through Pedagogical Progression

Juliet Hinrichsen

Introduction

This chapter introduces an instructional design model which is based on differentiating pedagogical methods aligned to a developmental structure of learning. This structure is proposed to both model and support a deep learning orientation. That is intrinsically motivated learning with an emphasis on extracting and constructing meaning (Bowden & Marton, 1998). The model proposes a cycle of movement through three qualitative pedagogical phases: Develop, Use and Extend (DUE). In each phase the pedagogic focus is different, providing a framework for the design and selection of learning strategies and methods. Progression is iterative and is focussed on the pedagogical design and planning of the learning curriculum with emphasis on the structure and focus of activity design.

In order to contextualise this model the chapter begins with an outline of the author's role as an instructional designer in a UK higher education setting, drawing out the key issues facing academics in curriculum design and delivery as they manifest themselves from an instructional design (ID) perspective. These issues are then reconstituted as principles underpinning the DUE model. The model will be described and two examples of application used to illustrate its operation. The chapter concludes with some reflections on the curriculum design and instructional design processes in an institutional setting.

Instructional design

My work as an Instructional Designer at Coventry University, UK, involves a variety of roles in the teaching, learning and academic development arenas. Sometimes this is at a broad level in terms of advice, workshops, production of exemplars or support materials. However, the real focus of this role is in the design of pedagogic strategies; that is, the specific methods that will be used for delivering a course or the detailed planning of a particular learning activity. This includes the ways in which materials or resources come into play and their most effective design and deployment; the role, type and timing of feedback strategies; and the choice of or improvement in assessment. Typical projects might be course redesign for e-learning delivery, diagnostic analysis to overcome a specific problem such as lack of participation in online discussions; support for the introduction of a particular method such as peer assessment; and participation in institutional-level applied research projects which involve learning methods, particularly with regards to e-learning. The aim in this work is to improve student learning. This is a complex and contested idea, as this volume indicates. However, I shall elaborate on a few principles on which I base this notion as these inform the model I am proposing. I shall also summarise the issues I encounter where I consider these to be typical and significant. Whilst these views will be necessarily bounded by my own perceptions and context, I have worked across faculties in two UK institutions and am partially informed by my own teaching experience in a third. Furthermore, they concur with the perceptions of an instructional design colleague, Amanda Hardy, with whom I have worked at Coventry and who has a background in the US higher education system. To illustrate the process through which these issues come to light I will give a short account of the approach we use in working with academic staff to improve their teaching and learning strategies.

The Instructional Design Conversation

Keppell (2007) argues that the instructional design role is partially that of brokerage between communities of practice (Wenger, 1998). Schwier *et al.* (2007:3) also suggest that the ID process can be a form of cultural or collaborative learning which promotes "*...new ideas and understandings through conversation*". One could therefore characterise the designs which emerge from the process as an expression of a sustained, professional, learning centred conversation.

The ID process begins with a reflective interview to 'knowledge engineer' the learning outcomes whilst fleshing out the learning dimensions and resolving topic order. This involves questioning the academics, using rough diagrams and summary-checks to reflect back and ensure that my own understanding of the issues corresponds to the academic's. Formal course documentation or example materials may be referred to intermittently. Learning methods are not focused on until the subject terrain has been explored and the pedagogical elements identified, thus the academic's teaching is not foregrounded. This helps to avoid a deficit model of educational development. Since particular approaches are not being advocated, value judgements are also minimised. Whether a practitioner wants to use lectures or discovery learning, the emphasis is not on changing their mind but on determining the degree of structure, possible techniques, implications for assessment, ordering of activities, sites and format of support etc which will lead to improved student learning. This process usually leads to constructive and exploratory changes by the academic. However, whilst the agency, expertise and individuality of the teacher is recognised, as well as that of the learner, the focus is neither on the teacher nor the learner but on the 'learning'. That is, the analysis is primarily centred around the intended learning outcomes, albeit sensitive to some of the inherent problematics associated with this term (Barnett, 1994; Nygaard *et al.*, this volume; Jordan & Carlile, this volume).

Issues identified

It seems to me that, increasingly, academics acknowledge that they require support in curriculum development and welcome it. Pressure to teach more people, in less time and to a better standard has contributed to this shift in attitude. However, they are confronted with a bewildering array of philosophical positions, learning theories and learning methods; this complexity and requirement for expertise is superimposed on their existing disciplinary expertise. How should they navigate this terrain? How select from the many ideas and techniques available? And how translate them into a rational plan that will help their students to learn? The instructional design process appeared to be helping with this set of questions; however, time pressures and resource limitations prevent this process from scaling up significantly. This pointed to the need for methodological support.

One overarching set of issues forms around an apparent disjuncture between the conceptions of academics and that of many students about the aims of and approaches to learning in higher education. It would be oversimplistic to suggest that the deep-surface distinction (Bowden & Marton, 1998) completely encapsulates this disjuncture. However, upper grading criteria and academic expectations do tend to cluster around attributes of deep learning. The QAA subject benchmarks for anthropology, for example, include: "*...independence of thought and analytical, critical and synoptic skills*" and "*...a realisation that knowledge is contested*" (QAA, 2008). Yet a typical academic complaint is that many students are too instrumental in their approach. For example, only undertaking work which is perceived as directly relevant to assessment. They also complain of students' tendency to be descriptive rather than analytical, too uncritical and lacking rigour and argument in their essays. These anecdotal observations of disjuncture are supported by recent studies on transition to university. Lowe & Cook, (2003) found evidence that a significant proportion of students struggle with the differences between the expectations, support and style of teaching or learning they have encountered in the past and those prevailing at university. Harvey *et al.* (2006) found that the diversity of student profiles on entry in terms of prior learning experiences, linguistic, literacy and numeracy skills, and personal, social and economic contexts could be disruptive to assimilating into learning communities.

Of course academics are concerned with student development, aiming for movement from where they are on entry to a profile of graduateness with all its implied sophistication (see benchmarking statements, QAA, 2008). I observe two common approaches to this. The first is in the organisation of the curriculum from introductory concepts to more complex theory; this is an epistemologically aligned organisation. The aim is to progress the student from simplicity to complexity by varying the content strategy. The progression is one of intellectual difficulty and the pedagogy tends to relate to that. For example, the lecture content becomes more complex, building on previous content, but the format of the lecture is fairly consistent. The subject of discussion in a seminar may require more depth and the student contribution is expected to be more sophisticated; yet the parameters of the seminar are usually similar to previous stages. Where pedagogical innovation is attempted (e.g. leading the seminar; setting the topic and reading for next week) it is not always developmentally anchored. That is, the student has not been incrementally prepared with the requisite skills.

The second typical scenario I encounter is where the academic adopts constructivist approaches, perhaps using discovery or inquiry methods such as problem-based learning, self-organisation and learner-responsible paradigms such as peer assessment. But they are often reluctant to employ overtly didactic methods which they may feel are incompatible with this philosophy. These are powerful and effective learning methods when appropriately designed. However, that design must reflect a pedagogical purpose and not merely a philosophical position. It is not uncommon for more unstructured or non-mandatory activities to fail through lack of participation or demands by students for the very transmission teaching the academic is trying to avoid. Many of us can relate to the experiences of Marsh *et al.* (2001:390) regarding the introduction of independent learning to a UK university. They write *"...the more we encouraged independence, the greater the support was demanded"*. My perception is that this is attempting too direct a correspondence between the desired characteristics of deep learning and the learning methods chosen. This fails to make a clear distinction between the end objective and the path towards it; that is, between the instructional objective and the instructional design. Kirschner *et al.* (2006:83) emphasise that *"...the epistemology of a discipline should not be confused with a pedagogy for teaching or learning it. The practice of a profession is not the same as learning to practice the profession"*.

Issue	Principle	DUE application
Packed syllabus leads to transmission teaching	Pyramidal learning: place emphasis on firm foundation	Active learning cycle to internalise knowledge → understanding
Lack of preparedness, 'curriculum squeeze' and over-assessment → students' instrumental or surface learning	Developmental curriculum planning	Pedagogical progression to leverage deep learning
'Learner-centred' over-focussed on independent learning	Foreground role of scaffolding in early stages	Frequent and iterative extension rather than summative or continuous extension
Disciplinary, personal or professional preferred methods	Hermeneutic, ideologically tolerant support	Not method specific; guidance framework, not prescriptive
Lack of formal rationale to support teaching & learning decisions	Explicit description of alignment between the syllabus and its delivery	Supports production of an articulated teaching and learning rationale
Lack of correspondence between outcome and methods chosen	Analysis of learning outcomes	Differentiated pedagogy to align methods to outcomes
Lack of time and expertise; need for pragmatic support	Easy to apply, intuitive methodology	Rubric using practitioner-oriented terminology but underpinned by theory
Granularity of pedagogic advice: curriculum design but also 'next week's class'	Flexibility and applicability of support for different curriculum purposes	Theoretical alignment, thus structure can be applied at macro or micro levels

Table 1: Underpinning principles of the DUE model

In both the above examples the learner may be left insufficiently supported or scaffolded; they are, in my view, *under*-didactic by failing to provide weaker students with the appropriate foundational subject and learning skills to develop into either expert practitioners or lifelong learners. Although apparently at opposite ends of the teacher-centred learner-centred spectrum, what these two teaching scenarios have in common is a lack of development in the pedagogic strategy aligned to the methods employed: a lack of pedagogical progression. Table 1 summarises the key issues I have encountered in my professional work, showing them reconstructed as principles underpinning the model and how these principles are applied in the DUE model.

Pedagogical progression

There are increasing calls in the literature for a developmental approach to curriculum design. Haggis, arguing an academic literacies perspective over deep-surface as a normative paradigm, notes that the skills and attitudes promulgated take academics many years and formative experiences to achieve and require explicit modelling in the curriculum (Haggis, 2003). The importance of targeting the first year in the development of graduate attributes is emphasised by Green *et al.* (2009). Thus the idea of transition need not be limited to the movement into higher education but could be extended to include the movement through it. The process of becoming literate within a particular disciplinary discourse is developmental and therefore the university experience should explicitly support such development in its curriculum delivery and design. My use of the term 'development' in this context is not intended to imply Piagetian structural or biological stages, merely a route on a learning journey; in this sense it is organic, more aligned with Dewey's concept of growth (Dewey,1938; Noddings, 2007). I suggest therefore that the 'induction' stage should be regarded as only the beginning of a process of transition which lasts throughout the university experience. The key to improvement of learning outcomes from this perspective, and embedded in the DUE model, lies in the idea of 'pedagogical progression'. That is, a pedagogy designed explicitly to develop and inculcate the kind of learning which can be expressed through competence but which is also fundamentally characterised by "...*a dispositional form of understanding [which] calls for lengthy processes gently encouraging the intended forms of intellectual development*" (Barnett,1994:108). In DUE such development is designed, planned, and unfolds over time.

Differentiating learning

Differentiation facilitates the management of complexity and is a hall-mark of instructional design. The use of the DUE model, as with most other ID models, begins with analysis of the intended outcomes. I have described this analysis as 'differentiation' to give clarity and purpose to this activity. This differentiation is both conceptual and procedural. Conceptual in that it pre-supposes a) that learning is of qualitatively different types, potentially involving different psychological processes (for example, psychomotor, affective and cognitive) and b) that therefore learning methods differ in their effectiveness for these classes of learning. Differentiation is also procedural in that when learning outcomes are deconstructed the sub-goals or stages often consist of a further range of types of learning. Thus, the pedagogic pathway to achievement of a learning outcome requires differentiated planning of learning and teaching methods. There are several taxonomies of learning, most notably Bloom's (Bloom *et al.,* 1956) and SOLO (Biggs, 2008). Whether these or more informal educational categories based on the language of learning outcomes are used, the important aim of this differentiation is to enable constructive alignment (Biggs, 1996) of learning method with type of learning. A simple example would be building longer chains of practice of a manipulative skill (repetition gives kinaesthetic feedback and reinforces neurologically efficient pathways) whereas an attitudinal outcome might require the development of empathy through exposure to authentic narrative accounts, role play etc.

It is also important to stress that, whilst deconstruction of learning outcomes to constituent skills and knowledge is usually the key to designing effective pedagogic strategies, more holistic interpretations of a learning outcome are amenable to facilitation through the DUE structure. This may particularly apply where interpersonal or creative outcomes are sought.

The DUE model

In practitioner terms the DUE rubric signals acquisition of basic constructs or techniques (Develop), application and contextualisation (Use), problematising, reflecting, creating (Extend). These terms are chosen because they are straightforward and part of the vocabulary of all teachers and academics. Furthermore, they are (almost) neutral in relation to teacher or learner perspective and focus instead on the structure of a potential learning event or course. At a theoretical level these terms represent ways of knowing which are seen in DUE as contingent and complementary. These are: the disciplinary content (epistemology), the so-

cially constructed community of practice (culture), and the transformative, identity-shaping learning experience (ontology) (see also Frick, this
volume). Teaching is organised around iterative progression through
these phases. That is, a cycle of learning which literally revolves around
the epistemological, cultural and ontological aspects of what is to be
learned. The integration of these conceptions of learning is also advocated by Dall'Alba & Barnacle (2007). This holistic but differentiated
pedagogical approach can improve student achievement by creating a
formative learning journey which models, in an integrated fashion, these
complementary ways of understanding. It further provides a focus for
instructional design by creating a framework for selecting methods and
organising content in a pedagogically logical way. The purpose of a
loop around a particular topic, concept or skill is to both promote understanding and model the process of acquiring it, enhancing the learner's
metacognition. Such metacognitive awareness characterises deep approaches to learning (Bowden & Marton, 1998). Explicit and planned
pedagogic reworking is a way of leveraging the student's current understanding in the development of deeper or broader understanding and to
prepare for concept or skill linkages. Dewey (1938:75) has suggested
that we: *"...must constantly regard what is already won not as a fixed
possession but as an agency and instrumentality for opening new fields
which make new demands... Connectedness in growth must be [the]
constant watchword."*

Type of Outcome	Develop	Use	Extend
Judgment	Given a workplace scenario, decide between two new job creation options and justify	Determine requirements of new position and needs of relevant departments	Choose a candidate for the post from several CVs; justify choice to committee
Organization	Identify the activities required to conduct field or market research and put into categories (administrative etc) and implementation order	Stage a small event or exhibition; identify issues and make improvements to plan	Identify problems in a workplace scenario; develop a plan to address problems; establish steps and roles required to implement
Communication skills (written)	Write academic or disciplinary equivalents of phrases relevant to essay writing	Write an executive summary from given key points	Write a press statement for a minister or company based on a headline event

*Table 2: Examples of pedagogical progression for different types of
learning outcome*

The idea of revisiting, reworking, or spiral organisation has been variously emphasised over time (Dewey, 1938; Bruner, 1960 in Driscoll, 2000; Davies & Mangan, 2007 in relation to threshold concepts; Wells & Ball, 2008). However, within the DUE framework such an approach is enacted pedagogically as well as in the content; that is, content is revisited and reworked in different pedagogical ways in order to develop understanding in a more complete sense as an outcome and in a more deliberately instructional process. Table 2 shows an example of how a learning activity in different outcome domains might evolve within a DUE structure. (Note that in each phase there could be DUE sub-loops; this is not necessarily a 'bottom level' design.)

Develop

This phase is not a direct attempt to inculcate deep learning but is a preparatory scaffolding towards it, a platform for constructing further knowledge and adding complexity; it is acquisitional in the sense that learners need to develop base knowledge which they can then augment through application and problematise through extension.

A key principle in Develop is the idea of modelling. This modelling can be thought of in structural terms such as schemata or in conceptual terms such as mental models but there are common elements which we could identify in terms of learners' need to develop a representation of what is to be learned. The use of analogical methods could be extremely useful for such modelling (see Branch, this volume). The focus on constructing a framework, whether theoretical, conceptual or procedural, is essentially epistemological. This is where many academics may resort to transmission ('telling') rather than development ('teaching'). Often they simply lack an appreciation of alternative ways of facilitating content knowledge and particularly fail to appreciate the inefficacy of passive learning. They may also feel that didactic methods are 'low-level' or politically incorrect in a climate of learner-centred and constructivist discourses. It is interesting in this respect to look at the work of Kirschner *et al.* (2006:83) who review empirical investigations into the effects on learning (as defined by factors such as comprehension and retention over time) of guided and non-guided methods – such as worked examples versus discovery learning. Their conclusion is emphatic: that guided instruction is of more benefit to novices: "*In so far as there is any evidence from controlled studies, it almost uniformly supports direct, strong instructional guidance rather than constructivist-based minimal guidance during the instruction of novice to intermediate learners.*"

Whilst there are critiques to be made of their assumptions, their plea for practitioners to take note of the well-established findings from cognitive psychology on areas such as memory, acquisition of new knowledge and its relationship to understanding is one endorsed within DUE. An illustration of how an appropriate guidance strategy can affect the way a task is approached by the learner, and their consequent deep or surface learning, is provided by Cerdan *et al.* (2009). They saw a positive effect on comprehension of a text by those students who were given high-level questions, designed to require inference across several paragraphs, compared to those given low-level questions whose answers required single propositions and had a verbatim relationship with the text. In DUE, the Develop phase is pedagogically geared to presentational structures or methods and learning through progressively designed activity with contextualised feedback.

Use

The Use phase is concerned with the application of skill, knowledge or theory to a professional or disciplinary domain and thus focuses on the issue of transfer of theory to practice and skill to context. Experiential approaches, progressive complexity and authentic context are key attributes of pedagogic planning. Increasing skill and 'discernment' through planned dimensions of variation (Bowden & Marton, 1998) is important to build the flexibility required for real-world competence. Learning activities with multiple dimensions, or employing skills in parallel, would also be an appropriate way to increase complexity in the application domain. However, application is not constrained by a narrow competence or performative interpretation; the term 'use' also implies a socio-cultural context and the Use phase involves initiation into communities of practice and associated discursive practices or literacies. Developing a professional or disciplinary 'view' of a topic, situation or problem (for example engaging with threshold concepts) is important, thus culturally contextualised and authentic learning situations are key dimensions of learning activity. The importance of a structured progression of knowledge development is supported in research into acquisition of threshold concepts (Meyer & Land, 2005). Such concepts are held to be transformative and paradigmatic shifts which underpin expert understanding of a discipline. Davies & Mangan (2007) found that introducing such concepts before students had sufficient pre-requisite knowledge caused problems of understanding. Whilst the Develop phase is more concerned with how the student 'sees' the subject, the Use phase fosters appreciation of how experts see it and how clients, users or society may experience it.

Extend

Two ideas are implicit in the concept of extension. One is normative: the promotion and demonstration of the set of characteristics of graduateness, deep learning or expert practitioner which are specified in the upper grading criteria of learning outcome statements and benchmarks. Although subject to disciplinary interpretation (Green *et al.*, 2009) they cluster around notions of critical thought and analysis, problem identification and resolution, expertise and creativeness. Depending on the overarching DUE phase this may be a smaller step such as finding a research question in a paper which has previously been worked in terms of comprehension, or it may involve improving or creating a complex artefact such as a professional best practice statement (see Table 3c). Extension requires minimising structure and migrating responsibility for learning to the student. This phase therefore lends itself well to non-guided methods and the cluster of practices and intentions described by the term 'independent learning'.

The other sense of extension is relative, personal and individual. This is about developing the relation between self and the knowledge acquired: opinion, values, judgment, self-awareness and responsibility. Extension is the curriculum element that pushes the student "beyond the limits of competence" (Barnett, 1994). In this sense it represents the ontological phase in the DUE cycle of instructional design.

Case One: Curriculum development with DUE

This example comes from a new planned module on health risk in the MA Health Communication. Students come from health-related areas in design or marketing, education and management. One of the overarching aims is to re-orientate students' initial understanding of the concept of risk to a more differentiated and complex appreciation of its political and cultural situatedness and to arrive at an informed understanding of their own view of risk and how this impacts on professional practice. The tables below indicate how the 'Develop Use Extend' structure underpins the learning methods chosen and shows an iterative loop in the Develop phase.

Topic area learning sub-goals	Learning method	Analysis
GLOBAL, ORGANISATIONAL, GROUP, INDIVIDUAL CONTEXTS • Grasp main theories • Identify & appreciate stakeholder perspectives	Locate concepts on concept map. Guided reading. Mini-lectures (20 minute summaries).	DEVELOP Simplified explicit structure to model field of study. Trade wider reading in Develop phase for secure reading: reduction in reading requirement weeks 1-3; requirement to articulate understanding through peer-viewed blog summaries; learning from other students' summaries; opportunity for tutor redirect and elaboration based on students' understanding of key readings.
RISK PERCEPTION, ASSESSMENT & EVALUATION • Perceive cultural situatedness of risk	International case; stakeholder analysis.	USE Reinforcing comprehension through immediate opportunities to recognise concepts encountered in abstract within concrete example. Use own notes to make analysis.
• Identify practical manifestations of risk • Introduce analytical framework	Discussion. Add entry to reflexive portfolio.	EXTEND Discussion introduces alternative viewpoints and conclusions. Requirement to defend own position, critique that of others. Reflection on learning and perceptions of risk.

Table 3a: Health Risk Management: Develop

This stage was the one requiring the most reworking from the initial plan of lectures and seminars. The reading list was extensive and was redesigned in several ways: 1) selection of key text from the essential bibliography (focused reading); 2) provision of question sheets to guide reading (integrative reading); 3) alignment of remaining bibliography to specific activities (distributed reading). The idea of a concept map of topics and issues was introduced (advance organiser, see Driscoll, 2000). This representational diagram will be revisited as a summative exercise in the extension phase when the student reworks their own version of the map, facilitating metacognition of their own learning process and reflection on understanding. The academic had a range of excellent case studies so the conversation was focused on drawing out and differentiating their importance and the principal learning points. The key to this phase, then, was on alignment of the pedagogical purpose of each case to the design of the case study activity. These learning points could then be applied to an authentic context (work based learning task).

Topic area learning sub-goals	Learning method	Analysis
RISK COMMUNICATION • Recognise factors of success or failure • Develop cultural awareness in communicating risk	Case study analysis. Apply analytical framework to examples.	Differential analysis of learning focus to design activity on case studies most effectively. a) choice of individual, paired or group activity (is learning intended attitudinal, analytical or creative?) (b) differentiated organisation of groupwork based on focus of learning i.e. same or different resource; same or different task (is focus of learning to widen perspectives, confirm issues or show effects of different approaches?) .
HEALTH COMMUNICATION CAMPAIGNS • Appreciate issue of trust in sources of health information • Work through process of communication • Raise awareness of ethical dilemmas	Develop a campaign plan. Document process in portfolio.	Apply principles to a professional situation (work-related topic).

Table 3b: Health Risk Management: Use

Topic	Learning methods	Analysis
BEST PRACTICE • Decision-making • Balancing stakeholder needs • Evaluation and judgment of risk • Personal and professional integrity	Create best practice statement. Develop own concept map of communicating risk and add to portfolio.	Alteration of penultimate activity from review of best practice (summative exercise) to create best practice statements (constructive exercise). Student re-work of concept map to reflect own perceptions, issues, relationships and questions (summative reflective exercise). Alteration of assessment to replace one of two essays (analytical or organisational assessment) with reflexive portfolio (reflective analytical, formative and summative assessment).

Table 3c: Health Risk Management: Extend

The Emphasis in the Extend phase was on promoting independent as opposed to merely advanced work by students. Thus two 'create' activities were introduced (best practice policy; personal concept map) supplemented by metacognitive activity (reflection).

Case Two: Diagnostic use of DUE

Here I was approached by an academic for some ideas on the assessment of a final year undergraduate module on Managing Change. This course was designed to challenge students' existing perceptions of the change process by problematising the macro, systemic approaches they had previously encountered and introducing a micro, holistic and ecologically framed approach; thus, a shift in their mental models of the consultancy role was a fundamental objective. These factors (final year, restructuring existing knowledge, focus on values, reflective practice) place the module in the Extend phase of the curriculum. The structure of the course consisted of a short lecture series shifting to use of learning sets. Seminar work was active and engaging and the academic demonstrated infectious enthusiasm, a sensitive appreciation of learner need and a good understanding of active learning methods. Much of the learning was concentrated on case studies and scenarios which were analysed and discussed. The last part of the module examined the role of consultants and the assumptions, implications and outcomes of various approaches to an organisational intervention, again through case analysis. The assessment consisted of one essay and a portfolio. The portfolio included various reflective pieces and a requirement to prepare three essay plans for the topics not chosen for the written essay. In addition to giving assessment advice about making the portfolio online, using a DUE framework I was also able to make the following diagnostic observations:

Diagnosis	DUE rationale
Early feedback on the essay plans (academic or peer) would be important.	Develop before Use and Extend
The skills component of the consultancy role being explored was underdeveloped both in the seminars (analytical, discursive) and in the assessment (textual). The introduction of role play and communication tasks, with feedback from other students and reflection-after-the-event, would give students a more experiential and therefore deeper understanding of the issues as well as provide insights into the impact of their own interpersonal and communication strengths and weaknesses. This is consistent with the consultancy approach being explored.	Differentiation of types of learning. Augment Use phase
An Extention activity was lacking. The final case analyses were progressive in terms of content difficulty but had the same learning structure as before. (Academic's) proposal: students produce their own consultancy plan for a given organisational scenario. This to be added to the portfolio.	Augment Extend with summative, constructive exercise

Table 4: Managing Change

The academic could not only see the benefit of these changes but felt that they created a better alignment with what she had been trying to achieve. This confirms that DUE supports what academics may be doing intuitively but without the benefit of an explicit structure and rationale which can guide their choices.

Applications

A DUE framework can be applied at programme level, course level or topic or skill level. It can be used as a structure to model a threshold concept or to design an activity or learning object. It also has potential to be used to aggregate learning objects into a learning design or pedagogical template, thus having indexing and metadata implications. Amanda Hardy and I have also used DUE effectively to design a staff development workshop on 'Designing for Active Learning'. Its use as a diagnostic tool has been illustrated and offers great potential to support the work of educational developers, learning technologists and academic writing or study skills advisors. It is also a methodology which would complement the use of curriculum mapping techniques (see Huet *et al.*, this volume). Further development of the model for practitioner application is planned, along with research on use and perceived effectiveness.

Discussion

Although not specifically a staff development intervention but rather a curriculum development process, DUE can have, in my experience, a fundamental impact on academic learning and professional development as a by-product of that process. The new ways of 'seeing' described as evidence of transformative learning in students (Bowden & Marton, 1998) is something I have noted anecdotally in academics. When a focussed discussion about learning grounded in the discipline takes place, my belief is that this has longer-lasting change consequences for the individual and more practical impact on the student than with conventional staff development workshops.

But how can processes such as these be implemented in a higher education institution? Clearly there are significant infrastructure issues, particularly with regard to the modularisation of courses, making it difficult to plan for student development or pedagogical progression (Green *et al.*, 2009). The analytical approach also results in a magnification of the learning process, with more concentration on each element; this is tricky when time is limited and has implications for the scope of syllabus, especially in year one. I have argued that it is necessary to have the intended learner transformation as a focus of design and not merely as a statement of output. Such a learning orientation needs to be explicit in the curriculum design process at the earliest stage: the validation or approvals process is therefore the key area to target improvements which will impact on the learner. Generating a focus on a development oriented curriculum at this early stage of course design would have a number of specific advantages. Firstly, the process of producing a detailed document or learning map requires choices of learning method to be rationalised, creating a shift from the attributes of the method to the reason for it in a specific context. Secondly, the ground is prepared for evaluation and quality enhancement activity as each course sets out its learning intentions in a way that enables research, reflection and improvement to take place. Thirdly, the requirement to produce an instructional design as part of the course documentation would create a focal point for a development intervention which would have maximum efficacy (time of need), impact (site of need) and least resistance (pragmatic, not ideological).

The indications are that the introduction of such a process could develop expertise, both in individuals and collectively, of learning methods, their appropriateness and effectiveness in different contexts, and broadens knowledge of the methods on offer and the learning theories behind them. In this way a community of practice can develop and a professional culture may be fostered which supports a developmental view of the curriculum. Schwier *et al.* (2007:3), in their review of instructional design practice in Canada, suggest that "*clients working with instructional designers in development projects are actually engaging, as learners, in a process of professional and personal transformation that has the potential to transform the institution*".

Acknowlegements
Amanda Hardy, Instructional Designer, Coventry University UK, for her collaboration on the practical application of DUE. Academic staff: Dr Sandra Harrison; Dr Ismail Ibrahim; Ms Tina Bass Critical reader: Professor Christopher O'Hagan.

About the author
Juliet Hinrichsen is an Instructional Designer at Coventry University, UK. She can be contacted at this e-mail: j.hinrichsen@coventry.ac.uk

CHAPTER 5

Developing a Coordinated Strategy to both Encourage Innovation and Improve Students' Learning Outcomes

Paul Bartholomew, Stuart Brand & Luke Millard

Introduction

The improvement of student learning outcomes is not something that emerges without the agency of faculty staff. In this chapter we describe how a coordinated strategy to support staff members within the Faculty of Health at Birmingham City University has provided enhanced opportunities for the development of new approaches to improve students' learning outcomes. This is a large faculty comprising 7000 students and 400 staff. We seek to demonstrate how, through policy-driven investment in innovation, we have created effective mechanisms to deliver on institutional learning and teaching development aims, including the improvement of student learning outcomes.

The four initiatives we report are the:

- Faculty Learning and Teaching Task Group
- Curriculum Innovation Fund
- Learning Partnerships Development Unit
- Module Makeover workshops

Table 1 provides a brief comparison between these four initiatives that underpin our strategy. As Table 1 demonstrates, we sought to provide a range of initiatives to attract staff at various stages in their own development in learning and teaching practice. We were also keen to offer opportunities that would allow even those with relatively less time to commit to participate in these supported initiatives.

Initiative	Description	Requirements	Parallel	Funding
	outcomes.		across the Faculty.	£1500 to fund project requirements.
Curriculum Innovation Fund	A scheme that makes funds available to support small project needs.	Application is via submission of a project proposal.	No effect on teaching commitment.	Each applicant can apply for up to £1500 to be spent over the life of the project.
Learning Partnership Development Unit	A new unit was set up and provides additional leadership in the development of innovations in learning and teaching.	Appointments have been through competitive application process.	New posts with a negotiated teaching load. The primary purpose of the role is to support Faculty staff in their academic practice.	The funding of four Senior Academic posts.
Module Makeover Workshops	A series of workshops designed to offer guidance on module redesign activity.	No require- ments, the workshops are open to all who wish to attend.	No effect on teaching or other commitments.	Modest funding for refreshments for participants.

Table 1: Comparison of initiatives in the coordinated strategy

We have found that the development by staff of innovations that yield improvement in student learning outcomes work best when supported by the agency of enthusiasts and some funds to catalyse such activity. This conclusion is echoed by Waite *et al.* (this volume) who note that innovations to support student learning are well served by these factors.

Developing a coordinated strategy

In order to explain the rationale for these initiatives, we need to offer some context. In 2000 the Faculty of Health was inspected, through subject review, by the Quality Assurance Agency (QAA), which identified a number of key problems. By early 2005, this same part of the University had been awarded, on behalf of the institution, a £4.2 million Centre for Excellence in Teaching and Learning (CETL) and in 2006 experienced a QAA Major Review inspection that revealed it to be the best provider of non-medical health care education in the region. *"Across all pre-registration and postgraduate programmes, in both academic and practice settings, a wide variety of innovative approaches are used to enhance effective teaching and learning"* (QAA Major Review, June 2006:Unpaginated).

This change principally occurred because the profile and resourcing of learning and teaching had been raised within the Faculty, through a sustained drive from the Associate Dean (Academic) who had convinced the Dean that focused funding on learning and teaching could transform the Faculty's ability to respond to students' learning needs. From 2003 onwards this Faculty funding was deployed to develop a coordinated strategy for the recruitment and support of staff to act as agents for the delivery of this agenda. A detailed description of the initiatives shown in Table 1 is provided below.

Learning and Teaching Task Group

Between seven and twelve staff, each of whom maintain a full commitment to the delivery of curriculum are selected each year as Fellows to form the Learning and Teaching Task Group. They are funded to spend 40% of their time on the Task Group developing specific projects and are expected to integrate this with their normal duties in the remaining 60% of their time. The goals to be achieved are agreed at the time of appointment. Selection of fellows through interview is on the basis of not only quality of proposed project or fit with a Faculty-commissioned project, but also commitment to engagement with colleagues. A further feature of the selection process is our desire to ensure interdisciplinarity.

The Task Group has monthly supportive meetings where progress is shared, ideas exchanged and common problems identified. An external consultant, John Cowan, proactively responds to issues and challenges raised or not raised in the discussions. However, Task Group Fellows retain the authority to reject any or all suggestions from colleagues or the consultant, since eventually they will be accountable for the impact of their project on the learning experience of their students in the Faculty.

Many of the issues and challenges that are declared and receive attention in Task Group meetings have been generic in nature. Examples have focused on immediate and long-term evaluation, provision of effective ICT support and other aspects of virtual learning environments, the use of flexible learning spaces and the assessment of cross-modular competencies. They thus have benefited from joint consideration and from general inputs from our consultant, during which members not only manage to offer helpful suggestions to colleagues, but have seen suggestions in regard to their own issues in the solutions offered to fellow members. This perhaps has assisted the intent for the Task Group to collaborate so that those working together produce products that are greater than the sum of their individual parts. The work of Gronn (2002), on concertive action talks about the additional dynamic that is the product of conjoint activity wherein people pool their experiences and knowledge for greater effect. This is a key component of our philosophy at the University and is actively encouraged through some additional cross-faculty tasks set for the Task Group.

As we have evolved the Task Group over four iterations, we have moved to a model whereby each Fellow is asked to identify from the outset fellow travellers with whom they will work. These are colleagues who are supportive of the project goals and willing to make some supportive commitment. This is an anticipatory variation of the networker/facilitator role identified by Clutterbuck (2003).

Through this mechanism, rather than solely through *post hoc* dissemination, we increasingly expect educational innovation to spread contagiously and contemporaneously and for all concerned to exploit personal and professional development opportunities. Sustained rates of uptake of an innovation in a way that is analogous to infection is also noted by Wallace (this volume) where she reports that recruitment onto a project was most successful where it was viral in nature. We also require all Fellows to specify the nature of the desired change that will occur within the typical twelve-month period of service to the Task Group. By way of a demonstration of this contagious spread, we have identified that the most recent iteration of the Task Group has directly: involved participation of 218 academic and support staff; affected 72 modules across 12 programmes; and impacted upon 3100 students.

The decision to require the identification of fellow travellers at the point of application was informed by our experiences of many of the projects within the earlier iterations of the Task Group. We had seen little evidence that even arguably effective *post hoc* dissemination of good practice had provided wide ranging or immediate effects in our Faculty. We therefore opted for the immediate support of innovators by relatively small units of teachers, who had displayed an interest from the outset in an innovative development to which they were sympathetic. It was our hope and expectation that these fellow travellers might be infected with some of the enthusiasm, methodology and expertise of the innovator with whom they are partnered; and that they might subsequently, and again contagiously, spread an approach of which they had first hand knowledge to members of their school or department, when they judged that it could be timely and relevant.

From the outset, iterations of the Task Group have been purposefully inclusive, with the opportunity to apply being made available to any member of staff who contributes to the students' learning experience. Successful applicants include administrators, technical support staff, librarians and clinical staff. This inclusive approach has been adopted as a means of ensuring wider engagement, for adding a different perspective to the project discussions and as a way to acknowledge the pivotal roles such individuals play in supporting the learning of our students.

Curriculum Innovation Fund

It is important, we believe, to offer real opportunities to those who are not in a position to make the more substantial commitment of applying to join the Task Group. The Faculty offers finance to support curriculum innovation funded (CIF) projects, through which staff acquire a small amount of funding to develop a curriculum innovation. These funds are used in a number of ways including to fund the creation of new resources or to fund a conference trip to inform or disseminate aspects of their practice.

Learning Partnerships Development Unit

The two initiatives above, particularly the Task Group, have contributed to the development of a creative and permissive culture with regard to curriculum development and delivery. This culture has inevitably become centred upon people and their practice. It became apparent to the Associate Dean responsible for these initiatives that the people who have been so empowered to engage in new approaches to improving students' learning outcomes might subsequently be diverted from such work. This could happen for example as they take on leadership roles within the organisation, or indeed as they take up senior positions elsewhere.

Consequently, a decision was taken to create a career path that would be attractive to these individuals, thus ensuring that career progression into a leadership role was not separated from an opportunity directly to support the learning and teaching agenda of the Faculty. In April 2004, four members of academic staff were appointed to a position of Senior Academic for Learning and Teaching; these individuals were convened along with a Project Manager within a new unit – the Learning Partnerships Development Unit (LPDU). Three of the four individuals appointed to the Senior Academic posts had been Task Group Fellows, as had the Project Manager (a Fellow who had been a member of the administrative staff when appointed to the first iteration of the Task Group). This LPDU acts as the principal focus for the University's CETL and manages the CIF projects. Additionally, chairing of the Task Group has been devolved to the Project Manager based within the LPDU.

Module makeover workshops

The fourth initiative underpinning our coordinated strategy to support improvements in student learning outcomes through the development of the learning, teaching and assessment competencies of our staff is the Module Makeover Workshop initiative. This initiative has run as a series of half-day workshop sessions, hosted by the Associate Dean in collaboration with colleagues drawn from the Task Group and beyond, whereby staff would bring particular curriculum design and delivery challenges for exploration and discussion. The role of the hosts has been to reassure, with expertise and most importantly authority, that the potential changes that emerged from the workshop are permissible. In Huet *et al* (this volume), the authors also describe how development workshops have helped staff to design well-aligned modules.

Facilitating a creative culture

The clear communication of permission, as described above, remains very important in stimulating innovation in curriculum design and delivery. Indeed, one of the factors we have identified as a potential barrier to innovative practice is an adherence to a culture of compliance, whereby staff feel inhibited to make changes to curriculum design or delivery for fear of encroaching upon some academic regulation or requirement of a professional, statutory or regulatory body. In our experience, such fears are just as likely to be based upon false assumptions as on reality.

The need constantly to reaffirm such permission has become apparent and this has underpinned, in part, a major, institution wide initiative to transform the design of curricula.

Supporting curriculum development

In pedagogical terms, higher education has advanced markedly in recent years. It has moved beyond the era in which the few expert practitioners in each institution gather together in a specialist unit, from which workshops are run to heighten general staff awareness, and whose advice is available to those individuals who seek it. Instead, there now exists the potential for distributed leadership in the development of practice with the potential to improve student learning outcomes. This arises from: the advent of specific postgraduate courses in learning and teaching in higher education; the encouragement to apply for well-planned National Teaching Fellowships (Higher Education Academy); and the engagement of most staff across the University in self-evaluation as a routine part of the processes of annual and long-term review. We might argue that this situation evidences the effectiveness of such central units and the programmes they deliver, in having led to significant institutional development.

We judged that, in our Faculty, we had many such potential leaders. We rated them well able to plan and undertake the next developments for which they were willing to be responsible, to seek out autonomously the external inputs which might assist them, and to support colleagues who might agree to join with them in such efforts. This notion of distributed leadership is enshrined within a 2003 report by the National College for School Leadership, which sees distributed leadership as "an emergent property of a group or network of interacting individuals". The personal transformation of the participants from workers or followers into leaders of change is an exciting by-product of this work.

It could be argued that one of the drawbacks of distributing leadership away from central units is that some opportunity to draw upon the experience of other disciplines across the whole university may be sacrificed. To avoid this drawback, strong links between the Faculty and the central unit have been maintained; indeed all three of the authors have migrated to positions at the centre in order that they can now actively develop University-wide networks that aim to ensure cross-fertilisation between those disciplines.

As a further feature of this work we have sought purposefully to embrace externality by securing the services of an external consultant to support our work. We find a number of advantages in this role, in reality that of a critical friend, who can offer advice and suggestions that may be accepted or rejected. Clutterbuck (2003) identifies this role as the empowering guardian, but we believe it goes beyond that. For example, in support of the Task Group, the consultant is able to argue his points more firmly than would have been the case were he to be the one to decide what decision would then be made regarding his proposals. Additionally, it frees the consultant to argue similarly with Deanery on behalf of individual Task Group Fellows, or the Group as a whole and again more freely than might otherwise be the case. In our example it is also worth noting that the critical friend has little knowledge of the subject area; however, he has the educational knowledge to guide and challenge participants.

Developing innovative approaches to curriculum delivery

In this next section of the chapter, we offer a context-rich, personal account from one of the authors, Paul Bartholomew who, as a result of being supported by the initiatives we have described, has successfully improved student learning outcomes and advanced his career as a consequence:

"I joined Birmingham City University in August 2001 and coming from a health care profession, my identity was initially centred upon my role as a clinical practitioner. This identity, once placed within a context of supported engagement with a focused learning and teaching agenda, shifted away from the specificity of a subject discipline to one which was centred upon the trans-disciplinary, scholarly activity of learning and teaching.

Fundamental to this transition was the opportunity to apply for a Faculty of Health Learning and Teaching Task Group Fellowship. My motivation to apply emerged from my exposure to the educational development programmes offered by the central education development unit. Through engagement with these programmes, I became aware of a need to develop my educational practice and developed a desire to bring to fruition ideas for curriculum development that emerged as a consequence of this activity.

As a consequence of a competitive application process, successful Task Group candidates were aware that the opportunities we had secured for ourselves came at the expense of those others who had applied but had been unsuccessful. This understanding, along with an appreciation of the significant financial support that bought our two days per week of remission from other duties, served to develop a sense of responsibility to deliver on our ideas.

We had been entrusted with accountability for the delivery of our innovation. This contrasts quite strongly with less well supported patterns of innovative practice in higher education, whereby lone enthusiasts must juggle a myriad of competing responsibilities with far less explicit expectation that their innovations in learning and teaching will be developed and deployed in a systematic way.

Given the journey that is being described it may be prudent, at this stage, to share the nature of and specific context for the innovation that I proposed at the point of application and that eventually shaped my career.

My example of an innovation supported through the Task Group initiative

The first module I 'inherited' when joining Birmingham City University was a 36 credit module in radiography. During my first year of coordinating and teaching on the module, I became dissatisfied with the traditional didactic model that was still dominant. I resolved to try to redesign this facet of the student learning experience so as to deliver the following improvements to students' learning outcomes:

- encourage a greater degree of independent learning;
- create curriculum space for introduction of problem solving activities;
- further align the 'classroom' experience with the clinical skills required for practice;
- capitalise on the social nature of learning by promoting exploratory talk, discussion and small group work.

The specific challenges for myself and close colleagues in achieving these goals were the relatively large size of the group (90 students) and the session delivery environment (a traditional lecture theatre). These challenges were addressed by developing two distinct phases to the innovation: information acquisition and knowledge construction.

Phase 1: The information acquisition phase – encouraging independent learning

The module required that certain indicative content be communicated to the student group; this had previously been done through reliance on didactic lectures, which left little room for the activities detailed above. I decided to use information and communication technology (ICT) to liberate the classroom from an information transmission model by shifting this process into the student study time. This shift was undertaken after full negotiation with and permission from the target student cohort.

This ICT innovation took the form of providing a CD ROM for each student containing a set of interactive multimedia presentations developed with the Microsoft Producer® software package. These presentations comprised an image rich PowerPoint® presentation, associated web links and a small video window that displayed the lecturer video narration. This combination of features is particularly suitable for diagnostic radiography due to its visual nature and intensive use of radiological images. Within the presentation, areas of interest are highlighted in real time in synchronisation with the narration and controlled by the student, who can pause, advance and review the material at will.

Phase 2: The knowledge construction phase
– making the best use of precious class contact time

Once I had facilitated the process of students acquiring information in their own study time, I was able to dedicate the classroom contact time to knowledge construction activities. Each classroom session followed on from a specific multimedia presentation and consisted of a series of activities that allowed the students to apply the information they had acquired to clinical scenario based problems. This allowed for explicit linkage of theory to practice and an opportunity to reinforce learning through problem solving and thus improve students' learning outcomes.

These scenarios and activities were designed to be undertaken in small groups, thus promoting discussion and initiating exploratory talk between peers. Since the module assessment includes answering questions based upon clinical scenarios these activities were always likely to appeal to the students' strategic instincts. This model of information acquisition followed by knowledge construction and application has been well received by the large student groups concerned.

My fellow travellers

Although the first iteration of the Task Group did not place as much emphasis upon early identification of fellow travellers as subsequent iterations, the most successful of the early projects did utilise this approach and so informed the decision to make this a requirement for applicants to later iterations of the scheme. In my case, ten out of twenty immediate colleagues engaged directly with the innovation; four of these went on to adopt a similar model for their own modules.

As the innovation matured and generated evidence of effectiveness this model of teaching began to be adopted across other courses and indeed other faculties.

As I now reflect upon the willingness of my colleagues to engage with me in this work, I believe that the sharing of evidence of effectiveness, though important, does not fully account for the degree of buy-in the project elicited. I have formed a view that an important factor in the dissemination of this work has been the advocacy of Faculty management as manifested through my membership of the Task Group. The fact that my innovation was a Faculty-sponsored project ensured that barriers to change were less rigid than may have been the case had I been perceived as a lone innovator.

However, the importance of accumulating and using evidence of enhancement was of crucial importance in other arenas. Just as the deployment of video lecture technology was my innovation, the Task Group itself was the innovation of the sponsoring Associate Dean and my evidence of effectiveness doubled as evidence of value of the Task Group initiative. At this level, such evidence has been fundamental in securing sustainable funding for this type of activity. As I reflect upon the role my Task Group participation had on my subsequent career, I regard the generation of credible evidence of effectiveness achieved by the investment made to be central in becoming regarded as an individual through whom investment for change could be initiated and delivered.

The innovative activity outlined above led to my selection as an institutional nominee for a Higher Education Academy National Teaching Fellowship (2004). This nomination was successful and I became the University's first National Teaching Fellow. This external recognition catalysed my transition from worker or follower to a leader of change as more of my time became devoted to the agency of change and the scholarly activity of learning and teaching. This transition is reflected and evidenced through my taking a central role in the authoring of the institution's successful bid for CETL status, appointment as a Senior Academic for Learning and Teaching within LPDU; appointment to the role of Senior Learning and Teaching Fellow for the Faculty and most recently a move to a University-wide role which has leadership responsibility for a redesign of our entire portfolio of undergraduate provision."

Evaluation and outcomes

Faculty Deanery has looked for a measurable and concrete return for its resourcing of the Task Group projects in terms of the tangible value added to the student learning, or to the student learning experience. It is thus necessary to judge every project, in accordance with the rationale for selection and funding, on the basis of the discernable impact on programmes within the Faculty, on Faculty staff including the project holder, and to a lesser extent by accepted conference presentations and publications in hand or accepted.

As a faculty that recruits staff primarily on the basis of their professional or vocational expertise, few applicants for appointment to the Task Group have come with much experience of educational evaluation, or of writing for publication in educational journals or at educational conferences. These demands are therefore aspects of working within the Task Group that have featured in the Group's monthly discussions together, and in individual contacts with the consultant, where these have been requested.

The importance of this development of capability for evaluation is clear: on the conclusion of each project, Deanery has expected project holders to include in their report, with brief details:

- The number and disciplinary spread of staff actively engaged with the project holder.
- The number and spread of modules or programmes affected or potentially affected in tangible terms which are specific to each particular project.
- Student module evaluations and improvements in student assessment outcomes.
- Improvements in some aspect of the working lives of staff.
- Papers published, drafted or in hand.
- Conference presentations.

Part of the agenda for monthly Task Group meetings has been to obtain oral accounts of progress under all of these headings, to offer supportive advice when certain items seem worthy of attention, and to arrange support from the consultant where that has been desired by the project holder. This monitoring and constructive oversight has developed from the early years of the scheme, when it was possible for some projects to slip off course, or to lack purposeful focus.

In the first section of this chapter we made the claim that the management practices described have led to the personal transformation of the participants from workers or followers into leaders of change. In this second section one of the participants from the first iteration of the Task Group has offered a narrative account that illustrates, and places into a personal-professional context, the transformation we have described.

What next?

This chapter was drafted in a period of change. A new Dean of Faculty has been appointed and the Associate Dean, who led these changes, accepted an invitation to become Director of Learning and Teaching for the University. This has provided an opportunity to take stock.

It is our view that the achievements of the current project holders, and their impact on the Faculty's programmes, speak for themselves. This justifies, we claim, the firm recommendation to others considering implementing such a programme, that much which is valuable in terms of an effective engine for change and enhancement would be lost if the scheme did not continue; perhaps in a wider context. We have already identified modifications or forward steps that we will recommend for the next round. These would be to:

- Extend the recently introduced practice of inviting project bids specifically in areas where there is scope and need for focused development, to ensure alignment with strategy;
- Extend and rearrange the project period, as we have partly done in the most recent round of projects, to commence before the beginning of an academic year, and to finish shortly after the end of the academic year. This would allow time for preparation of changes in curricula (where that is a feasible short-term feature of a proposal), and for some evaluation of delivered changes;
- Strengthen the assistance given with both formative and summative evaluation, and develop collaborations in learning communities involving project holders in formative evaluations. This on the basis of current arrangements for the offering of peer support that have been so effective in many ways in the Open University. This practice of peer support has been elegantly described by Cowan *et al.* (2004) as 'taking in each other's washing'.

Closing remarks from the outgoing
Associate Dean (Academic) and originator

We conclude this chapter with a second personal account, from another of the authors, the originator of the coordinated strategy, Stuart Brand:

"The transformation of a very average faculty into an excellent one took place at an accelerated rate primarily because of high level, managerial commitment and systematic dedication of resource to support learning and teaching innovation. This commitment needed a new focus that moved it away from the long-standing approach of merely supporting lone innovators in a notional way, albeit with some limited availability of funding. We had in the Faculty a good supply of talented and committed innovators but there were two further steps necessary before we could move toward real cultural change: I needed to offer the innovators protected time so that their work could flourish without the danger of overload and I had to demonstrate that senior management support was evident for those innovations, critically at this early developmental stage, but also at subsequent phases of wider implementation and evaluation.

The contagious nature of the developments of Task Group, CIF project holders, LPDU and module makeovers created a critical academic mass that has now prepared the Faculty to expect change and thus has supported innovation. The tipping point (Gladwell, 2000) has been achieved and the contagion may be becoming an epidemic. Consequently through an evidence-based paper, the new Faculty Dean has embraced the merits of these initiatives and will seek to carry this work forward in his own way, within the context of developments in the University's approach to the promotion of learning and teaching developments through the central educational development unit. I particularly welcome his commitment to align Learning and Teaching goals with Faculty strategy and to see this reflected in Task Group priorities.

I would also make special mention of the role of the critical friend. Without his prompting and challenging incursions, it is difficult to see how the Task Group would have been so successful. It has often led to challenges for the managers of those on the Task Group, and me as Associate Dean, as well as Task Group members. In many ways this appointment was a key step as it provided Task Group Fellows with the external validation they required further to believe in and embed their innovations.

I have now moved to the centre to become University Director of Learning and Teaching and am located in the central education development unit – the Centre for Enhancement of Learning and Teaching (CELT). This could be seen as a move from devolutionist to centralist, but I believe that it is not that simple! In the Faculty I led a programme aimed at cultural change. I firmly believe that it was observation of the impact of those Faculty developments that led the Vice Chancellor and Pro-Vice-Chancellor to seek a wider impact across the whole university. In turn this is already requiring some refocus of how CELT operates.

In the Faculty of Health we discovered a demonstrably effective way to encourage innovation, create better curricula and so enhance students' learning outcomes. Perhaps the opportunity has now presented itself for this model to be rolled out across the rest of the university. Already, the model of CIF in my previous faculty has been rolled out in two other faculties. Further the model has been adopted, as part of the University's CETL activity, to fund more than a dozen university-wide projects. Furthermore, new networks are being generated including: Senior Learning and Teaching Fellows in each faculty and Learning Technology Champions across the University. The model adopted in one faculty has thus now expanded and received wider adoption. It is indeed now at the centre of a substantial University-wide project to redesign the learning experience.

In summary, this chapter has argued the case for the location of educational support initiatives within faculties rather than within centrally based educational development units. I now believe that the two can co-exist if the central unit itself moves to a facilitative role, co-ordinating networks across the institution. To this end CELT will seek to support faculty initiatives and even assist staff to work across faculties and professional boundaries, rather than acting itself as the principal source of expertise."

About the authors

Paul Bartholomew is Senior Academic in Learning and Teaching in the Centre for Enhancement of Learning and Teaching at Birmingham City University. He can be contacted at paul.bartholomew@bcu.ac.uk

Stuart Brand is Director of Learning and Teaching at Birmingham City University. He can be contacted at stuart.brand@bcu.ac.uk

Luke Millard is Learning Partnerships Manager in the Centre for Learning Partnerships at Birmingham City University. He can be contacted at luke.millard@bcu.ac.uk

CHAPTER 6

How can Students' Conceptions of Learning Improve their Learning Outcomes?

Despina Varnava-Marouchou

Introduction

A major driver for exploring conceptions is the assumption that students' views on learning have an effect on the way they approach their learning, which in turn may influence the quality of their academic outcomes. Indeed, many studies (Marton & Säljö, 1976a, 1976b; Säljö, 1979) have aimed to identify and describe students' conceptions, whilst others have concentrated on students' outcomes. An attempt is made in this chapter to explore any possible connections between students' conceptions of learning and their learning outcomes. More specifically, possible relationships may shed light in understanding student outcomes within the context of higher education. Drawing on a 2007 study of Cypriot students' conceptions of learning, this chapter discusses the possibility of a link between these issues and outlines the importance of taking them into consideration when exploring learning outcomes, curriculum design and the development of lecturers.

The term 'conceptions' as specified in this chapter, describes the way a person conceives a phenomenon and this may influence an individual's actions (Freeman & Richards, 1993). Pratt (1992:204) stated that *"we view the world through the lenses of our conceptions, interpreting and acting in accordance with our understanding of the world"*. Consequently, conceptions may influence the way students act in their particular situation which is in accordance with these conceptions.

There is now a trend in the European Union to make teaching and learning more transparent and to facilitate the portability of university studies across the European nations. The development of the European Credit Transfer and Accumulation System (ECTS) is one such method that has been used across Europe to assist the design of the curriculum and to generally promote the quality assurance of learning within the EU. The importance of this system is that it is exclusively linked to the learning outcomes students are expected to achieve.

The point I will make within this chapter is that the design of effective learning outcomes, such as with the ECTS, especially for curriculum development, cannot be successfully achieved in the absence of the students' own experience of how they conceive learning to be, including the methods and approaches they use for learning.

My interest for this chapter was initiated by the findings of a research project undertaken in a local and private university in the city of Nicosia, Cyprus. My concern regarding the project was sparked by my personal experience in the academic life of the university during the last sixteen years. In my everyday job as a lecturer of Business Studies and as a student advisor, I was well aware of the issue of ever-increasing complaints made by faculty regarding their students' poor outcomes and, consequently, poor grades.

Our students go through what appears to be the same teaching exposure and yet have vastly different learning perceptions (Biggs, 1999) that inevitably affect their learning outcomes. This forms some of the most immediate challenges for lecturers, calling them to question the ways in which they teach. Thus, if teaching is about helping to make learning possible, the defining of effective learning outcomes may be derived from an understanding of what students conceive as learning and what they have actually learnt.

I have chosen to explore the learning conceptions of students studying Business Studies in the specific areas of Economics, Accounting, Management and Marketing.

Conceptions, approaches and outcomes of learning

The term 'learning outcomes' as used in this chapter and in wider educational circles, reflects a conceptual shift towards making learning more meaningful and effective for students. It mostly refers to the qualitative outcomes of student learning which emphasise understanding and obtaining meaning rather than quantitative outcomes of learning which have a focus on acquisition of factual knowledge. Indeed, it is important within the academic arena, that we should concentrate on learning from the students' own perspective and experiences about their courses, rather than concentrate on the teaching methods and what the lecturer does (Shuell, 1986; Biggs, 1990). There is an increasing need to understand what is involved in student learning from the students' own explanations of what learning means to them and how this relates to the quality of their learning outcomes (Entwistle, 1997). In the research literature, it is generally agreed that non-cognitive, individual differences, such as the conceptions and approaches to learning have been recognised as potential predictors of academic success (Cantwell & Scevak, 2004) and are thought to play a key role in the quality of student learning outcomes. A brief introduction of both these concepts is outlined below.

Conceptions of learning

Research on students' conceptions of learning was initiated by Marton & Säljö in the early 1970s. Marton and his colleagues argued that students at their initial stages of their university life bring with them their own beliefs regarding learning derived from their previous learning experiences, usually their school. Marton *et al.* (1993) divided these beliefs into six conceptions of learning as follows: a) learning as increasing one's knowledge; b) learning as memorising and reproduction; c) learning as applying; d) learning as understanding; e) learning as seeing something in a different way; and f) learning as changing as a person. The first three conceptions are referred to as 'reproductive' and were seen as lacking in understanding and meaning, whilst the last three were referred to as 'transformative' and are seen as being concerned with understanding and meaning (Marton & Säljö, 1976a, 1976b; Säljö, 1979). Many subsequent studies have confirmed the same or similar findings (Van Rossum & Schenk, 1984; Säljö, 1979; Van Rossum & Taylor, 1987; Morgan *et al.*, 1980).

The key point to be made within all these studies is that conceptions are not permanent and can indeed change from reproductive to transformative as students develop through university (Perry, 1970; Marton *et al.*, 1993; Hettich, 1997). The change will take place when the student is made to understand that his/her learning at the university can result in his/her changing as a person (Marton *et al.*, 1993). However, this transformation will depend on how the students perceive their academic activities which in turn, may determine the way they approach these activities (Trigwell & Ashwin, 2006). Indeed, a great deal of research on student learning has indicated that students' conceptions are possibly related to the approaches they use for learning, which in turn influence their learning outcomes. The following section addresses the issue of approaches to learning.

Approaches to learning

The term 'approaches to learning' is increasingly used to emphasise the importance of students and lecturers being aware of how they learn and how they teach. An approach to learning is, therefore, regarded as a key concept in teaching and learning, and describes a qualitative explanation of what and how students learn. According to Ramsden (1992:44) it: "...*describes a relation between the student and the learning he or she is doing"* by representing "...*what a learning task or set of tasks is for the learner"* (Ramsden, 1987; Prosser & Trigwell, 1999).

By acknowledging and understanding the approaches to learning we may be in a better position to recommend "...*appropriate solutions for improving student learning"* (Sharma, 1997:127) and consequently learning outcomes.

A number of researchers of students' approaches to learning have separated the initial approaches into two groups: namely 'surface' and 'deep' approaches (Marton & Säljö, 1976a, 1976b; Säljö, 1979; Marton *et al.* 1993). Students who employed surface approaches focused on the memorisation and reproduction of information, and generally viewed learning as acquiring knowledge merely for passing examinations, with little or no focus on the processes of learning. Students using deep approaches, on the other hand, aimed for understanding, forming a wider picture of how knowledge fits together and represents reality (Sharma, 1997). The actual learning processes and approaches students use are generally associated with the quality of learning outcomes.

Of the initial six conceptions by Marton *et al.* (1993), for example, the first three are normally associated with surface approaches to learning and the last three with deep approaches. According to Marton *et al.* (1993), the first three focused on 'quantitative' dimensions of learning, whilst the latter three are typically 'qualitative', and relate to gaining meaning and understanding. Even though some studies (Hall *et al.,* 2004) have criticised aspects of the deep/surface distinction there has been a general agreement about their usefulness in students' learning (Richardson, 1994).

The important point to be made is that research into both students' conceptions and approaches to learning has increased the attention given to how learning is experienced, understood, or conceptualised by learners themselves and remains a powerful influence on student learning in higher education (Entwistle, 1997).

The theoretical framework

Most of the traditional epistemological and methodological research frameworks regarded students' behaviour from the outside, as a separate and distinct experience (Marton & Booth, 1997). For example, the cognitive research tradition (Ryan, 1984a) does not take into account students' experiences of learning in formulating concepts of learning. Later, constructivist ideas were developed by merging various cognitive approaches with a focus on viewing knowledge as constructed rather than discovered (Marton, *et al.*, 1993).

Perhaps the most obvious distinction made within this framework is that rather than trying to examine academic performance and learning outcomes, an attempt is made to describe the students' own experiences of learning. In deepening our understanding of the theme of the present chapter we consider two main perspectives of students' learning: the meta-cognitive and the phenomenographic (Purdie *et al.*, 1996).

Meta-cognitive researchers explored students' epistemological conceptions about knowledge and learning (Ryan, 1984a; Schommer, 1990, 1998). Phenomenographic researchers, on the other hand, analysed the variety of meanings that learning has for people and the different ways in which they learn, using mainly qualitative methods (Marton *et al.*, 1993). Both the epistemological and the phenomenographic perspectives of learning are important in understanding the theoretical framework underpinning the current theme.

The epistemological perspectives of learning

Researchers since the early 1990s have begun to acknowledge the important role students' epistemological beliefs played in conceptual change learning (Driver *et al.*, 1994). The conceptual change model requires a central role for learners to actively construct and manage their learning. The link between conceptual change and meta-cognition has been noted by a number of education researchers (Driver *et al.*, 1994). Indeed, many of them have suggested that meta-cognition and conceptual change are 'totally intertwined' in such a way that may influence the change of ideas and beliefs about learning (Hewson, 1996; Gunstone, 1994).

The theory that underpins conceptual change learning was originally developed using Piaget's (1977) cognitive model and Perry's (1970, 1981) schema theory of epistemological beliefs. Perry attempted to clarify how individuals move from their 'common sense' conceptions to new more 'sophisticated' conceptions. During their time in higher education, students may gradually change from a belief in 'dualism' - where knowledge is concrete and provided by the lecturers - to recognition of 'relativism' (or non-dualism) - where they have to think and interpret meaning for themselves (Perry, 1981; Pillay & Boulton-Lewis, 2000; Pillay *et al.*, 1998). Higher education, therefore, may influence the students' epistemological development. Several studies have confirmed this (Alexander & Dochy, 1995; Perry, 1981; King & Kitchener, 1994; Schommer, 1998).

The overall assumption made in this section, is that students display increasingly sophisticated levels of development as they go through university, and that their development from one level to another arises as a result of their learning abilities (Hofer, 2001). Equally important is also the research evidence which indicates that if students conceive knowledge to be 'static' they will perceive learning as a process of accumulating information. On the other hand, if students conceive knowledge to be 'flexible' they will see learning as meaningful and something to be discovered. This is an important point since it maintains that there is a relationship between epistemological beliefs about knowledge, conceptions of learning and academic performance (Hofer & Pintrich, 1997; Dweck & Leggett, 1988).

The phenomenographic perspective

From the above argument it follows that from a non-dualistic perspective, if the learner has come to experience a phenomenon in a more complex and meaningful way, a change is implied and learning has taken place. In other words "*...learning is a response to a student's perception or way of experiencing his or her particular situation*" (Lucas, 2000:481). In the words of Ramsden*, et al.,* (1993:303): "*...there is only one world to which we have access to – and that is the world-as-experienced*". Knowledge and learning, therefore, lies within these experiences. Following from this rationale the phenomenographic perspective of learning implies that people act according to their interpretation of the situation rather than to an 'objective reality' which is emphasized in the positivist traditions (Watkins, 1996). It is within this framework that the phenomenographic approach is engaged in this study in order to identify variations in the experience of a phenomenon undertaken by a specific group of students.

The study

My own research (Varnava-Marouchou, 2007) aimed to identify and describe students' conceptions of learning within the undergraduate programmes in a university in Cyprus. More specifically, it aimed to develop an appreciation of how students in their initial courses conceive their learning and how this affects their studies and finally and, most importantly, how it may affect their learning outcomes.

Method

As already stated it is difficult for researchers to get a picture of students' conceptions of learning using quantitative methods. Consequently, for this study, I have drawn on the constructivist philosophy and employed a phenomenographic approach as the underlying framework of methodology. The data collected provide a detailed conceptualisation of learning which could only have emerged by using interviews as a method and I opted for semi-structured interviews. By using this method I hoped to gain a holistic rather than a disjointed understanding of the experiences and insights of the students who participated. The method used justified the small sample of participants engaged in the research which was made up of twelve students (five males and seven females). The students were all freshmen who had already taken or were studying one or more introductory Business courses. Based on the data analysis, a set of categories were developed and made up of six conceptions of learning. The findings of the study confirmed the results found by Marton & Säljö (1976a) and other researchers. Comparisons were then made between the categories.

Conceptions of learning – The findings

The research identified six categories of students' conceptions of learning. The categories were perceived as forming a kind of hierarchy in which each category included characteristics of the preceding conceptions (Byrne *et al.*, 2004). Furthermore, most of the beliefs were linked with each other and therefore could not be viewed as independent of each other. Table 1 provides a summary of the conceptions of learning as expressed by the students. It identifies each category in terms of its level, aim, orientation and learning activity.

From the Table 1 it can be seen that the conceptions of students' learning fall into two distinct divisions, described in the study as: 'higher-level' and 'lower-level' categories. Categories A, B, C and D represented learning as subject-oriented/lecturer-dependent activities and are seen as mainly dualistic activities. More than half of the participants saw learning as primarily acquiring subject knowledge directly from the lecturer with the aim of reproducing it in response to course assessment and exam requirements.

Levels of Conceptions	Aim of learning	Orientation of Learning	Learning Activity
Lower-level Conceptions	*Category A:* Receiving subject knowledge	Subject-oriented	Lecturer-dependent
	Category B: Receiving subject knowledge in a clear, comprehensible manner		
	Category C: Studying and memorising the subject knowledge with the aim of reproducing it at a future time		
	Category D: The lecturer as a role model in the process of learning		
Higher-level Conceptions	*Category E:* Learning through involvement and through understanding the subject knowledge	Learning-oriented	Student-dependent
	Category F: Learning as the self development of student into responsible human being		

Table 1: The levels of conceptions: Aim, orientation and activity of learning

The overall conclusion is that the student is seen as a passive follower relying on the lecturer whose responsibility, as an expert, is to hand down factual knowledge.

Students holding Conceptions E and F were found to take a more holistic view of learning. They viewed learning as centring on the concept of meaning or understanding. These categories convey a more constructive perception of learning (Van Rossum *et al.,* 1985; Marton *et al.,* 1993). Categories E and F suggested a higher-level of thinking that focused on learning outcomes as the exploration of meaning and the development of one's self. In other words, learning is undertaken for its own sake and students take responsibility for their own learning and advancement.

To conclude, the overall results of this study revealed that the subject knowledge, irrespective of the discipline, was mainly seen as external to students – being contained in notes and providedfor the express purpose of passing examinations and obtaining degrees.

Relationships between conceptions of learning, approaches to learning and learning outcomes

The influences that lead to a particular learning outcome are not always directly observable. According to Lucas & Meyer (2003:6) investigating and measuring learning outcomes should be seen as 'more an art than a science'. The qualitative measurement of learning outcomes, such as the 'deep understanding' of the subject, may be considered better indicators of student learning than quantitative measures such as examination performance (Trigwell & Prosser 1991; Ramsden, 1992, 2003).

This section examines the relationship between conceptions of learning, learning approaches and learning outcomes where the learning outcome is measured by the level of understanding of the concepts taught in the unit of study, rather than using performance based on formal assessment tasks.

Indeed, there is a well-established body of educational research which supports the debate that students' approaches to learning are related to their conceptions of learning and that the approaches adopted are linked to the quality of their learning outcomes (Ramsden, 1992, 2003).

Work by Dahlgren (1984), Van Rossum & Schenk (1984) and Marton & Säljö (1976a, 1976b) gave an inclusive summary of these relationships. These studies concluded that in order to arrive at a certain outcome, a particular approach to the learning activity must have been used. Hence the approach to a learning activity and the outcome of learning are joined in the overall experience and conceptions of learning. It could, therefore, be possible to identify the different learning conceptions of students over a particular topic within a subject (Bowden & Marton, 1998) that could be then be used to define their learning approaches and ultimately the quality of their learning outcomes and grades.

Furthermore, the students who viewed learning as understanding linked to their own personal growth showed that they wanted to appreciate, discover or gain meaning of the subject. According to Marton *et al.* (1993) these students adopted a deep approach to learning. Similarly, pioneering studies by Dahlgren & Marton (1978) conducted on the concept of 'price', for example, showed that students who use deep approaches had a deeper understanding of the concept of price. This result was concluded many times by different studies including the study on students' conceptions of mathematics conducted by Crawford *et al.* (1998). In addition the study by Purdie *et al.* (1996) of Japanese and Australian students' conception of learning and their use of self-regulated learning approaches could verify this.

Van Rossum & Schenk (1984) explored the relationships between students' conceptions of learning, their approach to learning, and their learning outcomes. Students using a surface approach never obtained more than a 'multi-structural' level of learning outcome, in which facts are presented in an unconnected manner. The majority of students using a deep approach reached the 'relational' level in which ideas are presented as a coherent whole.

This was also confirmed when the descriptions of the Cypriot students' interviews were examined. Students with conceptions E and F were found to aim for a complete understanding of the phenomenon in all their learning activities. From their descriptions it was discovered that they put emphasis on the 'whole meaning' of the learning task. When students grasp the meaning of a particular text they can put down answers in their own words. They will not choose to memorise the text. From this, one can assume that the approaches to learning and the conceptions of learning of these students are linked.

What is clear from my own study in Cyprus is that some students had begun to see learning as a continuous journey in which understanding their Business courses and understanding knowledge in general has a part to play in their general development. Thus, there was a clear indication that students were beginning to shift their conceptions of learning from merely 'acquiring knowledge' to that of 'understanding knowledge' and were starting to appreciate the use of deep approaches to learning.

Surface learning approaches, on the other hand, have been connected with beliefs that the learning activities require rote learning of factual material (Entwistle & Ramsden, 1983; Trigwell & Prosser, 1991a; Prosser & Trigwell, 1999; Lizzio, 2002). Ramsden (1992, 2003), for example, indicated that many students who attained 'low level outcomes' tended to memorise large quantities of information that were soon forgotten. These studies revealed that students who intended to acquire more knowledge without spending time to explore and understand the course material that has been taught in class undoubtedly diminished their learning outcomes.

From the findings of the Cypriot study it has emerged that students with conceptions A, B, C and D (see Table 1) are adopting the surface approach to learning. Indeed the analysis of their descriptions given in the interviews showed clearly that the students' main concern is concentrated on the quantity of knowledge and not in understanding knowledge. For example, a number of them stressed the importance of rote learning and memorisation through writing, rewriting, typing and reading over their notes several times.

Once again, the students emphasised their reliance on the lecturer to provide them with the subject knowledge using well-structured methods. In particular, the Cypriot students indicated their preference for well-prepared notes, well-illustrated slides and the use of real-life examples. Learning is perceived as receiving knowledge, and this is clearly the responsibility of the lecturer.

Furthermore, the study by Jackling (2005) examined the relationships between the learning approach used and the quality of learning outcomes obtained, by using questions intended to examine the level of conceptual understanding. The results showed that deep approaches to learning were generally connected with more meaningful responses to questions related to course content. Conversely, students with surface approaches showed a distinct lack of knowledge of the concepts that had been taught. In their studies, Marton & Säljö (1976b) found that students who used the deep approach not only had a more complete understanding but were also able to recall more facts. Other studies confirmed similar results (Dahlgren, 1984; Van Rossum & Schenk, 1984; Marton & Säljö, 1997). For example, Svensson (1977) found that students who used a deep approach were more successful in examinations than those who used a surface approach.

In addition, Prosser & Millar (1989) demonstrated that students with a deep approach to learning displayed a greater degree of conceptual change towards more sophisticated conceptions. Prosser and Millar maintained that in order to experience conceptual change, students have to actively participate in using a deep approach. Moreover, Marton & Booth (1997:158) concluded that "...*learning in the sense of changing one's way of experiencing a phenomenon is contingent on one's approach to learning*". Chin & Brown (2000) provided further evidence in their study of school students who were involved in science exercises. They found that those using a deep approach were more prepared to express their ideas, gave more extensive explanations, asked more sophisticated questions and engaged in more explicit theorising during the task.

So, the evidence from many years of research indicates the presence of a strong correlation between conceptions of learning and approaches to learning, with students at the lower level end of the conceptions of learning tending towards a surface approach, and those at the higher level end tending to a deep approach. These results provided evidence that there is indeed a link between these concepts of learning and the quality of student learning outcomes. The existing literature and my own study confirm that a relationship does exist between a student's conception of learning and his/her academic ability.

The importance of making both learners and teachers aware of the conceptions (or misconceptions) of learning cannot be underestimated (Marton & Ramsden, 1988; Hettich, 1997). It is not difficult then to understand how a student who comes to 'own' the knowledge through engaging with it personally and for its own sake, might be able to include what he/she has learnt into everyday life (Hodgeson, 1997).

Students' conceptions of learning: Implications for lecturer development and curriculum design

If we are serious in establishing a more student-centred curriculum in higher education in the EU and beyond, the need for educators to be aware of the experiences and beliefs every student brings to their learning environment becomes even more significant. The students we teach bring with them their own previous and personal learning experiences, some of which may have negative influences on their conceptions of learning and attitudes to study (Marton *et al.,* 1993; Hettich, 1997). Sadly, some students see higher education as a chore that they have to go through rather than something that could enhance their lives. However, as already mentioned above, such conceptions and beliefs are far from been fixed (Newble & Entwistle, 1986; Marton & Säljö, 1997) and could and should change during their study at university.

Therefore, one of the aims of university teaching should be to make education more meaningful for students by deliberately building educational experiences based on how students understand, conceive and experience knowledge including what students should be able to do with their knowledge. Educational agencies promoting reform and change should recognise and understand the importance of the conceptions of learning. For the majority of educators, this will require engaging with pedagogical issues and theories that might only have been of trivial importance in the traditional university. This brings to the fore issues regarding, first, the restructuring of the curriculum and, second, the training and development of lecturers.

Curriculum design

To begin with, an awareness of the conceptions of learning held by the students would be valuable to educators when structuring the course curriculum and course syllabus of the university. Educators may be able to design the curriculum in such a way as to promote deeper, more constructivist, approaches to learning and, by doing so, provide students with insights into how learning might occur. Such curriculum designs may facilitate the achievement of the desired high-quality learning outcomes.

By creating curriculum designs that encourage more reactive and creative teaching strategies we may raise students' awareness of the impact of learning on their education and lives in general. It may also be possible to assist the students with poor academic results to become better achievers by making them aware of the benefits of evolving to the higher level of conceptions. In the verses of William Butler Yeats (1865-1939) *"...education is not the filling of the pail but the lighting of fire"*.

Training and development of lecturers

Research has highlighted the important role conceptions play in the development of teaching practices and teaching methods. Gow *et al.* (1992:146) identified faculty development as an important part of their research on conceptions. They emphasise the significance of *"...mak[ing] changes in line with the practitioner's beliefs"*. Entwistle & Walker (2000) argued for faculty development which would support lecturers to develop more sophisticated conceptions of learning and teaching. Ho *et al.* (2001) provided concrete evidence that conceptions can indeed lead to improvements in teaching strategies and eventually in student learning outcomes. In addition, Marton & Ramsden (1988) have suggested several teaching strategies that promote conceptual change in students, enabling them to understand within their learning environment. In this regard, every educator should aspire to Rogers' (1969) philosophy of creating a 'community of learners'.

Whilst there are no direct relationships between lecturer training and student outcomes (Trowler & Bamber, 2005), there is an abundance of research linking teaching practices, learning conceptions and learning outcomes (Biggs, 1999; Dunkin & Precians, 1992; Kember & Kwan, 2000; Martin, *et al.,* 2000; McAlpine & Weston, 2000; Ramsden, 1992; Trigwell *et al.,* 1999). This leads to the conclusion that if we wish lecturers to adopt 'student-centred' approaches to teaching and students to adopt meaningful 'learning-oriented' approaches to learn-ing (Kember & Kwan, 2000), then it is important to direct lecturer de-velopment and training efforts towards engaging in teaching for under-standing (Ho, 1998). An appreciation of university teaching is there-fore incomplete without a consideration of the students' and also lec-turers' conceptions about learning and teaching and a systematic ex-amination of the relationship between those conceptions and actual teaching practices.

In practice, this would mean investing in specific training pro-grammes to tackle conceptions of both learning and teaching. Similarly, workshops and seminars can provide a good opportunity for 'conceptions awareness-building'. Indeed, Bowden (1989) designed workshops which focused on helping teachers to enable their teaching practices to match their intended learning outcomes for students. In his workshop, Trigwell, (1995) attempted to change participants' conceptions of teaching and learning by increasing their awareness of the existence of other conceptions which were more helpful to better learning.

These arguments, I believe, provide a good start to any future progress in both the curriculum design and lecturer training and development programmes. The conceptual change approach has developed as a way of achieving real progress concerning students' learning outcomes in higher education, even though the actual task of changing such conceptions remains enormous.

Conclusion

Both educators and employers have recognised the importance of students completing their university education with high-quality learning and have worked hard to achieve this. Even so, Boulton-Lewis (1995) reminded us that many graduates have little more than superficial knowledge once they have finished their studies. This chapter has aimed to re-address the lack of information concerning university learning and, in particular, the dynamic feedback that student conceptions of learning could provide to educators.

This chapter has set out to explore the impact student conceptions of learning could make on the quality of student learning outcomes. This information could provide educators and academics in general with valuable insights that can be used to review both the quality of the current curricula and the teaching methods and, by doing so, influence the development of new curricula so that their design assists the attainment of desired high quality learning outcomes. Hounsell (1997:241) sets out clearly our responsibility in this regard: *"The success with which students are able to achieve understanding may therefore depend critically on the capacity of the higher education teacher to recognise and build from students' existing conceptions and anchor knowledge in a meaningful framework".*

In other words, if educators are to provide students with educational experiences which promote the realisation of high quality learning outcomes, one factor about which they need information is students' views and beliefs on the nature of learning. We need to persuade and make students realise that learning their subjects should involve the adoption of more appropriate learning strategies which could contribute to their understanding and personal development that will eventually make a positive impact on their learning outcomes and life in general.

About the author
Despina Varnava-Marouchou is a senior lecturer at the European University, Cyprus. She can be contacted at this e-mail:
d.marouchou@euc.ac.cy

CHAPTER 7

Enhancing Mathematics across the Disciplines through an Institutional Initiative

Dorothy I. Wallace

Introduction

When college teachers define learning goals for subjects other than their own specialty, they frequently mention the difficulty students experience in transferring knowledge to a new context. Even students who master a body of knowledge and retain it for later recall may find that they cannot recognize the information when it appears in a new context in a different subject area, such as the use of calculus in an engineering class. The ability to transfer knowledge is necessary not only for success in college, but also for success in an increasingly interdisciplinary work place. It is a highly desirable student learning outcome. The push to introduce interdisciplinary curriculum at the college level is a response to this goal.

What is interdisciplinarity? Can it be taught? How can institutions create an environment that promotes interdisciplinary teaching and learning? Mathematics, which serves all sciences as well as economics and social science, provides an excellent example for reflection on these questions. This chapter will investigate the interdisciplinary teaching of mathematics from the point of view of various stakeholders and at different levels of granularity.

In the USA the National Science Foundation (NSF) recognized the value of teaching mathematics in the context of deep applications throughout the science curriculum by sponsoring a call for proposals in 1994 encouraging interdisciplinary applications. Both the justification for these projects and the kinds of projects sponsored illustrate an intervention at the national level intended to encourage institutions to develop interdisciplinary approaches to mathematics education, with the goal of improving the ability of students to apply mathematical knowledge to other disciplines. This initiative was not an isolated event, as the NSF sponsored related projects before and since. These initiatives represent a strategy for reform at the national level as carried out by professional scientists on behalf of the government. One official description of a collection of initiatives including one concerned with mathematics reads: *"The systemic initiatives share the goal of fostering reform of undergraduate science and mathematics education by encouraging institutions to reexamine the roles of each disciplinary department in the instructional program as a whole, to explore and exploit new relationships among disciplines, and to develop introductory and advanced courses, curricula, and materials that will benefit all undergraduate students at the participating institutions and have potential for national impact. Projects are expected to significantly involve faculty from several disciplines."* (NSF, 1995:Unpaginated).

One of the projects sponsored as a result of an early initiative was a broad intervention at a single institution. The "Math Across the Curriculum Project" (MATC) at Dartmouth College included courses across the sciences and in the humanities as well. In addition to a combined first year course in physics, chemistry and calculus, there were two courses in mathematics and music, two in mathematics and art, several in mathematics and literature and one in mathematics and philosophy. Further work included interdisciplinary modules introduced into existing courses, usually in the sciences. Dartmouth College is an elite institution, serving students who typically enter with a strong background in mathematics and science. As in other colleges and universities in the USA, Dartmouth students do not typically decide on their major area of study upon arrival, but rather take a variety of prerequisite courses before settling on an area of concentration. The NSF sponsors educational reform in order to attract undergraduates into scientific disciplines at this key moment in their education and to help them succeed in those disciplines.

The stated agenda of MATC was ambitious, including evaluation, dissemination and publication as well as curriculum development. Cumulative data reported in the fifth year include over 3,000 students affected, 186 faculty at Dartmouth and elsewhere, 83 modules, books and videos created, and 7 faculty development workshops directly sponsored serving 200 faculty in mathematics, literature, history, philosophy, art, art history, biology, geology, physics and engineering. All specific benchmarks stated in the proposal were met.

Five years of data are available, including student surveys, annual reports of the project investigators, NSF reviewers, and an external review committee. From these a picture emerges of how a massive attempt at curricular reform plays itself out inside an institution, affecting not only curriculum but also classroom pedagogy and the culture of the institution. We can also see how the ambient culture of the institution both assisted and hampered efforts to start and sustain such courses. The MATC project offers some useful lessons in educational reform at all levels.

In this paper we will consider four key aspects of the MATC case study. Foremost is student experience and change in one important learning outcome: the willingness to engage in mathematics in a wide range of contexts as a prerequisite to knowledge transfer. Second is the experience of faculty and their own willingness and ability to try new forms of interdisciplinary teaching in order to improve this learning outcome for students. Third is how the culture of the institution helped or hindered these outcomes. Finally we look at the management strategies used to guide the project and we see how they succeeded or failed in creating a sustainable intervention.

Knowledge transfer

Although the college had recently instituted an interdisciplinary requirement, the project proposed to NSF was very much a grass-roots effort on the part of faculty who expressed a general desire to have more mathematically able and aware students. Focus groups at the start of the project agreed upon goals and planned strategies for achieving them. About two dozen faculties were involved in these initial planning stages. Three of the goals of the project are presented here, taken exactly as stated from the MATC project proposal:

1. *Make mathematics welcome and even indispensable across the entire curriculum*
2. *Motivate students to take mathematics seriously*
3. *Increase the ability and willingness of students to use mathematics they already know to facilitate their understanding of other subjects and to draw upon other subjects to improve their mathematics*

It is clear from these goals that faculty was concerned with the issue of transfer of knowledge — the ability and willingness to carry material learned in one context to another one.

The fact that knowledge does not transfer that easily has lead some researchers to question to what extent it is even possible to transfer knowledge. The literature contains examples of subjects who, after training, fail to transfer specific skills, processes of abstraction, and even general problem-solving heuristics (Hayes & Simon, 1977, Pressley *et al.*, 1987). Perkins & Salomon, (1989) refer to problem-solving heuristics such as those made famous by Polya (1957) as "weak", because implementing them in a new context requires local knowledge of the phenomenon—"strong" knowledge that alone may be sufficient to solve the problem. It is clear from reading the goals set forth by the participating faculty that, although particular mathematical subjects are mentioned, the main concern is at the level of heuristics. They want students to expect to use mathematics as a way to study anything, and to expect to need the mathematics they have learned for subsequent work.

Salomon & Perkins (1989) make a further distinction between "high" and "low" roads to transfer. The "low road" requires sufficient practice that a skill or approach becomes automatic and therefore is likely to surface in a new context. The "high road" is characterized as "mindful abstraction", in which guiding principles or patterns relevant to one context are willfully summoned to study a problem in a completely different context. Although both roads are needed for masterful use of mathematics in a new context, the use of words such as "welcome", "willing" and "motivate" indicates that faculty members in this study were emphasizing the "high road" to transfer as an explicit goal of the MATC project.

Renkl *et al.* (1996) describe knowledge that cannot be used outside its original pedagogical context as "inert". In addition to metacognitive approaches, these authors mention the theory of "situated cognition", which postulates that knowledge is not a possession of the learner, but rather emerges in response to context. They conclude that a problem-based curriculum would be useful in triggering this emergence. One could view the goals set out by faculty of the MATC project as outlining a set of contexts that would offer a rich source of such problems. Tying this richness to the issue of motivation, the project proposal begins by pointing out that, for most students, the desire to learn mathematics would spring most naturally from existing interests in other areas.

The emphasis MATC placed on transfer of knowledge is remarkable because it differs from the way in which mathematicians perceive their own learning. Skemp (1987) was one of the first mathematicians to attempt to integrate the disciplines of mathematics, education and psychology. His work, familiar to mathematics educators and translated into 10 languages, provides a framework for understanding cognitive growth as experienced by a professional mathematician.

Skemp (1987) sets out an entire cognitive theory for learning mathematics, in which the emphasis is on passing from the concrete to the abstract, creating ever more abstract schemes for understanding correspondingly deeper mathematics. This description sounds right to a mathematician and fits the goals of advanced math courses intended to prepare students for further mathematics. However it is not a good description of most fields of scholarship, where the goal is to test abstractions against the nuanced particulars of reality, as often as possible. Neither does the constant building of abstract systems of thought produce in the student the habit of looking for these newly built systems across multiple contexts, which of course is exactly how most students might be able to make optimal use of their mathematical knowledge. The principal investigator for MATC was quite familiar with Skemp's work and aware of how the courses designed as part of the project would place an emphasis on learning that would elicit learning outcomes that were not usually a priority for mathematics courses. The project evaded this quandary by placing its effort in courses that were not, for the most part, in the traditional mathematics sequence.

One MATC course in mathematics and art provides an example of how this change in cognitive emphasis played out. A student majoring in mathematics would study the subject of group theory as a required part of the major, but few students other than those in the maths major would ever see this subject. Group theory is the study of "groups" which are a beautiful abstract mathematical structure that distills basic relationships common to a large class of examples. The mathematics student would become familiar with a few examples but would place the emphasis of study on proving properties common to all groups. By contrast, the student in the "Pattern" course would approach the subject by first creating repeat patterns using block printing techniques, then identifying common features of the patterns, then exploring those common features in depth and finally extracting the definition of a 'group' from this rich class of visual examples. One 'proof' might be presented by the instructor during the entire course, and it would be visual in nature and represent the culmination of understanding built upon lengthy exploration of visual examples. In the usual mathematics course this proof would be done in the first or second week of the course, based entirely on the abstract definition of a group. The mathematics student would emerge with a greater facility with abstract systems and proofs, but the Pattern student saw examples of groups everywhere.

The breadth of topics represented by MATC courses made any common analysis of content-based learning outcomes impossible. Each instructor was therefore responsible for assessing content mastery within a single course. It was possible, however, to establish affective learning outcomes that crossed all disciplinary boundaries. The importance of the affective domain is argued by Alias & Alias in this volume. Independent evaluators designed a study to address these outcomes.

Because the span of courses was large, and enrollments in any one of them likely to be small, the evaluators created an attitude survey using a Likert scale to measure change in students' beliefs about the utility of mathematics to other disciplines and other attitudes the project sought to affect. Salomon & Perkins (1989) recommend a strategy that establishes an "expectation for transfer", a statement about both pedagogy and student attitudes that describes very well what the general evaluation sought to measure. By using a broad attitude survey the impact of interdisciplinary courses with the sciences (such as math and physics or earth science) could be tracked with the same instrument as courses with the humanities (such as math and art, music or literature). The evaluators gave the survey the first and last weeks of class and approximately six weeks into the following quarter. The delayed third survey was intended to capture attitude changes that persisted. Due to the time frame and constraints of the grant, it was not possible to track attitude changes over many months or years.

The survey asked students how strongly they agreed or disagreed with statements such as *"Math helps me understand the world around me"* or *"Doing math raises interesting new questions about the world"*, as well as some scored in reverse such as *"I rarely encounter situations that are mathematical in nature outside school"*. A factor analysis of survey data identified redundancies within the questionnaire that produced the following four strong strands:

1. Confidence and ability to do mathematics
2. Utility of mathematics to life or career goals
3. Self-actualization (personal growth through studying mathematics)
4. Connections and relevance to other disciplines

Survey data was supplemented by interviews conducted according to a strict protocol, taped, transcribed and coded for responses. In this five-year project, the most valuable data to project investigators would necessarily be collected in the early offerings of courses. Three years into the project the evaluators had transcribed 130 interviews, running to 1000 pages of data. The interviews were meant to illuminate whether changes in student attitudes were indeed the result of the course they had just taken. For example, the prompt "Can you tell me something you learned in this course?" was a way to find out if the interdisciplinary aspects of it were important enough to surface spontaneously in the student's recall. When possible, evaluators also conducted interviews with a control course covering the same mathematics, and also tested content if a control existed.

By and large, students got the point. One student in a math/physics course described the "strength" of the course as *the way it ties together math and physics*" making it easier to learn. "*You understand it more thoroughly,*" the student states, "*and you understand applications.*" Another student from the same course described math and science as "*scary and messy and wonderful and exciting*". This particular course also had greater retention of students into science and engineering than the standard introductory sequence. In other words, students who had expressed an interest in majoring in these subjects at the start of their first year were more likely to continue in those subjects if they had taken the interdisciplinary course than the regular course sequence. Math and humanities courses drew students from a range of majors and these had a large spread in mathematics background. These were not courses "about math" but real mathematics integrated with real art/music/history/etc, and the mathematics could be a challenge at times. Students described this approach to mathematics as "*interesting and colorful*". One said it gave "*confidence about math again, but in a different way... I just learned its place in the universe... that it's always connected and that I can do it, I can succeed in math.*" Some mentioned learning to "*think more broadly*" and to "*look at things from different angles*". Asked to summarize years of data across all interdisciplinary courses, the evaluators reported three findings that address the transfer question directly.

1. Students' interest in mathematics is more important than their perceived math ability in determining whether they study more mathematics.

2. Real life applications make mathematics more approachable and more interesting.
3. Expanding the range of mathematics topics accessible to average college students increases their interest in mathematics.

The lead evaluator was also able to compare the experience of students in these interdisciplinary courses with that of students in introductory calculus courses. She concludes that although weak or uninterested students completed the calculus course discouraged about mathematics, their similar counterparts in the mathematics and humanities courses were having a productive learning experience (Korey, 2002a). She further suggests that the present emphasis on calculus for all students might be working against preserving the mathematical interests of these weaker students, who would benefit more from a more diverse selection of offerings.

One important lesson one draws from these statements is that transfer should not be treated as something that happens after learning the basic material. In the case of these students, the understanding that mathematics could and should be applied in unusual settings did indeed emerge in a context, as a true piece of "situated learning". We also see that asking students to use mathematics to some other end did not detract from their learning as long as they perceived the end to be a worthwhile goal. This finding underscored the successful strategy of offering a wide menu of academic choices. Students did seem to emerge from interdisciplinary math courses with a new willingness to use math to facilitate their study of other topics of interest to them. These students did not treat the deep applications they studied with the distaste usually reserved for "word problems". In short, the evaluators produced convincing evidence that a change in curriculum and/or pedagogy did indeed produce a measurable change in affective learning outcomes.

It is important to place these findings in the context of traditional content-based learning outcomes. If a student is completely successful at learning something but has concluded on the basis of his or her experience that they never wish to think about the subject again, then educators may have won one battle but they have certainly lost the war. In mathematics education, this war is the crux of the problem, as lack of a mathematics foundation effectively shuts the door to the academic pursuit of science and engineering. Preserving student interest in mathematics and their willingness to use it in other classes is a key to success across all of the scientific disciplines.

Interdisciplinary curriculum

The courses influenced or created through MATC did indeed span the curriculum. Four years into the project one finds eight new courses intersecting with the humanities, eight new courses intersecting with the sciences, and thirteen existing courses across the disciplines on which the project had an influence. Most of these were co-taught by at least two professors from different departments, who regarded these courses as interdisciplinary. The project as a whole both supported and benefited from a recently instituted interdisciplinary requirement within the college. An independent college committee approved courses as suitable for fulfilling the interdisciplinary requirement. As it struggled with these decisions, this committee searched for a suitable definition for "interdisciplinary" teaching. The literature on 'interdisciplinarity' reveals the difficulty of making a definition, with various authors splitting the concept into many levels depending on the level of integration of the two (or more) disciplines (Kockelmans, 1979; Stember, 1991; Finkenthal, 2001; Lattuca, 2001; Paxton, 1996). Even the concept of a 'discipline' requires elucidation (see Jordan & Carlile, this volume). Unable to deduce the degree of integration of content from a mere syllabus, the committee had to rely on rules of thumb: each course had to have two instructors from different departments. All faculty creating new courses through MATC submitted their courses to this committee for approval. Almost all of them earned "interdisciplinary" status on the first try, although the committee did hesitate on math/physics and math/computer science combinations.

The change in faculty perception of how teaching and learning are supposed to work was an important aspect of MATC. It is unreasonable to expect much improvement in student learning outcomes if there is no change in the classroom. However, two instructors co-teaching could take different strategies. They might present their perspectives sequentially, in relative isolation from each other. Alternatively they might attempt a thorough integration of their subjects in advance of the course, with room for dialogue between these subjects built into the strategy.

The evaluators tracked faculty progress as they invented, gave, and talked afterward about their courses. Teams that relied on a tag-team approach to lessons (first this subject, then that one) had less positive student response than those who constructed an integrated content platform from scratch. Those undertaking a full integration of material found that they had to overcome the very different linguistic styles of different disciplines, needing to explain to each other things they had previously taken for granted. Co-teaching required open discussions about pedagogy and a willingness to learn the material from the unfamiliar field. One student remarked, *"If we can learn it in ten weeks, why can't they?"* Faculty remarked on the time commitment involved in designing a good interdisciplinary experience for the students but were, on the whole, enthusiastic. They described their experience variously as *"stimulating intellectually"*, *"very exciting"* and *"humbling in a very good sense"*. In an early project report, the principal investigator remarks: *"Rubbing our faculty up against each other in this way breaks the cycle of the classroom as the instructor's private fiefdom; it allows one to see new possibilities, and increases our options for change."*

Having identified learning outcomes and created a strategy that reliably produced them, the project investigators were then faced with the question of sustainability. Ultimately, some aspects of the sustainability of both courses and continued innovation would depend upon the culture of the college.

The culture of the institution

Nissani (1997) makes the point that interdisciplinary courses could be in competition with standard courses for resources. Because the college had put separate resources towards its interdisciplinary requirement, this competition was postponed for a while. Ultimately, decisions about resource allocation would affect this rich collection of courses at various levels in the institution, but especially at the department level, where the administration ultimately placed the responsibility for support. So in the beginning these courses benefited from their designation as "interdisciplinary" because they could draw on separate resources from the college. In the end the designation worked to the disadvantage of the project because departments were asked to pick up the tab for courses that were typically twice as expensive as a regular course.

Interdisciplinary teaching and learning do not always fit in well with the academic culture of a particular institution (Nissani, 1997) (Korey, 2002b). Overcoming conflicting goals for student learning is certainly the first step in making interdisciplinary teaching possible, but teaching also occurs in the larger context of college departments, divisions, and requirement structures, which may also work against innovation. Program officers visiting the MATC project were clearly aware of this obstruction to the potential sustainability of new courses being developed and made culture change one criterion upon which they based the success of the project. Internal transformation of the culture of the college was not explicitly stated as a goal of MATC, but the National Science Foundation demanded that MATC principal investigators address this issue explicitly in annual reports.

The way in which an institution successfully goes about changing its course offerings, requirements, and more, is highly dependent on its culture (Kezar & Eckel, 2002). Typologies of college and university cultures characterize a given institution as "collegial, managerial, developmental or negotiating" (Bergquist, 1992), "strong" versus "weak", or "internally" versus "externally" oriented (Cameron & Freeman, 1991; Sporn, 1996).

The culture of the institution in which MATC grew could be characterized as collegial, strong, and internally oriented. Bergquist's "collegial" culture is characterized by scholarly engagement and shared governance and decision-making, in which the faculty as a body would have a considerable say in curriculum requirements, tenure, etc. Dartmouth fit this description perfectly. Although administrators had considerable power in the institution, a single vote of "no confidence" from the faculty would almost guarantee the end of term for an individual. Sporn (1996) identifies a "strong" culture as one whose cultural values, internal structure and strategic plans are aligned well with one another. In spite of considerable internal debate about the balance of cultural values inside the institution, Dartmouth faculty members were very aware of how it sought to place itself in the academic spectrum, how it aspired to be different from other similar institutions. Alumni, faculty, students and administrators all expected certain viewpoints, policies and traditions to continue indefinitely into the future. Finally, the college was "internally oriented" in the sense that change of any sort would always be measured against the image or vision the faculty, students and administrators held of who they, as a body, were. This measurement could easily outweigh other, more outwardly directed, considerations.

No aspect of MATC was designed or intended to affect any of these broad characterizations of the culture of its institution. But these characteristics may be applied at any level of granularity. A single department may be externally oriented to the college as a whole, or it may be internally oriented to its own singular interests and concerns. In return, the administration may encourage or discourage such an orientation. A transformation in the orientation of a single department may persist or wither in the face of responses from the administration. The same relationship pertains between a single course and the department in which it is offered. These are the relationships MATC sought to transform, making departments more externally oriented to the intellectual habits of other disciplines and simultaneously more supportive of courses with the same goal, and proving the worthiness of these courses to the administration with the goal of earning its ongoing support.

Starting with the first visit of representatives from NSF, MATC had the issue of 'culture change' on the table. For all other aspects of the project the proposal included specific goals, outcomes, benchmarks and even timetables for achieving these. The principal investigators found it easier to meet the scheduled outcomes stated in the proposal (courses invented, modules written, publishers contacted, workshops held, etc.), than to grapple with the slippery notion of culture change. The reports of the project's external steering committee mention the issue annually, stating emphatically that the college needed to recognize the project financially by committing to the ongoing support of certain aspects of it after government funding ended. It is a telling observation that, over the course of five years the annual project report does not emphasize culture change at all until the final project report done, due to rollover funds, two years after the projected end. Financial support from the college after MATC funding ran out was never mentioned in the original project proposal, but the request for this emerged as the project grew and showed success. While waiting for this large gesture from the institution, the project investigators could not identify other short term markers of institutional change, nor could they make such change happen. The external steering committee wanted culture change incarnated in a center devoted to the continuation of the project, including course support. This did not happen.

Sporn (1996) makes the point that a "strong, internally oriented" academic culture is difficult to change because it is not responsive to outside forces. The general outcome of MATC fits this description well. However, even in such a culture there may be groups that behave differently, especially in a "collegial" culture where the faculty has great autonomy. In the case of MATC, the department of mathematics actually became more externally oriented towards other departments in the institution. Even now, almost 10 years after the end of the project, this department actively supports and continues to invent courses that are intrinsically interdisciplinary, even though they are taught without a second instructor from the partner discipline. Occasionally funds can be found to support that second person. The institution as a whole abandoned its interdisciplinary requirement entirely, so these courses no longer depend on it for enrollments, yet they succeed and persist.

The MATC project also built strong ties between mathematics and humanities faculty that continue.

Managing change within the culture

In order to make a lasting impact on its institution, MATC had to consider three issues. These were (in order of necessity) recruitment (of faculty to the project and students to courses), sustainability (of funding for successful new courses) and infrastructure (to support courses, publishing, new funding initiatives, outreach, and so forth).

The ability of the principal investigators to involve a growing number of faculty in the project varied across disciplines and had great, but uneven, success. Collaborations inside the science division were usually negotiated with departments either through committees devoted to the task, through individuals who wanted permission to pursue a course, or via emissaries - usually project principal investigators from that department. In the humanities division negotiations were always with individuals and were generally the result of an invitation extended by a mathematician over lunch. The collegial culture of the institution made the step from eating lunch to proposing a new course to the college committee for approval, and usually funding, an easy step. In the social sciences the strategy was to collect all interested individuals and attempt to reach some consensus about how the teaching of statistics, in particular, could be improved. This last strategy was not successful. By the end of its funding period the project could boast accomplishments in science and humanities, but had only minor interventions to report in the social sciences. Inside the mathematics department there was no overt recruitment to the project, which had such a large impact on the department that it was already a frequent subject of discussion. Recruitment inside the mathematics department was strictly viral in nature and generally successful in sustaining both the number of faculty interested in teaching interdisciplinary courses and also the general attitude of acceptance towards these courses.

Sustainability was a far greater issue. The college had mechanisms for supporting a handful of interdisciplinary courses in one guise or another, but only on a sporadic basis. Courses developed as integral parts of a major could not depend on these mechanisms for survival and were supported in the short run directly by MATC funds. In the long run they would have to be paid for by either departments or through special funds set aside by the administration. New infrastructure could exist for the duration of MATC through project funding but would need support from the administration to continue beyond the funding period.

Sporn (1996) makes the case that, in addition to functional approaches stressing costs and benefits of change, there is also the possibility of using the culture to change the culture itself. She specifically mentions the role of symbol in the second strategy. Academic life is full of rituals that confer symbolic importance to activities that would otherwise be invisible. Thus the principal investigators and the administration had, broadly speaking, two strategies at their disposal. On both sides costs and benefits were certainly weighed and the project provided copious reports and data documenting the success of courses developed through MATC. Although the data were clearly of interest outside the college and were used effectively to motivate faculty from other institutions, inside Dartmouth the data were only sufficient to prevent interference while the project was in progress. Indeed, one could make the case that Dartmouth was sufficiently prestigious that the data carried symbolic weight at other institutions.

From the start, MATC was to have an external steering committee. The NSF requested that it be enlarged from its original three members to eight, embracing a variety of disciplines. The chair of this external committee was a member of the National Academy of Science, as prestigious a position as could be desired. From the start, the principal investigators attempted to use this committee to establish the importance of the project to the president of the college, deans, and other administrators. The reports from this committee consistently include portions directly addressed to institutional leaders, requesting both support for courses and the creation of a center to continue the work of the project. These requests were argued from data, but also on the grounds of symbolism. The center, in particular, was to engage in outreach and be a national model (and hence a valuable symbol of the institution itself). Often the case was made, not only in writing but also face to face with the president and other administrators and in the company of program officers from the National Science Foundation.

As mentioned before, none of these recommendations came to fruition. The project created a small, underfunded center that continues to exist but has never been officially recognized by the institution. Sporn's observations, and the characterization of the college culture as collegial, strong and internally focused, may help to explain why.

The fact that the external committee consisted of individuals who were very highly regarded in their field and was chaired by a member of the National Academy of Science made little impression on administrators. Like the collegial institution in Kezar & Eckel's (2002) study, administrators at MATC's institution regarded outside influences as interference. In that study, change was successful based on a top-down plan overseen by a respected faculty member who was promoted to vice president for this purpose. Note that this is exactly the opposite strategy from the one used by MATC. Although administrators were invited to planning meetings by the principal investigators early on, it soon became clear that they would not come to these.

Similarly, the idea that Dartmouth would be a leader of national change was not compelling to an internally focused institution, especially one that did not embrace "change" as part of its strong self-image. The institution led a change in spite of all this, as the growth of interdisciplinary proposals to NSF during the next decade was partly due to a host of faculty development workshops in which MATC took part. In the last year of the project the principal investigator read approximately 50 files of job applicants for a position in mathematics (by no means all of them). Two of the 50 mentioned MATC directly as a reason to come to Dartmouth, and one recommender also mentioned the project, as noted in the annual report to NSF. It is very unusual for job applicants to indicate awareness of curriculum projects in their application letters, and the principal investigator took this as an indication of successful dissemination, at the time largely unaware that a large project at a prestigious college functions as a symbol outside that institution whether one intends it or not.

It is clear from annual reports that the principal investigators were not aware of the possibility of using symbolic gesture to guide MATC to a permanent place in the institution. It seems unlikely that administrators consciously refused to make any symbolic gestures (funded or otherwise) in support of the project. It is more likely that the fit between the vision that investigators and steering committee had for MATC simply didn't fit with the vision administrators held for the institution, a vision reinforced regularly by the strong culture of the college. One should not conclude from this discussion that changing the situation was impossible, merely that the principal investigators could not figure out how to do it.

The reader is invited to contrast MATC's bottom-up approach with that of Bartholomew *et al.* (this volume), or Huet *et al.* (this volume). Coupling sustainability of change with measurably improved student learning outcomes proved difficult for MATC.

Conclusion

There are quite a few lessons to be drawn from the MATC case. First of all, we see that meaningful change in curriculum and pedagogy is very implementable provided participants have a clear sense of the goal for student learning outcomes (attitude change in this case) and a tool to measure success (survey instruments and interview data). Most full size courses were successful by these measures. Those that were not were instantly discontinued. Short-term interventions in existing courses were expected to have too small an effect to be worth measuring. From evaluation data (Korey, 2002a) we also see the value of interdisciplinary learning to students, both intellectually and motivationally.

We also see that several kinds of change are facilitated by collaboration across disciplines, and that faculty as well as students can benefit from this effort. Changing what happens in the classroom is a prerequisite for improving student learning outcomes. Interdisciplinary teaching requires one to re-evaluating the language, boundaries and defining questions of one's own discipline. It also provides a platform for re-evaluating pedagogy that otherwise might be taken for granted. Faculty members involved in the MATC project made both of these observations repeatedly to evaluators. They also found that co-teaching with a faculty member from another discipline appears to be a useful form of faculty development.

MATC is also an illustration of how the goal of culture change may be met or not at a variety of levels of granularity. Deep and persistent change at the departmental level may exist in a wider institutional context that is resistant to change. The presence of a relatively large proportion (a quarter to a third) of mathematics department members involved in the project surely contributed to what seems to be a lasting cultural shift inside that department, suggesting that the notion of "critical mass" would be worth studying across a variety of educational reform projects. It may be a good strategy in some cases to concentrate effort inside a smaller cohesive cultural unit, rather than scattering effort broadly (and therefore thinly) across a wider range. It would be useful to know if "critical mass" is a measurable phenomenon.

It is also clear from MATC how the presence of easily verified benchmarks kept the project on track and how the absence of these led to difficulties. In particular, the culture of the institution was not taken fully into account by the principal investigators. The external steering committee and the National Science Foundation were aware of the need to address culture change explicitly and set project goals of institutional buy-in that would have made the project productive far beyond its end date, had they been met. But there were no intermediate, lesser benchmarks set that would naturally lead to the larger goals. In particular there were no intermediate benchmarks of the symbolic sort that could mark a clear path from an enthusiastic faculty movement to an institutionally recognized and supported effort.

In summary, this case study illustrates how one project attempted to address a single learning outcome broadly across many courses and sustainably within one institution. Integrated institutional and pedagogical change requires strategies, evaluation, and benchmarks that address all levels of granularity, from the student experience in the classroom to administrative response at the highest levels.

About the author

Dorothy Wallace is Professor of Mathematics, Dartmouth College, USA. She can be contacted at this e-mail:
Dorothy.Wallace@dartmouth.edu

Chapter 8

Putting Humpty Dumpty Together Again: Learning as Integrated Performance in Context

Anne Jordan & Orison Carlile

Introduction

Our experience as academic programme managers in Waterford Institute of Technology in Ireland has led to our growing unease about the use of learning outcome statements as the basis for the design and delivery of postgraduate education programmes. In particular we are concerned about the way learning outcomes may ignore the integrative approach and broader purposes and values associated with postgraduate programmes. Improving students' learning outcomes is therefore of key interest to us. A learning outcomes approach to curriculum is not solely of interest to those involved in postgraduate or professional education – it is also of interest to those working in most types of post-compulsory education, at undergraduate and in further education levels. Learning outcomes are widely used and are in accord with educational trends over the past century, where the higher education curriculum has experienced a process of gradual subdivision of its goal of producing the generally educated person to that of producing specialists in a range of separate disciplines.

Figure 1 illustrates how, historically, disciplines have been subdivided into smaller programmes which are then delivered in smaller subsections called modules which are again subdivided into a series of precise learning outcomes. In order to establish if our concerns were shared by other academics, we reviewed the literature on learning outcomes, looking specifically at the claims made for and against them. We followed this by a small scale research project that explored the perceived advantages and disadvantages of statements of learning outcomes from the viewpoint of teachers and participants on our postgraduate programmes. This led to an understanding of the most important features of learning outcomes that we needed to address.

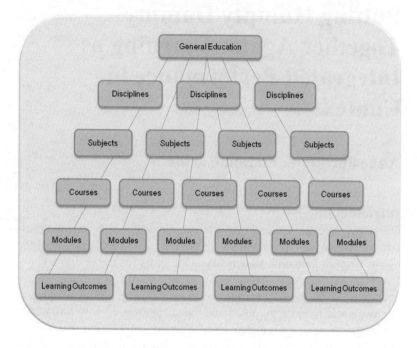

Figure 1: Subdivision of education

We then sought a solution which would retain the best features of learning outcomes while addressing the identified deficiencies. This resulted in some practical implications for the programmes we deliver, so that our students' learning outcomes could be improved.

Theoretical background

A learning outcome has been defined in the Bologna Process as a *"...written statement of what the successful student/learner is expected to be able to do at the end of the module/course unit or qualification."* (Adam, 2004 cited in Kennedy 2007:19). Over the past fifteen years, a number of authors and researchers working within higher education have signalled the possibility of an improvement to student learning through the use of a 'learning outcomes' approach. Typical of these was an early influential article by Barr & Tagg (1995) entitled *"From teaching to learning: a new paradigm for undergraduate education"*.

They argue for the need to move from a traditional teacher-centred paradigm to a student-centred learning paradigm, based on explicit learning outcomes, clearly linked to assessment.

A range of authors have also attested to the value of a precise description and statement of learning outcomes. According to Baume (2009:9), a good learning outcome is:

Active	it describes what students can do
Attractive	students want to achieve it
Comprehensible	students know what it means
Appropriate	to the student's current goals and career plans
Attainable	most students will mostly meet it, with due effort
Assessable	we can see if it has been achieved
Visible	in the course booklet and in the VLE

Maher (2004) claims that the value of focusing on the outcomes of education, rather than on inputs, is that such outcomes can meet the needs of all higher education stakeholders - the student, the teacher and external bodies if these are properly considered and articulated in the curriculum. Their use can add value to the educational process, if they are used flexibly to guide student learning and curriculum development and involve both learners and teachers as active participants in their development (Hussey & Smith, 2003:367).

Biggs (2003) argues that assessment is fairer, more transparent and reliable when teaching, assessment and learning activities are 'constructively aligned' with learning outcomes. In her chapter Isabel Huet proposes a curiculum tool that can aid the constructive alignment process. According to Biggs (2003:27), this alignment 'entraps' students within a consistent web of learning, obliging them to engage with the learning outcomes.

Learning outcomes provide mechanisms for obtaining credits, exemptions and advanced standing on the basis of experience or prior learning that would otherwise go unrecognised, unmeasured and unrewarded. A number of our students have gained admission to our programmes on the basis of their demonstration that they had achieved the relevant outcomes through prior learning and experience.

On a broader front, learning outcomes, when used with national and international frameworks of qualifications, can aid student mobility by the recognition of their qualifications, demonstrate their transparency, and simplify credit transfer (Adam 2004).

However there are both conceptual and pedagogical objections to a learning outcomes approach. Hussey & Smith (2003:358) assert that the clarity, explicitness and objectivity claimed for learning outcomes is largely 'spurious'. They argue that a tight focus on pre-specified outcomes fails to promote good learning, good teaching and the empirical experiences of teachers and of learners. *"The most fruitful and valuable feature of higher education is the emergence of ideas, skills and connections which were unforeseen even by the teacher"* (Hussey & Smith, 2002:228).

In "The McDonaldization of Higher Education" Hayes & Wynward (2002) attacks the technicality and instrumentalism of learning outcomes claiming that they exemplify the key characteristics of 'technical rationality' of modern society.

Characteristic	Learning outcome implication
Efficiency	Outcomes specified
Predictability	Predetermined
Calculability	Number of learning outcomes specified
Control	Teaching methods directed
	Assessment methods directed

Table 1: Technical rationality of learning outcomes

Table 1 illustrates the characteristics of specificity, pre-determination and direction. A serious problem with learning outcome statements are that they address only isolated behaviours but integration is an important aspect of higher education programmes such as ours. Higher order learning requires a connected and deep understanding. Hussey & Smith (2003:359) claim that the development of knowledge is better represented as an iterative and expanding spiral, rather than a linear process which implies that once the learning outcome is achieved, it need never be revisited. At a practical and pedagogical level, an uncritical acceptance of prescriptive, pre-specified outcomes can lead to an instrumental *"...reductionist approach where students simply aim to meet the minimum threshold requirements, as specified in the learning outcomes, inadvertently stifling creativity and originality in both staff and students."* Moreover, if learning outcomes become the driver of classroom interactions, they may prevent the discussion of ideas or questions that do not clearly relate to the set outcomes, creating what Ecclestone (1999:29-36) calls a *"...subtle form of closure on ideas about what is important in learning"*.

The above literature suggests a balance between what academics perceive as the positive and negative aspects of learning outcomes. A number of the views given above accord with our own experience of administering and teaching on these postgraduate programmes: in particular, the claims that learning outcomes ignore the deeper knowledge that comes from an understanding of knowledge and of values.

However, we did not wish to set out an open and shut case in relation to learning outcomes. We wished to ascertain the salient aspects of learning outcomes, positive and negative, as they were perceived by staff and participants on our MA in Learning and teaching (MALT) and MA in Management in Education (MAME) programmes, and to establish the extent to which they reflected the balance of views presented by the literature.

Research project

The research questions we identified were: in the perceptions of our staff and students:

- what are the salient aspects of learning outcomes?
- how are these aspects categorised, positively or negatively?

This research was carried out in the autumn and early spring of 2008/9 in the Waterford Institute of Technology. The population investigated was composed of the students (n=56) and staff (n=7) from the MALT and MAME programmes. The methodology was based on thematic interpretation of the views of course participants, teachers and administrators. Specific methods used for data collection included focus group interviews with teachers and students; a follow-up quantitative survey of course participants on the use of learning outcomes based on the themes identified in the focus groups and our own reflections on the literature and our own experience in teaching in higher education.

Focus groups

Our MALT and MAME participants (N=36) generally liked the fact that learning outcomes were explicit targets for what they would need to achieve at the end of a designated module. Participants approved of the emphasis in learning outcome statements on what they would be able 'to do', rather what they would 'understand'. They saw learning outcomes as useful at several levels: at lecture level, module level and course level. Learning outcomes were also seen to be useful in preparing for assessment by taking away uncertainty.

However, participants felt that learning outcomes did not take account of insights that might have occurred and that although the learning outcomes show the final result, they don't show the route to its achievement.

Our students felt that there was no incentive to do more than the amount needed to pass the assignment or module, and no point in undertaking extra unnecessary work.

Teachers

Our MALT and MAME teachers (N=19) also liked learning outcomes, but for different reasons than the course participants. Teachers welcomed the explicitness of learning outcomes and the fact that they provided a clear focus for curriculum and session planning. Teachers also favoured the assessment focus to learning outcomes claiming they made assessment comprehensible to students, and so gave them some responsibility for their own learning. Teachers were also aware of the role of learning outcomes in facilitating the recognition of prior learning in applicants to advanced programmes.

However, there was a feeling that learning outcomes should be used with caution, because they lose sight of the whole and do not foster higher order cognition or holistic professionalism. As one of our focus group members remarked about an accountancy student: *"He's passed all his accountancy exams and was awarded his degree, but I'm not sure he is competent to practise as an accountant"*.

The comment was made that in some humanities areas such as Art and Design, the language is alien to the discipline. It was thought that ultimately, learning outcomes are more helpful to course designers than to teachers. Some teachers claimed that because there is no reward for exceeding the minimum threshold, they could lead to the 'dumbing down' of knowledge.

Focus group analysis

The simplest form of thematic analysis was the division of thematic items into the positive and negative aspects of learning outcomes, with a consideration of the weighting accorded to a learning outcomes-based approach.

Positive aspects	Negative aspects
Explicitness	No incentive
Use as targets	No attention to unintended learning
Predictive nature	No attention to process
Practicality	Emphasises strategic learning
Emphasis on behaviour	
Setting of clear thresholds	
Can be used at different levels	
Useful for assessment	

Table 1: Categorisation of student themes (N=36)

Table 2 shows that the positive aspects of learning outcomes were recognised and appreciated at a number of levels. The negative themes appear to relate to the indifference to process.

Positive aspects	Negative aspects
Explicitness	Lose sight of the whole
Focus for lecturers/curriculum planners	Don't foster connected understanding
Linked to assessment	Language of LOs alien to some subjects
Give student responsibility own learning	More helpful to course designers than teachers
Useful for recognition of prior learning	Do not represent or foster higher order cognition
Comprehensible to students	Could lead to 'dumbing down'

Table 2: Categorisation of teacher themes (N= 19)

The teachers took a balanced view of the benefits of learning outcomes. As would be expected, there was a stronger awareness of the bigger picture and the dangers of the disintegrating effect of learning outcomes, a recognition of their suited-ness to some subject areas over others and a concern about a lowering of academic standards.

Follow-up survey

The themes identified above were used in the construction of a one-page questionnaire consisting of a number of closed questions eliciting the respondents (N=35) experience of learning outcomes and their perceptions of the advantages and disadvantages of a learning outcomes approach.

Experience of learning outcomes as a student or teacher	
Used them as targets in covering a course/module	21
Read them in course documentation	16
Teachers used them as stated objectives for sessions/courses	13
They were given as criteria for assignments	10
Other	4
None	4

Table 4: Experience (N=35)

Advantages of learning outcomes	
Targets for students and teachers	25
Assist designers of modules and programmes	21
Assist students in making course choices	16
Signpost essential elements for students and teachers	17
Help the teacher to assess individual students	15
Assist teacher to evaluate overall student mastery of programme	13
Help students to be strategic in their learning	13
Precise and unambiguous in stating what student will be able to do	8
Other	3

Table 5: Advantages (N=35)

Disadvantages of learning outcomes	
May not be understood by students until end of programme	21
May not address core values or philosophy of a subject area	18
May be seen as irrelevant and ignored by students	16
Fail to take account of unintended outcomes of learning	16
May be seen as administrative technicalities by teachers	13
Attempt to limit learning before it occurs	13
May break down a subject into too many separate parts	13
Not suited to subject areas where outcomes are open-ended	11
Do not take account of cumulative learning	9

Table 6: Disadvantages (N=35)

Our analysis of the data we collected indicates that students appreciate the value of learning outcomes as a focus for learning and assessment. However, in spite of proponents' assertions that learning outcomes make knowledge more comprehensible, students may not understand how they relate to a course or programme overall, and consequently may see them as irrelevant. This suggests to us that while useful as pedagogical targets, students are failing to see the big picture.

This data also confirms the misgivings in the literature that learning outcomes may ignore core philosophies and values, promote strategic learning at the expense of a broader philosophy and fail to take adequate account of cumulative learning or of valuable yet unintended outcomes.

Improving learning outcomes for students

Two problematic themes need to be addressed:

1. How learning outcomes are perceived and conceptualised given their:

- fractional epistemology
- behavioural emphasis.
- lack of student understanding
- possible perception of irrelevancy for achievement
- failure to see the big picture.

2. How, as designed in curriculum and presented to students, learning outcomes:

- are discrete, limiting and behavioural in nature
- promote strategic learning
- neglect cumulative or unintended learning.

Having identified these two problematic aspects of learning outcomes, we conducted an investigation of alternative pedagogical strategies, which, whilst retaining the positive aspects of learning outcomes, would address their deficiencies and so improve the ultimate learning of our students. Given their nature, it is clear that the issues need to be integrated holistically. Our search for a means of overcoming atomisation led us to look for pedagogical models that stressed 'understanding'.

Teaching for Understanding

Developed in Harvard by the Howard Gardner and the Project Zero team, the Teaching for Understanding Movement (TfU) stresses the concept of 'understanding', outlawed in behaviourist learning outcome usage. 'Understanding' here is defined in a constructivist sense which stresses the importance of meaning in learning, rather than isolated behaviours. According to the cognitive scientist, David Perkin understanding is "*a flexible performance capability*" - the ability to think and act flexibly with what one knows (Wiske, 1998:40):

> "*To gauge a person's understanding at a given time, ask the person to do something that puts understanding to work – explaining, solving a problem, building an argument, constructing a product...what learners do in response not only shows their current level of understanding, but very likely advances it.*" Wiske (1998:41).

According to the TfU philosophy, such understanding is composed of knowledge and skills, where *knowledge* is: information brought to bear in a particular context. The learning of facts can be crucial to learning for understanding, but learning facts is not learning for understanding, and *skills* are: routine performances brought to bear in a particular context leading to an integrated understanding and competence.

The 'Teaching for Understanding' Movement stresses the importance in curriculum of identifying four key elements:

Element	Characteristic
Disciplinary knowledge	Main topics that are central to the discipline and need to be understood
Understanding goals	Public statements of what teachers want students to understand
Performance	Methods and opportunities for developing performances of understanding
Assessment	Ongoing assessment of understanding

Table 7: Key elements of teaching for understanding
Based on McCarthy (2009)

This approach is similar to that of statements of learning outcomes, but goes beyond them, since it demands active engagement and student performances that develop and demonstrate understanding. Such performance should be varied, complex and often collaborative.

Dimensions of understanding
Teaching for understanding involves a combination of particular disciplinary knowledge and appropriate pedagogical methods. Hinrichsen (in this volume) points out that the epistemology of a discipline is often confused with its pedagogy. Understanding occurs within a particular discipline and cannot be separated from it. The teacher is the expert in the discipline and needs to analyse and present topics in line with the understanding required. In their chapter on analogical learning, Branch *et al.* (in this volume) explore how instructors can use of analogy to improve student learning outcomes. The dimensions of understanding framework developed in line with TfU, suggests a way of analysing and organising topics in a discipline.

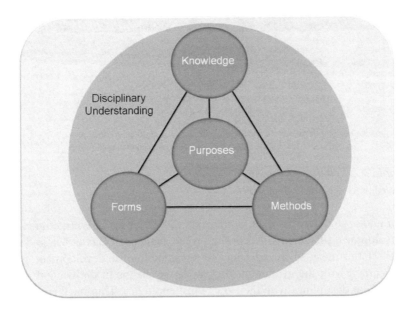

Figure 2: Dimensions of disciplinary understanding

Figure 2 illustrates four dimensions of understanding:

Knowledge What is the material?
Forms   How is it expressed?
Methods   How it is done?
Purposes   Why it is done?

All of these four dimensions co-exist within an overall framework of disciplinary understanding. Within a discipline area are concepts vital to progress, but which frequently cause students difficulty. Meyer & Land (2003) refer to these as 'threshold concepts'. Threshold concepts are vital because they represent a transformed way of understanding and involve an ontological shift, irreversible once understood (Graham & Potter, 2008).They are integrative in that they expose the hidden interrelatedness of phenomena and troublesome knowledge. Some-times they are counter-intuitive, bewildering or incoherent until grasped. For example, one threshold concept in our postgraduate pro-gramme on education management is the idea that management is con-cerned not about managerial actions but with the world view and val-ues of the manager.

Attribute	Evidence
Transformative	Ontological and conceptual shift
	Changed perception of self and subject
Irreversible	Paradigm shift not forgotten
	May be modified or refined later
Integrative	Exposes hidden interrelatedness of phenomena
	Reveals new connections from new perspective
Bounded	Defines the boundaries of a subject area
	Clarifies the scope of a subject community
Troublesome	'Troublesome knowledge' may appear counter-intuitive, alien,
	incoherent or absurd (Perkins in Meyer & Land, 2003:7)

Table 3: Attributes of threshold concepts
Based on Graham & Potter (2008)

An understanding of threshold concepts facilitates the epistemological development of students. According to the analysis of Baxter Magolda (1992) the most advanced stage of epistemological development is concerned with the evaluation of knowledge claims in the context of particular disciplines with their own epistemologies. This stage is integrative - concerned with the bigger picture, with values and with disciplinary knowledge.

Integrative performance in context

The development of integrated 'performances' of knowledge, skills and values rather than the achievement of individual outcomes is necessary as an aid to understanding. The coordination at institutional levels required to support such performance is discussed by Bartholomew *et al.* (in this volume). TfU's constructivist methods of teaching stress relevance and context, active learning, problem-solving and reflection. Expert understanding enables the learner to carry out a variety of performances that can both demonstrate the understanding of a topic and advance that understanding in an authentic practice-based context. For example, our participants are required to relate course concepts to their own experience offering them an awareness of the social embeddedness of professional knowledge, skills and values.

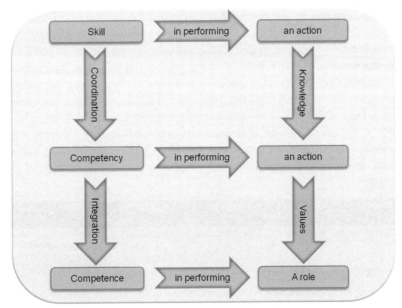

Figure 3: Role integration of skills and task performance
Jordan *et al.* (2008:204)

Learning can be viewed as a process of increased sophistication of understanding displayed in sequenced performances. This involves a reorientation and transformation that can only truly be recognised in relation to a holistic view of a topic. Such an integrative approach involves a combination of skills, competencies, knowledge and values. Skills are the abilities to perform particular activities successfully and consistently. If a set of skills are integrated with appropriate knowledge and attitudes then it produces competency in the performance of a complex task. If a range of competencies are then combined the result is competence in the performance of a role in context.

The performance of an action is integrated through the coordination of skills and knowledge to perform certain tasks which in turn are integrated with values, in context to arrive at competence in a role. The three horizontal parts of Figure 3 emphasise performance; the vertical parts illustrate increasing sophistication and integration as one progresses from skill to competency to competence.

For example, in our management in education programme financial leadership requires that technical skill and knowledge in balancing accounts needs to be integrated with good educational values to produce competence in the performance of the managerial role. The integration of knowledge, skills and attitudes in performance in requires integrated programmes of study and the coherence and connectedness of modules. One of the problems with our programmes lies in the tension between the demands of administrators and prospective students for shorter courses and our awareness that integrative understanding takes time in order to progress through competency levels from novice to master.

Stage	Naïve Pre-engaged	Novice	Apprentice	Master
Performance	Intuitive	Based on ritual	Based on disciplinary knowledge	Integrative, creative and critical
Concepts	Seen as directly available and unproblematic	Simple rehearsed concepts seen in performance	Seen as complex	Flexibly related to criteria and purposes
Student view	Learning is not connected to life. Purposes not considered	Knowledge is step-by-step mechanistic	Following procedures of domain experts	Complex driven by conflicting frameworks
Validation	No ownership no reflection	External authority	Connects knowledge, performance and life	Emerging from public argumentation of practitioners

Table 9: Gradual progression through competence levels
Based on McCarthy (2009)

The move from novice to master is a progression to sophistication of understanding displayed in performance. To achieve this requires time and deliberate practice and goes through a progressive sequence of stages from naïve to novice to apprentice to master. To achieve this sophistication takes much time. The research experience supports the need for time in the process very clearly. *"The emerging picture from such studies is that ten thousand hours of practice are required to achieve the level of mastery associated with being a world-class expert – in anything"*, Levitin (2006:197).

The Levitin reference above is to music where practice is only to be expected, but practice is required for mastery in any field. Gladwell (2008) in his hugely successful book *Outliers: The Story of Success* offers example after example from computers programming, chess, music, academic study and sports that confirms the efficacy of consistent and deliberate practice.

Implications for our practice

Our exploration of the ideas of 'teaching for understanding' and 'integrative performance in context' led us to view them as ways of addressing the problematic areas identified by our reflection and small scale research project Table 10 pinpoints the identified issues drawn from the data and show how these may be addressed.

Problematic issue	Solution
Flawed perception and conceptualisation of learning outcomes	• Teaching for understanding • Threshold concepts
Flawed design and presentation of learning outcomes	• Integrative performance in context • Progression from novice to expert

Table 10: How the two problematic issues are addressed

Implications for teaching

Teaching for understanding differs from a learning outcomes approach by having as its centre the purpose and the values which are embedded within the particular domain, but are absent in learning outcomes because they are not behaviours, but intentions. It also requires considerable attention to the different forms in which knowledge is represented in a particular domain, and to the epistemology and methods used. Interdisciplinary interactions between domains are discussed by Wallace (in this volume).

Although the movement stresses 'understanding goals' as a guiding principle in teaching and curriculum design, as course administrators we are constrained by the existing bureaucratic system in our college that require behavioural learning outcome statements to be used as guiding principles. One benefit of the TfU approach is its stress on the specific purposes and values underpinning the discipline and the knowledge. We intend to lay more stress on these in course documentation, in professional development training for lecturers and in induction sessions for new participants.

Through the use of TfU we believe that it is possible to incorporate a greater element of meaning-making as displayed in performance in our programmes.

Implications for assessment

In the 'Teaching for Understanding' paradigm, the purpose of assessment is to indicate what students do and do not understand and to help students to develop deeper understanding. This requires ongoing self,

145

peer and teacher assessment of student performances, with criteria based on understanding goals. We already encourage performance in our current assessment methods. In the pedagogy module assessment methods include a micro-teaching element where participants are filmed teaching a short lesson to their peers followed by debriefing and critique. It also involves peer observation of a real lesson. Some modules use posters as an assessment method and participants also make presentations that are assessed. However, it would be fair to say that the majority of the assessment is of the essay-type.

As part of an action -research cycle we plan to introduce a new improved assessment method based on sequenced performance followed by an evaluation. Authentic performance and authentic assessment require that active learning in the major concepts within a discipline is embedded within a specific learning community and a realistic environment. The assessment therefore will involve the everyday scholarly activities of an academic. These activities include teaching, writing articles and producing posters and making presentations – all under the scrutiny of review and the community of peers.

In order to arrange a sequenced realistic performance we propose to organise the assessment around a mini-conference which will be a fitting display of understanding in performance in the form of a final public event in front of peers as colleagues and lecturers as choreographers. In this way the assessment will be situated in a community of practice. As they participate in the conference, students will be required to:

- make a presentation employing PowerPoint and handouts;
- produce a poster;
- produce an academic paper of publishable standard.

In preparation for this conference, there will be some preparatory assignments for example the construction of a 'wiki' page and mini-research proposals that will be used to assess and to guide the student so that the final conference is as successful and rewarding as possible. There will also be a debriefing and discussion session as part of the conference so that students can share their evaluations of the process as part of the action research cycle.

Conclusions

There is a well-rehearsed debate about the pros and cons of learning outcomes. We too enter into that debate but we can also see a possibility of improving students' learning by marrying learning outcomes to more recent preoccupations of the scholarly community. These include an awareness of the importance of contextual and disciplinary knowledge, of understanding demonstrated in performance and of the nature and development of mastery.

About the authors

Anne Jordan is Programme Director of the MA in Learning and Teaching in Higher Education at Waterford Institute of Technology, Ireland, and Honorary Professor at Lev Tolstoy Pedagogical University, Russia. She can be contacted at this e-mail: ajordan@wit.ie

Orison Carlile is Programme Director of the MA in Management in Education at Waterford Institute of Technology, Ireland, and Honorary Professor at Lev Tolstoy Pedagogical University, Russia. He can be contacted at this e-mail: ocarlile@wit.ie

Chapter 9

Analogical Learning in Higher Education

John Branch, Huai-Mei Chiang & Ivan Goenawan

Introduction

The use of analogy in education is arguably as old as education itself. Indeed, in early Greek thought, for example, analogy was the fundamental tool in the articulation of cosmological theories, in the development of the natural sciences, and in the rhetoric of ethical and political debate (Wiener, 1973). According to Hall (1987:302), the key to the teachings of Confucius is understanding his use of allusive analogy, a type of analogy which "...*attempts to set up resonance between poles of a modeling relationship*". And the world's best-selling book, the Bible, is replete with analogy - consider how 'God as Father' or 'God as Lord' conjure up images of a paternalistic and benevolent guardian.

The scientific study of 'analogical learning', however, is a relatively new phenomenon; theoretical and empirical research on analogy in learning only really took off in the early 1980s among cognitive psychologists, and today remains unknown to many educators. Likewise, discussion of the use of analogy for improving student learning outcomes occurs mostly within the context of primary and secondary schools, and is isolated to a few disciplines, namely physics, chemistry, and other 'hard' sciences.

The purpose of this chapter, therefore, is to explore analogical learning in higher education. Specifically, it aims to 1) elucidate the theory of analogical learning, and 2) examine the use of analogy for improving student learning outcomes within the context of higher education. The chapter begins by defining the concept of analogy. It then summarises the theoretical and empirical research on analogy in learning. Finally, it presents several specific analogical curricular models and study methods which can be used by instructors in higher education to improve student learning outcomes.

An analogy is like a. . .

The word analogy is derived from the ancient Greek αναλογια (*analogia*) which meant proportionality. Like its Latin derivatives *proportio* and *proportionalitas* suggest, it referred to the relationship between any two ordered pairs, mathematical or otherwise, and is understood most easily in the logical form A:B::C:D — read as "A is to B as C is to D". For example, 'source' would be analogical for spring and sun, because a spring is to water as a sun is to light.

In the Middle Ages, *analogia* took on various other meanings (Ashworth, 2008). In Biblical exegesis, for example, analogy involved the reconciliation of conflicting passages of scripture. Grammarians used analogy to settle doubts about a word's form. And for theologians, analogy judged a person's capacity for divine perfection.

It is the original Greek sense of analogy, however, which today has not only influenced the 'word on the street' but has also become the basis for theoretical and empirical work on analogy. At the most elemental level, therefore, an analogy is understood to be the similarity between two concepts. It usually takes the form "a T is like a B", as in "a battery is like a reservoir", implying not that a battery is a reservoir, but that there is some similarity between the two concepts.

Gentner (1983) is often acknowledged for bringing a formalism to the concept of analogy which, until then, had largely been a philosophical and linguistic exercise. Indeed, her structure-mapping theory presented a framework which both clarified the concept of analogy and provided a construct for empirical research. The theory responded directly to Tversky's (1977) contrast model of similarity which proposed that the greater the intersection of the attributes of objects T and B (T∩B) and the smaller their complement sets (T-B and B-T) — the attributes of T which are not shared by B and vice versa — then the greater the similarity of T and B.

According to Gentner (1983:156), however, an analogy does not rely on the degree of similarity of object attributes. Instead, the central idea of an analogy, she argued, is "*...that a relational structure that normally applies in one domain can be applied in another domain*". Indeed, the essence of the analogy between electricity and gravity is derived from the notion that both objects store energy and can be harnessed for power, which is neither strengthened nor weakened as a consequence of object attribute similarity.

In brief, the structure-mapping theory of analogy states that the analogy "a T is like a B" defines a mapping of the base domain B onto the target domain T, written as

$$M: b_i \rightarrow t_i$$

where b_i and t_i are the conceptual nodes which together comprise knowledge about domains B and T. Fundamental to the theory, therefore, is not the similarity of attributes of conceptual nodes

$$M: A(b_i) \rightarrow A(t_i)$$

but the relationship between these conceptual nodes

$$M: R(b_i) \rightarrow R(t_i).$$

Additionally, Gentner suggested that higher order relationships — systems of existing relationships — also play an important role in analogy. She called it the systematicity principle; it can be written as

$$M: R'[R_j(b_i)] \rightarrow R'[R_j(t_i)].$$

The structure-mapping theory of analogy, therefore, makes a firm distinction between literal similarity and analogy. Literal similarity maps both base attributes and relationships to the target domain (An automobile engine is like a motorcycle engine). Analogy maps only base relationships to the target domain (An automobile engine is like a pendulum).

As an example, see Figure 1 which illustrates the greenhouse effect, a concept which is the subject of much conversation and debate in higher education and everyday life. It is a relatively complex concept, and consequently, a common analogy has surfaced among science educators. . . "The greenhouse effect is like a pinball game".

In Gentner's (1983:162) words, the foundation of analogy is "...*that it conveys a system of connected knowledge, not a mere assortment of independent facts*". The intended inferences of this analogy, therefore, concern the relational structures of a pinball game and the greenhouse effect, not the attributes of either domain. Indeed, a partial interpretation of the analogy, according to the structure-mapping theory (see Figure 2), demonstrates clearly that the strength of the analogy is derived from the similarity of the relationships between the elements of a pinball game (plunger, bumpers, ball, etc.), and the relationships between the elements of the greenhouse effect (energy, greenhouse gases, atmosphere, etc). The attributes of a pinball game do not map to the greenhouse effect whatsoever.

It is important to note, however, that not all relationships are equally likely to be preserved in analogy — that is to say, not all relationships will necessarily map 1:1 from the base domain to the target domain, and vice versa. In this analogy, for example, a pinball machine has a 'backglass' which keeps score of the action and often has novel pictures or attractions. There is no obvious equivalent in the atmosphere. Similarly, a pinball which does not have enough energy does not 'enter' the pinball machine. Energy which is reflected back into space by the atmosphere does so randomly, not because of its impotence.

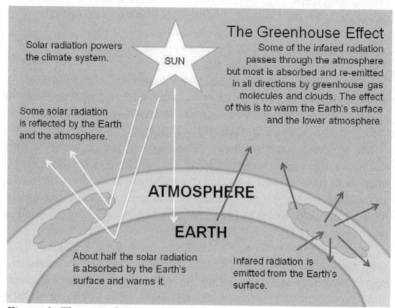

Figure 1: The greenhouse effect
Source: http://www.global-greenhouse-warming.com/images/GreenhouseEffect Diagram.jpg

Additionally, as suggested by the systematicity principle, higher-order relationships also add to the strength of the analogy. In a pinball game, for example, flippers add energy to the pinball, and re-direct it (somewhat randomly) back into the pinball machine where it encounters bumpers, some of which will reflect the ball, others of which might 'capture' the ball, only to release it later. Similarly, the earth radiates infrared energy which it had absorbed from the sun. This energy might return to space, be reflected randomly by greenhouse gases, or absorbed by greenhouse gases and re-emitted later in some random direction.

In summary, the example "The greenhouse effect is like a pinball game." evinces the intuitive nature of the structure-mapping theory of analogy. It also underlines Gentner's insistence that the interpretation of an analogy is constructed from the meaning of its parts, using syntactic rules for characterising the relationships between these parts.

And it delineates clearly the concept of analogy, distinguishing it from other kinds of domain comparisons.

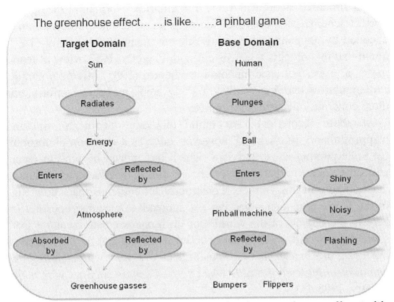

Figure 2: Structure-mapping analogy of "The greenhouse effect is like a pinball game"

It ought not be surprising, therefore, that much empirical evidence also exists in support of the structure-mapping theory of analogy, as the psychological mechanism by which people interpret an analogy [See Gentner (1977, 1980), Gentner & Gentner (1983), Markman (1997), and Markman & Genter (1997), for example.]. An important issue which remains, however, is the role which analogy plays in learning.

Analogy in learning

Linguist and cognitive scientist George Lakoff, using the term metaphor instead of analogy, believes that metaphor is at the very core of human learning. Indeed, he contends that the development of human knowledge relies on the development of better metaphors — that the application of one domain of knowledge to another provides new conceptions and new understandings of reality.

The principle idea of Lakoff's 'theory' is that metaphors are a conceptual device, and thereby essential to human thought. *"Our ordinary conceptual system in terms of which we both think and act, is fundamentally metaphorical in nature... the way we think, what we experience, and what we do every day is very much a matter of metaphor"* (Lakoff & Johnson, 1980: 315).

In a similarly theoretical vein, Rumelhart & Norman (1981) developed a schema perspective of learning, in which new information is encoded by appealing to existing schema using analogy. Duit (1991) noted that this process is consistent with Piaget's (1953) view of learning as a process of accommodation. Shapiro (1985) offered a parallel explanation of learning — that analogy helps make new information more concrete and easier to visualise.

All these theoretical viewpoints (including Gentner's structure-mapping theory of analogy), however, have as a common philosophical underpinning constructivism, which has indeed become in recent years the scientific 'paradigm of choice' for many educators, including most authors in this volume. Constructivism contends that knowledge of the world is neither objective nor subjective; meaning does not inhere in the objects of the world, nor do humans create meaning from some netherworld. Instead, constructivism claims that the *"...objects of the world are indeterminate. They may be pregnant with meaning, but actual meaning emerges only when consciousness engages with them"* (Crotty, 1998:43).

Knowledge, therefore, is not discovered, nor is it created, but instead constructed at the nexus of subject and object. Indeed, *"[k]nowledge of the world is not a simple reflection of what there is, but a reflection of what we make of what there is"* (Schwandt, 1997:20). This construction of knowledge depends on the recognition of similarity between conceptual domains, which emphasises the central role of analogy in learning.

Empirically, this central role is borne out. Studies of a variety of students suggest that they often try to make sense of scientific phenomena by using analogy [see Duit (1991) and Pfundt & Duit (1991), for overviews.]. Undergraduate chemistry students, for example, using the 'classic' waterfall entropy analogy which attempts to explain the second law of thermodynamics in terms of a waterfall (Herrmann, 1989), showed remarkable ability to recognise the analogy, and, more importantly, to create new terms and relationships in the target entropy domain (Kaper & Goedhart, 2003).

Similarly, Clement (1987) found that both novices and experts employ analogy frequently when solving physics problems. Pre-service teachers improved their grasp of scientific knowledge when using analogy in a study by Paris & Glynn (2004). In a competitive debate environment, participants who used analogy to compare previous cases showed a better understanding of the cases and, in turn, performed better in the debates (Loewenstein *et al.*, 2003). And work by Gentner & Gentner (1983), Glynn (1989), Shapiro (1985), and others all point to the same conclusion — analogical reasoning facilitates learning.

Other empirical research on analogy in learning, however, has taken this central role of analogy in learning as a given, and instead investigated the effects which various factors have on the process of analogical reasoning. This research can be summarised (see Table 1) in three broad categories which correspond to the three key stages of analogical reasoning which were identified by Falkenhainer *et al.* (1989): 1) access, 2) mapping, and 3) inference.

Access

Access refers to the retrieval from memory of knowledge about the base domain (Gregan-Paxton *et al.*, 2002). It is obvious that a learner must be familiar with the base domain for the analogy to function (Gentner & Holyoak, 1997). Gabel & Samuel (1986) discovered, however, that it is also necessary for the learner to see the connection to the target domain. Tenney & Gentner (1985) added that familiarity also affects the power of the analogy.

Research also emphasises that the learner's attention must be directed toward the analogy. Indeed, spontaneous analogical reasoning is not that common, argued Glynn *et al.* (1989). And consequently, instructors ought to allude to the analogy for it to trigger access by the learner (Hayes & Tierney, 1982; Reed *et al.*, 1974; Tenney & Gentner, 1985).

Finally, recall that the structure-mapping theory of analogy distinguishes analogy from literal similarity in terms of relational structures and not domain attributes. Access to analogy, however, appears to be influenced by both (Gentner & Landers, 1985; Holyoak & Koh, 1987), although in their studies, only "*...structural similarities affected students' ability to make use of an analogy once its relevance was pointed out*" (Duit, 1991:656).

Mapping

In the mapping stage, learners identify the structural similarities of the base and target domains, and then align the domains in terms of these similarities (Gentner & Markman, 1997). Royer & Cable (1976) found, however, that analogy is only employed when the target domain is difficult to understand — that is to say, when the problem is 'sufficiently novel and challenging' (Gick & Holyoak, 1983). Complex target domains also intimate that multiple analogies might be needed by learners. Indeed, research suggests that analogies only appear to support the learning of specific conceptual nodes of a target domain (Dupin & Joshua, 1989; Gentner & Gentner, 1983; Rumelhart & Norman, 1981). In the words of Spiro *et al.* (1989), multiple analogies, therefore, might function as antidotes for analogy-induced misconception.

Stage	Factor and effect
Access	• the learner must be familiar with the base domain for the analogy to function • the learner must see the connection between base and target domains • the learner's familiarity with the analogy affects its power • the learner's attention must be directed toward the analogy • the learner's access to the analogy is influenced by similarities in both relational structures and domain attributes
Mapping	• the target domain must be difficult to understand • complex target domains demand multiple analogies • visual material in the analogy improves learning • summarisation of both base and target domains increases transfer • overemphasis of differences renders differences meaningless • presentation sequence of base and target domains impacts learning
Inference	• the learner's ability level is linked to the complexity of the target domain • learners use misconceptions of base domains • learners mix inferences • the duration of the analogy reflects the learner's conception 'strategy'

Table 1: Summary of empirical research on analogy in learning

Visuals — pictures, graphics, photographs, etc. — also appear to aid analogical reasoning. Studies by Dreistadt (1969), Rigney & Lutz (1976), Royer & Cable (1976), and Shapiro (1985) all found that the addition of visual material in the analogy improved learning.

With respect to the identification of structural similarities specifically, Catrambone & Holyoak (1989) discovered that learners who summarised both the base and target domains showed significantly higher rates of transfer from base to target than those who summarised only the base domain. In a similar vein, Ross & Kilbane (1997) revealed that learners who highlighted many differences in the two domains often overlooked the important differences, thereby making those important differences no more salient than the irrelevant differences.

Finally, Lim (2007) showed in her work that the presentation sequence of the base and target domains has an impact on analogical learning. Indeed, although instructors prefer a T-B sequence, learners show a marginally better grasp of the target domain following a B-T sequence. Similar conclusions were made by Goldstone & Son (2005) and Royer & Cable (1975).

Inference

It is the alignment of the base and target domains in the mapping stage which leads the learner to inferences about the target. The most obvious factor which impacts this inference stage is the ability level of the learner. Analogical learning in early years (pre-school) is intended more for cognitive development rather than the introduction of new conceptual domains, and the focus, therefore, ought to be on analogical mapping skills (White & Caropreso, 1989). Lim (2007) suggested that in secondary school, the identification of patterns through sequence and connection is crucial to establishing a learner's analogical reasoning.

Overall, however, the ability level of the learner seems to be linked with the difficulty of the target domain. Students *"with high cognitive abilities benefited more from creating their own analogical connections, whereas students with low abilities benefited more from having the teacher help them make the analogical connection"* (Duit, 1991:657).

There is also concern over a student's use of an existing misconception of a domain as the base for analogy [See Gentner & Gentner (1983), for example.]. In this case, analogical reasoning will not remedy the misconception, and will perhaps even reinforce it. Similarly, Krawczyk *et al.* (2005) worried that mixed inferences — a violation of 1:1 mapping — might occur among students. Their research indeed revealed a small rate of this phenomenon.

Finally, duration of the analogy in the learner's mind has been a topic of interest, resulting in the concepts of 'fading' and 'popping' (Gentner & Medina, 1997). Fading occurs when conceptual understanding of the base is replaced with the conceptual understanding of the target. Popping, on the contrary, occurs when the conceptual understanding of the base remains and a 'pop-up window' of conceptual understanding of the target emerges. In the case of popping, the learner attempts to maintain both concepts for a period of time, visualising both conceptual domains simultaneously. In Lim's (2007) research, fading showed a marginally stronger mean result than popping, supporting Markman & Gentner's (1997, 2000) conclusion that fading could improve analogical memory and problem-solving.

Analogy in practice

Despite the central role of analogy in learning, it might be surprising that analogies are relatively rarely in both textbooks and the classroom. In a survey of 43 elementary-, secondary-, and university-level science textbooks, for example, Glynn *et al.* (1989) uncovered some examples of 'simple' analogies, such as "cells are the engines of life", but 'elaborate' analogies were less common. Curtis & Reigeluth (1984) found similar results in their sample of 26 science textbooks.

The formal research which has been conducted in classrooms points in a similar direction. Teachers who were observed by Tierney (1988) used analogies in only a limited manner. In an interpretive study by Treagust *et al.* (1990), participating teachers seldom used analogies, a result which was buttressed by his interviews with them which revealed that most have a paltry repertoire of analogies.

The more disturbing observation, however, given the theoretical and empirical research on analogy in learning, is that in both textbooks and the classroom, no attempts were made to describe the analogies or how to use them strategically. When analogies were used, they were seemingly uninformed and unsophisticated, assuming that students already possessed both the skills to reason analogically and the requisite understanding of the base domain.

Several analogical curricular models and study methods, however, are available to instructors in higher education to improve student learning outcomes. They attempt to provide sophisticated approaches to analogy in practice, and are generally based on a solid understanding of the theoretical and empirical research on analogy in learning. They are presented here from instructor and student perspectives.

Instructor-centred

Given the apparent risk of creating an 'analogy on the fly', several curricular models have been developed — albeit, primarily with science teaching in mind and primarily for the classroom— which can be used by instructors in higher education to improve student learning outcomes. Four common models are summarised.

The first is called the 'Teaching-With-Analogies' model and was developed by Glynn (2004, 2007), based on both theoretical and empirical considerations.

It consists of a six step process for creating an elaborate analogy.

1. introduce target concept
2. recall base concept
3. identify similar features of the concepts
4. map similar features
5. draw conclusions about the concepts
6. indicate where the analogy breaks down

The process indeed provides a valuable framework for creating an analogy, although, as admitted by Glynn, it lacks detail in each of the steps and, therefore, requires that the process be followed 'in spirit' (Duit, 1991). It is also imperative to verify in steps 2 through 5 that the student has interpreted the analogy as the instructor intended.

Zeitoun (1984) offered a nine step process (see Figure 3) which mirrors the schema theory of Rumelhart & Norman (1981). Entitled the 'The General Model of Analogy Teaching', it likewise provides a pragmatic approach to creating an analogy, but ignores salient theoretical considerations such as the importance of existing knowledge and the possibility of misconceptions.

A third analogical curricular model is the '5E Model' by Orgill & Thomas (2007). Unlike the previous two models which are focused on analogies, it focuses squarely on student learning. Students are encouraged first to *engage* in their own learning process, then, in active mode, *explore* their current conceptual understanding and misunderstandings. The instructor has the opportunity to *explain* and then *elaborate* on the analogy. Finally, the student's learning is *evaluated*. The model lacks specific details in each of the stages, but is rooted firmly in the constructivist paradigm.

The fourth model was developed by Clement and his colleagues at the University of Massachusetts (Brown & Clement, 1987, 1989; Clement, 1987). It attempts to remedy misconceptions which students have as a consequence of analogical reasoning by providing 'bridging analogies'. The idea is for instructors to identify very carefully the base domains which are most apt - those most likely to be interpreted correctly. These are called 'anchors'. But even then, there is the possibility for misconception because the jump from anchor to target is too big. The authors, therefore, suggest bridging analogies which provide intermediate steps for the learner.

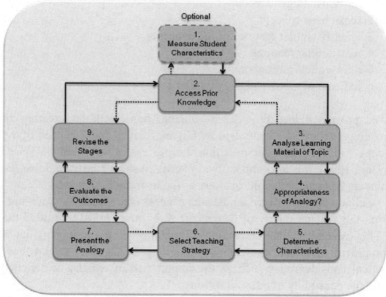

Figure 3: The General Model of Analogy Teaching
Source: Zeitoun (1984)

Experiments using the 'Bridging Analogies' model demonstrate its efficacy. It ought to be questioned, however, if anchors can indeed be found for all students, especially given the research which notes their varying pre-conceptions of the world. Success of the model, therefore, might require the instructor to fix the anchor for the students as a precursor to analogical bridging. In summary, therefore, the 'Bridging Analogies' model reinforces the notion that "...*much more effort than usually allocated should be focused on helping students to make sense of an analogy*" (Clement, 1993:1241).

Student-centred

In contrast to the previous instructor-oriented analogical curricular models in which learners worked with an analogy in a more passive manner, Loewenstein *et al.* (2003:394) proposed a student-centred study method which they called 'Analogical Encoding'. In this study method, rather than mapping from a base domain to a target domain, learners compare two concepts, and "*by doing so come to understand the underlying structure common to both*". Clearly, the 'Analogical Encoding' method puts students in an active role, and because they must examine the structure and characteristics of both concepts in or der to draw conclusions, rather than transferring knowledge from a base domain to a target domain, deeper learning ought to occur. Indeed, investigating the effectiveness of analogical encoding, Loewenstein *et al.* (2003) found not only that students develop schema which contained more elements of the key structural relationships, but also that they were more likely to transfer these relationships to new conceptual domains.

Possible Lesson Plan

1. Learning Objective: Upon completion of the course, students will understand the greenhouse effect.

2. Student Assessment: Students' understanding of the greenhouse effect is assessed by their ability to teach others about the greenhouse effect. As part of a service learning component of the course, students will work with a local elementary school over the course of the semester in an after school science program. Students must create an original interactive lesson to use with the elementary students, which will also serve as evidence of conceptual understanding. Lessons will be assessed prior to working with the elementary students, so any misconceptions can be addressed.

3. Development of elaborate analogy: The analogy "The greenhouse effect is like a pinball game" will be used in class. Questions to consider: Is the analogy engaging? Is it relevant to the students? Is it contextual? Does it scaffold their learning effectively? What is the existing knowledge of pinball games? Does a pinball game serve as an anchor? Are there bridging analogies which could work?

4. Prior to session: Instruct students to play pinball game on a computer or at a local arcade, recording their observations about the game and its operation.

5. Use of the analogy in session (base domain): Divide students into groups, and instruct them to describe their observations about pinball games. As a class, combine their observations and draw a visual model of a pinball game. Questions to consider: Are there any misconceptions about the pinball game? Do the students need to explore the concept in more detail? Additional instructional tools to consider: A simulation using basketballs and students as bumpers. An analogical encoding with another domain which is analogous to a pinball game.

6. Mini-lecture on greenhouse effect.

7. Continuation of analogy in session (target domain): Divide students into groups and instruct them to describe the greenhouse effect. As a class, combine their observations and draw a visual model of the greenhouse effect. Questions to consider: Are there any misconceptions about the greenhouse effect? Do the students need to explore the concept in more detail?

8. Continuation of the analogy (mapping): Begin with the question "Does this remind you of anything?" Divide students into groups, and instruct them to attempt a mapping of the pinball game to the greenhouse effect. As a class, combine their observations and draw visual links between the pinball game and the greenhouse effect. When completed, ask them where the mapping falls apart. Highlight the analogical differences.

9. Assign students the original interactive lesson to use with the elementary students.

10. After assessing the lessons, evaluate the analogical learning process and adjust accordingly.

Figure 4: Possible Lesson Plan for Teaching the Greenhouse Effect

Integration
As an illustration, a possible lesson plan for teaching the greenhouse effect in an undergraduate geopolitics course using analogy is outlined (see Figure 4). It integrates the theoretical and empirical research on analogy in learning with the analogical curricular models and study methods which were presented.

Conclusion
The use of analogy in education is indeed nothing new. But to many instructors in higher education, analogical learning is still relatively unknown, in terms of both the theoretical and empirical research on analogy in learning, and the many analogical curricular models and study methods. This chapter responded, therefore, by 1) elucidating the theory of analogical learning, and 2) examining the use of analogy for improving student learning outcomes within the context of higher education.

About the authors
John Branch is Lecturer of Marketing at the Stephen M. Ross School of Business, and Faculty Associate at the Center for Russian and East European Studies, both of the University of Michigan, USA. He can be contacted at this e-mail: jdbranch@bus.umich.edu

Huai-Mei Chiang is an elementary music educator in Portland, USA. She can be contacted at this e–mail: huaimeichiang@yahoo.com

Ivan Goenawan is a graduate of the College of Engineering at the University of Michigan, USA. He can be contacted at this e-mail: igoenawan@gmail.com

CHAPTER 10

Reflective Teaching: A Tool to Improve Students' Learning

Saretha Brüssow & Annette Wilkinson

Introduction

Our initial teaching approach was based on the traditions and practices of direct instruction where curricula are designed with a focus on content rather than learning processes, thus a syllabus-driven didactic paradigm. Challenged by student-centred teaching, a need arose to investigate the effectiveness of student-centred approaches in the learning-based paradigm in our own teaching environment. In striving to support the improvement of students' learning outcomes, we made use of reflective teaching practices to explore students' feedback by means of an action inquiry to identify changes that need to be made in our teaching. We focused the feedback on academic instruction because contact time with students lends itself to the improvement of students' learning. Acting on the following two questions helped us to adapt and correct instructional practices:

- What did the students perceive to be positive or negative actions or interactions in class?
- How did these actions or interactions influence students' learning and learning outcomes?

This type of reflection on how students perceive teaching is the basic philosophy behind reflective teaching since students and their perspectives play integral parts in choosing educational approaches. Varnava-Marouchou (this volume) also emphasises the significance of students' own experience of how they conceive learning and how this relates to the quality of their learning outcomes. Reflective teaching presents valuable ways to capture positive or negative learning experiences because it provides an opportunity for both student and teacher to reflect. The purpose of the action inquiry on which this chapter is based was twofold, namely to look into teaching practices by means of reflective teaching to identify negative or positive actions that advance or obstruct learning; and to make teaching more responsive to students' preferences and/or needs to improve student learning outcomes. The objectives were thus to:

- identify shortcomings encountered during academic instruction;

and

- encourage best teaching practices during teaching that enhance the quality of learning and as a result students' learning outcomes.

In the ensuing paragraphs we discuss the potential value of reflective teaching in an effort to get closer to an understanding of how students' learning outcomes can be improved in higher education. The chapter first outlines various aspects of reflective teaching, namely the concept, the process, and the advantages. It then explains the philosophy underpinning reflective teaching and its contribution to teaching effectiveness. As a final point, we also share the value of reflective teaching based on the mentioned action inquiry in the first author's own educational environment (Brüssow, 2007) in an effort to present an alternative route as we move from a discipline-based to a learning-based view on higher education.

The concept of reflective teaching

Reflective teaching has become a widely used approach in HEIs (Schön, 1990; Fendler, 2003; Hoffman-Kipp *et al.*, 2003; Atherton, 2005a; Korthagen & Vasalos, 2005; Green, 2006; Graves & Jones, 2008; Dana & Yendol-Hoppey, 2009; Webster, 2009). Reflective teaching entails *"thinking about one's teaching"* (Parker, 1997:8) and involves classroom observation and reflection aimed at refining teaching theories and adjusting teaching practices (Ferraro, 2000). Reflective teaching approaches based on students' feedback create a platform for both students and teachers to reflect on learning as well as the quality of teaching.

We gained a better understanding of the term "reflective teaching" by first looking at the meaning of "reflection". Bailey (1997:2) defines reflection, among others, as *"a thought occupying the mind"*, while Birmingham (2004:321) sees reflection as an image that implies a *"personal inspection of oneself"*. Both the concepts of "thought occupying the mind" and "personal inspection" have been influential in not only individualising the process of reflective teaching, but also in providing us with a frame within which to situate *"thinking about one's teaching"* put forward by Parker (1997:8) in his book about reflective teaching in the post-modern world. To better value reflective teaching as such, we reviewed the literature on reflective teaching to gain insight into perspectives on reflection in teaching and to become acquainted with models of reflection used in educational environments.

The process of reflective teaching

Although "reflective teaching" is a concept that has various meanings (Adler, 1991), the general opinion is that a problem sets in motion the process of reflection, which steers the development and understanding of teaching and learning practices (Loughran, 2002). Reflective teaching, also called inquiry-oriented teaching, is seen as a process that provides structure in which insight into the complex nature of teaching is improved (Green, 2006; Schmuck, 2008; Hedberg, 2009). Black (2005) encourages teachers to make use of reflective teaching in an attempt to advance their own teaching and to explore new teaching strategies. She further points out that critical reflection upon practice leads to teachers taking responsibility for their own professional development.

Both reflective teaching and action research are processes in which teachers investigate teaching and learning to improve their own and their students' learning through self-reflective practices. The course of action generally associated with action research is a reiterative cyclical process of different phases that pass through planning, action, observation, and reflection and back to planning and action (Zuber-Skerritt, 2001; Tripp, 1990), a process that inevitably entails a more extended approach. Reflective teaching, on the other hand, can be a single action (Bailey, 1997), an inquiry that places emphasis on a constructivist approach to teaching which brings theory and practice together (Kuit *et al.,* 2001). The current study can best be described by Tripp's explanation of the term "action inquiry". Tripp (2003) describes it as an umbrella term that encompasses any investigation that purposefully takes a cyclical approach that includes planning, acting, describing and reflecting. According to Tripp's action inquiry continuum an additional difference between reflective teaching and action research is that reflective teaching is more personally focused, while action research to some extent includes a broader public involvement (Tripp, 2003). Different types of action inquiry exist that include – among others – thoughtful action, reflective practice and action learning. Since this study embarked on action and reflection as a means to improve teaching and hence learning outcomes, reflective teaching was regarded as the most appropriate approach.

The advantages of reflective teaching

The main advantage of reflective teaching practices is that a better understanding of one's teaching style ultimately leads to greater efficiency in teaching (Dirkx, 2006; Ferraro, 2000). A culture of inquiry and the exploratory nature of reflective practices increase the probability of successful teaching and learning – where successful learning refers to the achievement of expected outcomes. A second advantage is that teachers who explore their own teaching through reflection adjust their teaching based on developed thoughts to improve the kind of support they provide their students to become better learners.

The philosophy behind reflective teaching

Although various theories and models of well-known reflective practice researchers were studied we used insights from the Colton and Sparks-Langer's Model to establish the appropriate actions used in this action inquiry.

Colton & Sparks-Langer's model

Colton & Sparks-Langer's model focuses on teacher reflection and consists of three dimensions, namely action, knowledge and disposition (Colton & Sparks-Langer, 1993; Goff *et al.*, 2000). The action dimension of the model includes the "doing" dimension of the teacher. It is a cyclical process leading to the creation of meaning. According to Colton & Sparks-Langer (1993), meaning is created when the teacher collects, analyses, reflects and acts on information gathered through inquiry. This part of the model shares the views of Dewey (1909) and also encompasses the four stages of experiential learning developed by Kolb (1984), namely concrete experience, reflective observation, abstract conceptualisation, and active experimentation (Colton & Sparks-Langer, 1993; Kuit *et al.*, 2001; Atherton, 2005b). We realised the value of Kolb's learning cycle in this model, since teaching was the concrete experience while reflecting on the experience led to transformation and, in turn, knowledge construction.

Within the knowledge dimension, the model includes six types of knowledge, the supposed "knowing" dimension, concerning knowledge of:

- self as a teacher;
- the discipline;
- teaching and learning;
- students;
- the context in which education takes place; and
- higher education in societal contexts

These knowledge types are important to teachers and address teaching and learning theories in general and were pivotal to the use of reflection to improve teaching in the action inquiry under discussion.

The third dimension, namely the disposition or the "being" dimension of Colton & Sparks-Langer's model includes qualities believed critical to effective teaching (Goff *et al.*, 2000). The model takes account of social responsibilities that include the moral and ethical side of teaching; caring which is the positive relationship with students; efficacy which refers to the belief that one's efforts will make a difference; consciousness – the thinking about one's own thinking; and, lastly, flexibility is the ability to use a variety of teaching and learning activities to fit the diverse needs of students (Goff *et al.*, 2000). These different dispositions also emerged as a result of the action inquiry since we started with an initial theory of teaching and learning, based on personal experiences as students, studying educational theories, and formal educational training. This theory entailed the perception that all students in higher education know how to learn, are motivated, self-regulated, use specific study skills and learn independently. During the process of the action inquiry into reflective teaching we applied this theory during academic instruction, observed and reflected on the results, and ultimately had to change the theory.

The structure of the action inquiry

The action inquiry was conducted in a natural setting, namely the first author's own teaching environment that is the radiography learning programme at the Central University of Technology, Free State (CUT) in South Africa. The target group, a convenience sample, included 26 second-year students from the programme Diagnostic Radiography at the CUT in the learning unit Radiographic Practice II in 2006. The focus was on interpretation rather than quantification because the feedback on learning experiences during teaching points towards interpreting the phenomenon of learning to create or build new theory. The educational research approach used in this study is therefore based on the paradigm of interpretive research. The purpose of this kind of research is to inform decisions as a basis for improvement. The inquiry included a Critical Incident Questionnaire (CIQ) and a Teaching Assessment Poll (TAP). Areas of concern were factors that enhance or obstruct learning.

The Critical Incident Questionnaire

The CIQ is seen by various authors as a valuable tool to determine how students experience their learning and how they perceive teaching in general through "critical incidents" (Brookfield, 1995:114). In addition, Waite *et al.* (this volume) in agreement with Adams (2001) indicate that if students actively share perspectives and experiences they can build the educational environment to fit their needs.

The construction of knowledge that leads to learning is caused, among others, by students asking questions. Thus the intention of using questions was to facilitate thinking – in this case, the thinking about teaching that enhances or obstructs learning. The CIQ, developed by Brookfield (1995), was used to incorporate these questions and perspectives. The CIQs were used to provide frequent, anonymous chances for students to reflect on their experiences in class by means of critical incidents. The students had to respond on their reaction to classroom actions and/or activities or anything else that happened or occurred to them.

The CIQ consists of five open-ended questions that ask students to reflect on their experiences during academic instructions. The CIQ's questions were included after changing them to fit the needs of the module under investigation. Students were asked every two weeks to describe events in class that most engaged, distanced, helped, confused or surprised them. The following questions, adapted from the CIQ of Brookfield (1995:115), were included:

1. At what point in the lecture today/or any lecture did you feel most engaged with what was happening?
2. At what point in the lecture today/or any lecture did you feel most distanced from what was happening?
3. What action that the teacher took in this lecture did you find most affirming and helpful?
4. What action that the teacher took in this lecture did you find most puzzling or confusing?
5. What about the lecture today/or any lecture surprised you most?

The Teaching Assessment Poll

The second data source, namely the TAP, consists of only three questions. The TAP questions invited the students to reflect on either actions that most helped them to learn or which for the most part obstructed their learning. It was also expected from them to make suggestions for improvement.

1. What most helped you to learn in this class?
2. What impeded/obstructed/hampered your learning?
3. What suggestions do you have for improvement?

Analysis of the data sources

These collected CIQs and TAPs were read and answers summarised under the different questions. These answers were then categorised according to similar responses and specific patterns were searched for. Since the feedback occurred on a two-weekly basis, the students tended to react and reflect on recent issues encountered during specific contact sessions.

The overlapping questions of the two surveys allowed the identification of specific areas of concern and also triangulation of the feedback to make it more reliable. The triangulation not only confirmed certain patterns, but also validated findings through revealing common issues which the students experienced as positive or negative actions in class. The feedback provided valuable insight into the students' preferences and needs and also emphasised that experiences differ from student to student. These data sources revealed that what most helped the students to learn in class were practical demonstrations and examples, the visual images of *PowerPoint* shows and the provision of structured information, together with the use of concept maps.

Learning was mainly obstructed by long sessions which caused concentration levels to drop. Suggestions for improvement included that all lectures should include practical demonstrations and that regular mind breaks should be built in to improve concentration. Most students commented that too much knowledge or information was included in one contact session. The question into what they find most affirming and helpful also revealed that practical demonstrations, PowerPoint visuals and structured handouts should be maintained. The students also suggested that there should be more interaction.

Reflection on feedback

The next phase in the process of reflective teaching was to reflect on the feedback. As certain patterns became obvious during the data collection phase, we became aware of aspects of teaching that the students experienced as negative. We looked for specific reasons that caused students to feel distanced, for example going through the learning material too fast or providing information without interaction and not giving outcomes and learning tasks in advance. We assumed that all students prepare for class sessions and as a result we only touched upon key concepts during the lessons. The students perceived this as going too fast through the learning unit and conveying too much information. These findings had to lead to changes to fit the needs of the students. The students' responses not only provided an insight into what they perceived as constructive to their learning, but also revealed that their perceptions were diverse.

We realised, in accordance with Adams (2001), that the CIQ provided for the most part an opportunity for students not only to construct knowledge, but also to actively shape the education environment to fit their needs. See Raiker (this volume) for a deeper discussion of giving students control of their own learning. The advantages we experienced in using these data sources were, first, that they provided a platform for us and the students to reflect. The students used the data sources to convey their point of view and express their needs, while we used the opportunity to reflect on the feedback and acted in response in an effort to improve teaching and learning during instruction.

Second, the data sources offered confirmation that specific teaching and learning strategies were positively perceived, for example the practical demonstration, structured interactive activities and the use of tables and concept mapping as note-taking techniques. Third, after communicating measures of improvement as a consequence of the students' responses, a positive attitude developed which became evident in the students' responses in later surveys. The initial CIQs included some inappropriate and negative answers, while later responses included mostly personal reflection on how learning could be improved through collaboration.

Responding to feedback

The "doing" dimension, based on Colton & Sparks-Langer's model, was to act upon students' responses once the feedback was analysed and reflected on. Students were informed about the most prominent issues that had emerged from the surveys. Possible pedagogic changes

were discussed and, where appropriate, justified or adapted after negotiation. We also used the feedback time to explain the use of certain
non-traditional teaching strategies and the potential benefits they held
for improved learning, for example self-directed activities and group
work. It was not possible to react on all issues raised, but the opportunity to give feedback provided a chance to explain the reasons for not
being able to react or change. These feedback sessions also offered
time for discussion and this facilitated the reinforcement of certain
teaching strategies which the students had viewed negatively.

The teaching changes that flowed from perspectives gained from the
action inquiry included a more pragmatic application of learning
strategies during academic instruction. Teaching strategies were developed to include the proactive use of practical demonstrations and application, tangible information and skills, as well as handouts, learning
tasks and learning goals that were better structured and provided two
weeks in advance. A more interactive way of teaching through collaborative learning was also pursued through more structured group
activities which encouraged everyone to participate equally.

Discussion

Many teachers teach the way they were taught. The biggest challenge
that teachers thus face is to move from traditional teaching to one fo-
cussing on learning without losing the disciplinary focus. Over and
above the fact that it is the responsibility of the teacher to create and
structure a learning environment conducive to learning, we need to
ask, how do we improve students' learning outcomes in practice? We
therefore need to explore aspects involved in teaching through inquiry
and reflection to reach higher levels of professional effectiveness and
proficiency in teaching since a better understanding of the complex
ways in which students learn will ultimately result in improved teaching. Through this awareness teachers can, as a result, scaffold students
to become more effective learners.

This action inquiry allowed the students to communicate their perspectives and needs with regard to teaching events and the resulting
impact on their learning. Reflective teaching provided valuable information on constructive classroom conduct. It caused a better understanding of the learning process and, in addition, assisted us in shaping
teaching and learning approaches to the students' needs. This process
not only allowed informed choices to be made, but also enabled the
justification of teaching and learning alternatives. In relating teaching
theory to teaching practice and the feedback from students, we also re-

alised that students are diverse in their perceptions of good teaching. Reflective teaching was also found worth doing because it forced the students to become active participants in the learning process see also Nygaard *et al.* (this volume) who emphasise the importance of students to own and define their individual learning processes through active participation. Inquiry is at all times an active course and is seen by Tripp (2003:15) as action learning, a process he explains as *"...doing something one wouldn't otherwise do in order to learn from doing it".* The students were engaged as collaborators in the action inquiry into reflective teaching and were thus encouraged to think for themselves about their own learning (also apparent in Alias & Alias, this volume). Increased motivation on the part of the students was also a positive experience. Considering their views and involving them in decisions caused this increased motivation as well as an improved level of conversation between us and the students. These increased levels of motivation and conversation led to a more positive attitude towards student-centred learning practices.

We are aware that using an action inquiry into reflective teaching as a means for improving teaching practices and, ultimately, students' learning depends on identifying the quality of the inquiry as well as the desired end. To validate the quality of the inquiry we looked into the three phases of reflection presented by Van *Manen* (1977), namely technical, practical and critical. The first phase, which is the technical rationality, focuses on what is considered effective teaching based on the reflection on the success or failure of teaching-learning strategies used in the classroom. The second phase of reflection is seen as practical action and centres on the learning experience of the student. During this phase the effect of teaching and learning practices are evaluated with a definite commitment to learning theory. These two phases were pivotal to this action inquiry. The critical and third level entails justice and equity as ethical standards of education practices and also determines the quality of the inquiry (Hatton & Smith 1994). Van *Manen* (1995) proposes that teaching is not only directed by effectiveness but also by ethical or affective disposition. The critical level is linked to the reflective model of Colton and Sparks-Langer (Goff *et al.,* 2000) that forms the basis of this action inquiry. The disposition dimension of the model, which includes the social responsibility that embraces the moral and ethical side of teaching, thus confirms the quality of the inquiry because this action inquiry into reflective teaching is fundamental to the inclusion of student diversity and embraces a willingness to adjust instruction practice in the pursuit of improved learning.

Valuable insights were gained through this action inquiry and used to support students during academic instruction to learn better see also Nygaard *et al.* (this volume) who argue that reflective processes are generally valuable. Reflective teaching is seen as the process in which thought determines change and the intended change in this action inquiry is to improve the quality of teaching along the shortest possible route from the ineffective to the effective or preferred end. Parker (1997) points out that the process of acting on information received to reach specific teaching outcomes is depicted as well-judged behaviour, which he calls rational teaching. Parker explained rational teaching as a quantitative process that involves observation, data gathering, analysis and the intention to reach a desired end. This course of action was also followed in this action inquiry with the desired end result of effective teaching, a process that adheres to the criteria that require that the action inquiry be performed systematically and based on reason.

In validating the claim that knowledge should be constructed and justified, we depended on the experience gained by this action inquiry which falls within the "pedagogical tact" described by Van Manen (1995:39), who states that reflective teaching allows an understanding of *"the nature of the experienced reality of teaching"* when interacting with students, which does not necessarily entail the development of a new knowledge base. However, this action inquiry contributed to developing a metacognitive awareness within our own educational environment, since the feedback on the success or failure of teaching methods and strategies led to the gaining of knowledge about the students' perception of what instruction methods or actions most facilitated or impeded their learning. We thus developed a knowledge base in two areas, namely how students learn and how to create an educational theory which supports the shift to a learning-based paradigm.

Concluding thoughts

This chapter has attempted to show how reflective teaching can be influential in the development of more effective teaching practices. Reflective teaching allowed us to take both the needs of students and those of ourselves as teachers into consideration, since the reflection took part in us and the students. By exploring, evaluating and modifying teaching practices as well as seeking reasons for specific behaviour we were able to refine our own teaching philosophy and create our own 'living' educational theory. To better understand the concept of living theory, we identify with the explanation provided by De Long & Whitehead (2006), namely that a living educational theory is an account of one's educational influence on one's own learning and the learning of others. As a result the theory born from the perspectives gained is that any action taken during academic instruction, to be of normative significance, should have productive pedagogical value and positive consequences for learning. We concur with Hedberg (2009) that reflection has the potential to influence deeper learning, it challenges embedded theories and viewpoints while in devising one's own teaching-learning approach has a clear ontological significance. To situate this action inquiry into reflective practice within the book as a whole we propose that reflective practices have the potential to improve teaching competence, a gain that will ultimately lead to improved student learning.

About the authors

Saretha Brüssow is the Head: Teaching, Learning and Assessment at the Planning Unit of the University of the Free State, Bloemfontein, South Africa. She can be contacted at this e-mail: sbrussow.rd@ufs.ac.za

Annette Wilkinson is Professor, Researcher and Head: Division Higher Education Studies and Research of the Centre for Higher Education Studies and Development of the University of the Free State, Bloemfontein, South Africa. She can be contacted at this e-mail: wilkinac.rd@ufs.ac.za

CHAPTER 11

A New Focus on Assessment of Student Learning Outcomes

Hesta Friedrich-Nel

Introduction

Student assessment at many South African universities has traditionally been based on written assessment at the conclusion of a semester or sometimes even the year. In 1995 the South African Qualifications Authority (SAQA) was established through the SAQA Act No 58 of 1995 (RSA, 1995) mandating the Outcomes-based education and training (OBET) approach for educational organisations in South Africa. A major thrust within OBET is the concept of student learning outcomes (SLO) (SAQA, 2001:21). Written assessment, however, is limited in terms of SLO assessment and indeed suggests the need for a new focus on student assessment.

The purpose of this chapter, therefore, is to document how the School of Health Technology at the Central University of Technology Free State (CUT) in South Africa appraised current assessment practices of student learning. A project to survey assessment practices was introduced. Based on the outcomes of the survey specific development actions and appropriate assessment practices were implemented to align assessment practices with curricular and instructional design with the aim to improve on SLOs.

The chapter begins by outlining the assessment requirements associated with the new learning environment. It then continues to describe the project to survey assessment, the quantitative and qualitative results obtained by the survey as well as the actions and interventions to improve on students' learning outcomes. Steps to align assessment with SLOs as well as a tool used to facilitate assessment feedback to students are highlighted. Finally, the outcomes of the interventions are presented together with the challenges created by the new focus on SLOs in assessment. Although OBET implementation impacts on the wider educational environment, the center of attention of this chapter is on the assessment of SLOs.

Assessment requirements in the new learning environment

The principles of the OBET approach as prescribed by SAQA are based on SLOs (SAQA, 2001:21). Embedded in the OBET approach is the emphasis on student-centred teaching and assessment practices where the student needs to provide appropriate evidence that SLOs have been attained. SLOs are statements outlining what the student should know (cognitive), be able to do (competence and skills) as well as values and attitudes (affective) reflected upon after completing a specific learning module or unit (Bloom *et al.,* 1956; SAQA, 2001:21). To offer the appropriate evidence that students attained the learning outcomes, assessment has to be aligned with the learning outcomes of knowledge, competence and skills and attitudes (SAQA, 2001). Since the aforementioned assessment practice with the focus mainly on written assessment did not specifically relate to assessment of student learning outcomes (SLO) as emphasised by the OBET approach, it was deemed necessary to adjust assessment of learning.

SAQA also draws attention to the principles of good or "credible" assessment referring to fairness, validity, reliability and practicability in assessment (SAQA, 2001). The literature on assessment of learning use the term "assessment culture" (Peterson & Vaughan, 2002:45) when referring to environments of meaningful assessment. Requiring a meaningful approach to assessment, assessment has to be focused on outcomes that matters (Angelo, 2006), in a manner that involves students in their learning. In the context of this chapter meaningful assessment refers to assessment aligned with student learning outcomes to improve SLOs.

Underpinned by the OBET and student-centred approaches, administrators, facilitators and students had to abandon the familiar "examination" system focusing mainly on written assessment. Facilitators therefore had to think about and practice assessment with a different focus. Students were automatically drawn into the process of change in assessment since they were involved in assessment as prescribed by the facilitators. Based on the aforementioned, facilitators were exposed to new challenges in assessment. One such a challenge was for the facilitators to unlearn the principles associated with "traditional" assessment, shifting the emphasis away from written assessment and towards the principles associated with assessment in the OBET and student-centred approaches. An additional challenge was to assist the facilitators in implementing innovative assessment methods, instruments, strategies and practices so as to align assessment with SLOs. Huet *et al.* (in this volume) refer to "curriculum maps" to assist facilitators with the alignment of assessment.

	Facilitators' assessment methods (n = 32)	Students' assessment methods (n = 195)	Facilitators' assessment methods (n = 32)	Students' assessment methods (n = 195)
	Often used %	Preferred method %	Often used %	Preferred method %
Formal tests and exams	88	78	98	90
Practical exams in clinical practice	38	63	57	57
Assignments	65	66	80	55
Objective structured clinical assessment (OSCA)	25	25	33	27
Oral presentations	28	50	57	30
Reflection report	31	31	35	24
Simulations	28	28	28	26
Demonstrations	34	34	50	45
Peer assessment	34	34	59	44
Self-assessment	13	28	30	30

Table 1: Assessment methods of facilitators and students in 2005

The innovative assessment strategies and practices potentially prepare students in health technology for their tasks in clinical practice due to the fact that there is a focus on the assessment of their knowledge, competence and skills as well as attitudes. Leinster (2002:15) point out that the performance of health care professionals depends on the attainment of learning outcomes based on clinical competence and communication skills rather than the memorisation of facts. Meaningful assessment practices that consist of innovation in assessment are thus necessary to provide evidence that students in health technology attained the required SLOs. Examples of appropriate and innovative assessment methods in this context are available in Table 1.

A project to verify assessment

Since written assessment did not specifically relate to assessment of student learning outcomes (SLO) as emphasised by the OBET approach, it was deemed necessary to change assessment of learning. Almost three years after OBET and the student-centred approach were implemented the need was identified to verify the status of current assessment practices in the health technology programmes. Furthermore evidence for the different programme portfolios on how well assessment aligned with student learning outcomes as well as with the educational environment, was necessary. Programmes also had to report in the programme portfolio on innovation in assessment. As a result a project was initiated in 2004 to verify and appraise assessment practices. The project to verify assessment was lead and managed by a programme head in health technology with an educational background. Facilitators as well as third and second year undergraduate students in six programmes in health technology namely Biomedical Technology, Clinical Technology, Dental Assisting, Emergency Medical Care, Radiography and Somatology were requested to participate in the project. Second and third year students were targeted specifically because of the experiences in assessment of learning outcomes that they could share. Students from the Dental Assisting programme were excluded initially since there are only first year students in the programme. The focus was specifically on student learning outcomes at the undergraduate level, referring to the students' first three years at university. It is at this level that students have to display knowledge, competence, skills as well as the necessary attitudes and values expected from health care workers in the variety of fields offered by the School of Health Technology.

The project was twofold and consisted of an initial survey followed by assessment interventions based on the results obtained. The purpose of the project was explained as such to the programme heads under the guidance of the director of the School. The commitment from each programme was required initially. However in the roll-out of the project it was necessary for the various programmes to document information on the respective assessment practices and to participate in workshop sessions and focus group meetings.

The survey on assessment

By means of the survey information about facilitators and student assessment preferences in assessment were probed. Two separate questionnaires were designed for the survey for facilitators and students respectively so as to capture information regarding knowledge level and attitudes towards assessment, to determine if changes in assessment have occurred and identify future assessment interventions that may be required. The questionnaires were also designed to create awareness concerning innovative assessment among facilitators and students. Both closed and open-ended questions were included in the questionnaires, providing quantitative as well as qualitative responses.

The questions directed at the facilitators were formulated in order to acquire information on assessment methods commonly used and their preferred methods. Students also had to report on the assessment methods commonly used in class and the methods they preferred, mirroring the use of assessment methods by the facilitators. "Commonly used" intended to verify if changes in assessment have indeed occurred while the preferred methods could establish the buy-in of facilitators and students in the changed assessment environment. Since participants were not limited to a single choice for each assessment method, the percentages in Table 1 do not add to 100%. The open-ended section of the questionnaire facilitated feedback on facilitators' and students' general assessment practices and attitudes.

The assessment methods included in the questionnaires were formal written and practical examinations, assignments, Objective Structured Clinical Assessment (OSCA), oral presentations, reflection reports, simulations, demonstrations, as well as peer and self-assessment. The "OSCA" refers to structured assessment tasks related to the clinical environment where students obtain practical experience. This assessment method, as well as reflection reports, simulations, demonstrations, peer- and self-assessment were specifically included in the questionnaire to determine if the required alignment between assessment and the student learning outcomes of competence, skills and attitudes indeed existed. Internal validity of the questionnaire was secured by attaching a detailed and explanatory cover letter to each questionnaire. Permission to approach facilitators and students to participate in the project was obtained from the director of the School of Health Technology. Although participation was on a voluntary basis, questionnaires were distributed to and feedback received from the majority of full- and part-time facilitators as well as second and third year students within the school. The participants included 55 full- and part-time facilitators and 245 second- and third-year students.

After collecting the completed questionnaires from the participating programmes, questionnaires were coded and quantitative responses entered into a computer using the SAS system. The Department of Biostatistics at the University of the Free State assisted with the calculation of the results. Open questions were summarised using a thematic approach. Themes were clustered and collapsed in identifying similar patterns in the qualitative responses.

Quantitative responses

In Table 1 the assessment methods often used, as well as the preferred methods by both facilitators and students, are displayed. The trends identified show some development as well as changes in assessment practices. However it also points to factors restraining assessment practices in a changing educational environment. As expected the results in both the facilitator and student groups showed similar trends in the "often used" and "preferred" method categories.

Formal tests and examinations were often used by the majority of the facilitators, while assignments were often used as well as the preferred assessment method of more that two thirds of the facilitators. Practical examinations in clinical practice were preferred by two thirds of the facilitators. It is noteworthy that the majority of the facilitators who participated in the project did not use or prefer to use the OSCA, reflection reports, simulations, demonstrations, peer-assessment and self-assessment. This shows evidence that assessment and SLOs were not yet aligned and consequently did not provide the expected evidence on assessment of learning. Further investigation on the possible reason for facilitators not using the specific assessment methods showed that they were still unfamiliar with a number of assessment methods so they did not take any notice of these methods.

The majority of the students reported that the assessment methods formal tests and exams were mostly used. The students also mentioned that assignments were often used but were the preferred method of just more that half of the students. The oral presentation and peer assessment were not often used and were also not the preferred methods of the students. The results displayed in Table 1 for students show a pattern similar to that of the facilitators, namely that the assessment methods such as OSCA, reflection reports, simulations and self-assessment were not frequently utilised at the time of the investigation. The students mentioned that they did not prefer the aforementioned assessment methods, most probably because they were not yet exposed to these methods to the extent that they are confident in using them.

Qualitative responses

The qualitative results collected by means of the open-ended questions in the questionnaire also showed that some changes were already evident in assessment practices, even though small. Some of the responses recorded that agree with the changed assessment environment and mentioned by the majority of the facilitators will be mentioned first, followed by areas in assessment that still require improvement and action. Assessment was scheduled on a time-table as part of the learning process and was no longer an "add on" activity in the respective programmes, showing that assessment has become part of the learning process. Facilitators assessed their students more than once per term in each module/subject, pointing to more frequent assessment practices. The majority of the facilitators timeously outlined the purpose of the assessment to the students and explained what they expected from students in the assessment (the criteria) before the actual event. Higher order thinking was reflected in the use of appropriate action verbs of Bloom *et. al.* (1956). Peers were asked for feedback when the assessment papers were designed, showing transparency and a sense of quality awareness that developed. Feedback on the assessment was provided to students within a reasonable duration of time after the assessment had been completed. "A reasonable time" was flexible and negotiated with the students. According to the majority of the facilitators the students could use the feedback to improve on their academic performance.

Some of the responses in the questionnaire point to areas in assessment that still require improvement and action. Although all the facilitators claimed that students were provided with a timetable for assessment when the academic year commenced, a small number communicated the specific assessment method to be used with the students. Since transparency in assessment is a priority, this is an aspect to be addressed. While all the facilitators reported that students could use assessment as a learning experience, it was thus almost contradicting that only a third of the facilitators emphasised assessment as a learning opportunity. It helps the students when the facilitator creates the link between assessment and the learning outcomes.

The students on the other hand reported that they had been assessed more than once per term in each of their modules/subjects, showing the move away from the "single event assessment". Some of the students reported that they received a timetable for assessment at the beginning of the year and therefore know the assessment method that will be used for assessment. The majority of the students said that they took assessment seriously; used assessment as a learning experience; and used the feedback to improve their academic performance and the SLOs, providing evidence of the student-centred approach in assessment. Also in agreement with the student-centred approach was the fact that half the students mentioned that they wanted to be assessed with more that one assessment method and/or instrument.

Aspects in assessment that were not in agreement of the student-centred approach were also identified with the survey. Almost all the students reported that they studied only to pass their assessment. They also mentioned that they still preferred assessment via written tests/examinations. This evidence shows that development in a student-centred environment was slower than anticipated and that students may still focus on the surface approach in learning.

The results collected by means of the questionnaires showed how facilitators used assessment methods and what students preferred in their assessment experiences. The objective to raise awareness and obtain buy-in from facilitators and students on a variation of assessment methods was also attained, since facilitators and students requested explanations based on the survey. The quantitative results in Table 1 as well as the qualitative responses provided evidence that some change and innovation in assessment was already evident. Since the change and innovation had not yet reached the expected level, the need for specific actions to address assessment in general was also evident. Therefore the results obtained with the survey were instrumental in indicating the way forward in assessment developments because it was used as the starting point to design specific assessment interventions to enhance the identified assessment strengths and address the shortcomings in assessment. This will be outlined in the next section.

Actions and interventions to improve students' learning outcomes

In planning the assessment actions and interventions, it was noted that a changed educational environment was not viable without the underpinning knowledge of the theory and practice of the OBET and student-centred approaches. Exposure to knowledge of the theory and practice of the assessment methods and how to use it expanded the variety of available assessment methods. It was also noted that a specific effort was necessary to outline student learning outcomes, teaching and assessment practices accordingly. For this reason, facilitators in health technology participated in formal and informal learning opportunities at appropriate workshop and seminar sessions (Table 2). Guidance, direction, knowledge and skills to assist facilitators in creating a changed educational environment were facilitated at "in-house" workshop and seminar sessions, presented by on-campus experts. Specific information sessions for students were scheduled focusing on learning outcomes, facilitation and assessment so as to bring students on board with the new educational developments. Additionally, an external consultant was invited to participate in the project. The consultant led a series of workshop sessions for facilitators and students to enable the school to refine its work in assessment. The schedules of the participants were considered when these interventions were planned and presented.

The consultant also assisted in creating a discussion trend among facilitators and students, focusing on how to align assessment with SLOs, emphasising meaningful assessment in this context. In an effort to maintain the motivation of academics and students, "Brown Bag lunch" sessions to discuss assessment were organised and facilitated on an ongoing basis. It was at these sessions that informal learning regarding a variety of assessment instruments, methods and strategies occurred. These sessions also assisted with facilitator the buy-in. Although the actions impacted on the time-schedules of the participants, the provision of snacks dealt with the issue.

The involvement of a consultant as part of the project was one of the reasons why facilitators and students were motivated, encouraged and convinced to invest in and use innovative assessment practices and strategies. The consultant, a professor in Health Sciences from the United States of America, visited at regular intervals and helped to identify areas that may have required specific interventions, so keeping alive the assessment movement in both facilitators and students. Bartholomew *et al.* (in this volume) also refer to a co-ordinated strategy in the university as a requirement to impact on student learning outcomes.

Actions and Interventions	Purpose	Audience
Workshop sessions	Provide underpinning theory in assessment	Facilitators Students
Workshop sessions led by the external consultant	Align learning outcomes and assessment Obtain buy-in on assessment	Facilitators Students
"Brown Bag lunch" discussions	Discuss a variety of assessment topics to increase confidence in assessment	Facilitators Students Support staff working with assessment of student learning
Focus group meeting	Obtain dynamic feedback	Facilitators Students

Table 2: Actions and interventions in the School of Health Technology to improve SLOs

Outcomes of the interventions

Student focus group discussions as well as facilitator assessment discussions became trends in the School of Health Technology. Agenda items in these discussion sessions included the benefits of using for example, student presentations, portfolios and reflection reports in assessment. Discussions focused on how to integrate these assessment practices into student learning and, by doing so, highlighted the importance of meaningful learning. Academic environments in which innovative assessment methods and strategies are discussed and tested provide evidence that the culture of learning and assessment in this particular academic environment was changing and becoming a meaningful measurement of learning.

Facilitators reported that they made specific efforts to expand on the variety of appropriate assessment methods and strategies used to assess student in health technology. This specific approach in assessment was particularly relevant to assess the knowledge, competence and skills of health professionals and, by doing so, improve students' achievement of learning outcomes (Crossley *et al.*, 2002). Crossley *et al.* (2002) further emphasise assessing the competence and skills of students in health rather than that of knowledge only. In the same way Atkins *et al.* (1993) caution that traditional assessment practices may encourage surface learning. Thus, a wider variety of assessment instruments was implemented including assessment in clinical practice, assignments, simulations, OSCA, portfolios and reflection reports rather than being so heavily reliant on traditional written examinations. The portfolio, designed in the correct manner, has proven to be an assessment method used to assess a variety of knowledge and skills outcomes as well as meta-cognition and attitudes, specifically aimed at assessing the health professional (Friedman Ben-David, 2000). Friedman Ben-David (2000) also claims that the OSCA is the ideal assessment method to assess the knowledge, competence and skills and attitudes of a health professional to be. The specific advantage of the OSCA is that all the students are subject to exactly the same assessment tasks addressing the reliability and validity of the assessment. In this way assessment becomes meaningful.

Assessment aligned with SLOs

The larger variety of appropriate assessment methods and strategies also included methods and instruments that developed and assessed the transferable competencies of the students. Transferable competencies are linked to critical outcomes that include communication skills, collaboration and research skills, and preparing students for the world of work in clinical practice. The exposure to a larger variety of assessment methods and instruments in an attempt to scaffold an innovative attitude in assessment and align assessment with the SLOs also engaged students in deep learning (Biggs, 2001; Entwistle, 2001; Huet *et al.*, this volume). Likewise, action verbs according to the taxonomy of Bloom *et al.* (1956) were included in the assessment in order to focus on application, evaluation and creation and, thus, addressing the higher order cognitive skills in assessment (Table 3). Furthermore, the idea that the end of the year assessment is the ultimate gave way to a formative and continuous model in which assessment becomes part of the student learning. Consequently students had more opportunities to attain academic growth, development and success. Peer-assessment and self-assessment were introduced to help students gain knowledge and skills from peers while also learning from their own strengths and shortcomings.

More emphasis and attention was invested in the planning of assessment strategies as part of the course of study. Careful planning and scheduling of assessment can assist facilitators in making the shift from assessment awareness to the integration of the methods in their daily teaching and assessment practices (Gray, 2002). Effort was put into communicating the timing, purpose of and rubrics used to grade assessment. When students know the purposes and expectations of assessment, and receive feedback on assessment, it has the potential to improve their learning (Angelo, 2006), since the aforementioned impacts on the motivation and self-regulation of students in a student-centred environment. Changes in assessment were balanced by facilitating structured interactive sessions with the potential to engage students and to assist in the internalisation of the learning material, and so stimulate higher order thinking (Steinert & Snell, 1999). The use of constructive learning styles – such as interactive sessions and group work – fosters interactions between students. It also promotes communication skills, cultural sensitivity and teaching the students skills so as to manage themselves in a group. Wigen *et al.* (2003) confirm, in a study involving medical students, that activities such as group work correlate positively with academic success and improving student learning outcomes. Facilitators can therefore play an active role in improving student learning through assessment (Angelo, 2006) and, consequently, enhance the quality of the experiences of undergraduate students (Kuh, 2006). For this reason facilitators should make the necessary efforts in creating a challenging, co-operative, collaborative and

185

supportive learning environment for students (Barr & Tagg, 1995). In this kind of environment, facilitators are expected to portray the desire to learn more about assessment and constantly work on improving students' learning outcomes (Borland, 2002). Students, on the other hand, also have to start looking at assessment as an opportunity to enhance their skills and knowledge (Sutherland & Peckham, 1998) as well as to promote deep learning (Entwistle, 2001).

SLO aligned with	Action verbs	Assessment instruments / methods
Knowledge	Discuss Describe Explain	Written assessment Integrated assignment Case report
Competence and skill	Show evidence Design / Evaluate / Create Interpret	Clinical assessment Simulation Case study report Presentation
Attitudes	Reflect Critical reflection Meta-cognition	Evidence of learning portfolio Clinical assessment Presentation

Table 3: Specific assessment methods to align SLOs

A tool to facilitate assessment feedback

The increased use of innovative assessment methods and strategies also necessitated the design of rubrics as tools to facilitate formative feedback on assessment for students in order to help them address their academic performance. Rubrics were designed to capture the performance levels as well as the required assessment criteria and standards. Not only were the rubrics developed as handy assessment tools with which facilitators scored the students, it also evolved as a versatile method used to facilitate formative feedback on assessment to each student. Hinrichsen (in this volume) encourage facilitators in using tools to align teaching methods and assessment.

Thus the feedback to the student offered the possibility to link a performance level such as "revise", "task accomplished/meets minimum standards" or "exceptional" to specific assessment criteria for each of the student learning outcomes. This tool captures, summarises and displays at a glance to the student where to enhance strengths, as well as to address and improve on shortcomings pertaining to the specific assessment task completed (Table 4). An additional advantage of this feedback system was that facilitators also noted that assessment results provided a means to reflect on and revisit their own teaching and assessment practices, including the contribution that they make to improving student learning outcomes.

Criteria	Performance levels			
	Not done	Revise	Meets minimum standards	Exceptional
Description from the literature	Task not performed	"Academic" language from textbook	Own interpretation added to text	Text comprehensive, Shows creativity and judgement
X-ray examination requested	Task not performed	Included	Included with reasons	Included with reasons and additional information

Table 4: Example of a the criteria and performance levels in a rubric

Outcomes of the interventions

Progress in assessment in the School of Health Technology was monitored by observing the quality of the discussions and feedback during ongoing "Brown Bag lunch" discussion sessions, the evidence provided in the respective programme portfolios and feedback obtained via reflection reports of students, verified during focus group meetings. The project did not aim to quantitatively compare the overall academic performance of the student groups neither did the researcher assess the grades of each student as evidence of improved student learning outcomes.

After the implementation of the assessment interventions and actions the level of facilitator discussions on assessment during "Brown Bag lunch" discussion sessions changed from "how do I?" to "these are my experiences in assessment". Discussions focused on how to best align assessment and learning outcomes to attain the best and most appropriate evidence that students have attained the required learning outcomes. Assessment terminology used by facilitators reflected that they now speak with confidence and use the appropriate assessment terminology.

Programme portfolios are used as a tool for self-evaluation and institutional evaluation of programmes contained evidence pointing to success of assessing student learning outcomes. The ability of students to effectively function in clinical practice was obtained via assessment of skills and competence learning outcomes as well as feedback from the clinical staff with which students interact. Positive and encouraging reports were received on the ability of students to integrate theory into clinical practice, emphasising the focus on the assessment of student learning outcomes of knowledge, competence and skills and attitudes.

Student	Quotations from the students' reflection report
	Communication
1	"I have done two presentations in class and that taught me to stand in front of people and express myself"
10	"Since we started with presentations I have acquired a lot in the process. It has helped me to improve my skills of communication, the power to believe in myself, confidence, the ability to have better study skills and to have a thorough subject knowledge"
	Confidence to present work
2	"I have attained a lot of confidence in presenting before a crowd of people"
6	"I have attained much confidence, courage and commitment"
8	"Because of my confidence I found that I could interact better with the class, I could contribute to group discussions, I could voice my opinion without stressing myself whether I was right or wrong and most importantly I can address my class mates with ease e.g. presentations, announcements and speaking"
	Motivation
8	"Any chance that I have to do something, I will do it to the best of my ability with 100% dedication"
	Ability to execute tasks
4	*"We have learnt the necessary skills so that we can be more independent in executing tasks in practice."*
5	*"I also achieved my goal this year of attaining the skill of time-management"*
1	*"I have learned to work under pressure because I have to prepare for assessment and also prepare for class. I think the skills that I have attained this year have made me a better person ....."*
	Advantages of assessment
1	*"With these various approaches to assessment everybody is being assessed fairly"*
3	*"The different assessment e.g. group work, written assessment and others helped me to achieve my academic goals"*
7	*"The different assessment modes have contributed towards attaining learning outcomes. I could identify my strengths and weaknesses and has helped me to achieving my holistic development"*
9	*"The manner in which we are assessed, i.e. the variety presentation (listening skills for peers and teaching skill in the presentation); writing skills like the formative assessment and the assignment to see how good a person is in doing research. So with all these methods everybody is accommodated therefore chances of failing are less".*

Table 5: Selection of quotations from ten student reflection reports

The most valuable evidence on the success of the assessment intervention came from the students themselves. Students were requested to complete structured reflection reports so as to reflect on their assessment experiences as well as their own academic growth and development. In the reflection reports students had to substantiate the statements as well as provide evidence of their learning experiences associated with specific assessment opportunities. Actions such as these encourage students to become active participants in their own learning process. Brüssow & Wilkinson (in this volume) outline the potential of reflective teaching to accommodate student participation in their learning.

So it was encouraging to read in the reports how students reflected on their learning experiences (Table 5 provides a random selection of quotations from 10 student reflection reports). The information from the reflection reports, although regarded as sensitive and personal, was verified during follow-up focus group discussions with students Particular areas that were noted include improved communication skills (students 1 & 10), confidence to present work (students 2, 6 & 8), motivation (student 8) and the ability to execute tasks (students 1, 4 & 5). The larger variety of assessment methods and specific focus on meaningful assessment in this specific group of students pointed towards improving the students' transferable skills in addition to their professional or subject knowledge (students 1, 3, 7 & 9). Evidence of attaining the transferable skills outcomes of students is beneficial in the clinical environment because employers are keen to make use of graduates who can communicate effectively, collect information and manage their working environment effectively.

However, the fact that assessment and learning facilitation are interrelated the new focus on assessment also impacted on teaching practices. Facilitators therefore have to be innovative in teaching practices as well to confirm that student learning outcomes are attained. This emphasises once again the importance of assessing student learning outcomes in a meaningful manner so that the right kind of evidence regarding the attainment of outcomes becomes available.

Challenges in attaining the desired outcomes

Even though the outcome eventually showed positive results, a number of challenges were experienced that reflected initial resistance to the changing educational environment. Facilitators and students were not always familiar with the particular assessment methods and instruments, or did not have the necessary confidence to use certain assessment methods and strategies, in particular the OSCA, portfolios and reflection reports. Additionally, both groups reported that using innovative assessment strategies was time-consuming. Students complained about "over-assessment", since they were used to one "end of the year" assessment.

Although the majority of the students could identify the advantages of the larger variety of assessment methods and interactive facilitation methods used, there were also those who complained. Feedback from students revealed that their preferences and knowledge about assessment strategies varied. Some students expected to be assessed by a variety of methods while other students believed they can best be assessed best through the traditional written work. Initially the idea of peer-assessment and self-assessment was uncomfortable for some students. Students also confessed that they were not always prepared for interactive sessions. Although it is possible that factors such as fear for the unknown as well as time constraints prevent interactive learning (Steinert & Snell, 1999), it is also essential that both facilitators and students buy into a new educational approach and accomplish ownership for successful implementation of new trends in teaching and assessment (Gray, 2002).

An additional area that needed to be addressed in order to move to meaningful assessment was in feedback to the student regarding their assessment and students' reactions to the feedback. Although the students reported that they found the feedback helpful, students must follow up on the feedback appropriately. Unless they do they will be unable to benefit from their learning experiences and improve on student learning outcomes.

Conclusion

The initial aims of the project were to verify assessment, align assessment with SLOs, and increase the variety of appropriate assessment methods. By doing so the focus on assessment of student learning outcomes changed to become meaningful with the potential to improve on student learning outcomes. Since ongoing assessment discussions with both facilitators and students have become a trend within the School of Health Technology, possible challenges and needs addressing innovative assessment were used to fuel future assessment discussion sessions in creating the ongoing growth in the desired assessment culture. Both facilitators and students were willing to consider assessment methods and strategies that were also new to them. However, students also stressed the importance of timely assessments accompanied by relevant, positive and well-timed feedback. These are essential steps in developing a learning-based curriculum with the potential to improve student learning outcomes.

About the author

Hesta Friedrich-Nel is an Associate Professor in the School of Health Technology and Programme head of Radiography and Dental Assisting at the Central University of Technology, Free State, Bloemfontein South Africa. She can be contacted at this e-mail: hfried@cut.ac.za

Chapter 12

Improving Students' Learning Outcomes via Teamwork & Portfolios

Antigoni Papadimitriou

Introduction

There are many ways to improve students' learning outcomes in higher education. I teach a management course in a Greek university. My ambition is to improve students' learning outcomes using teamwork and portfolios. Teamwork happens in class when groups of students work together to solve a case or problem. Teamwork is an integrated part of my teaching and all students who show up in class, will participate in teamwork exercises. Johnson & Johnson (1989) states that learning to work effectively in a team may be one of the most important interpersonal skills a person can develop since it will influence employability, productivity, and career success. The literature supports the importance of teamwork, which is ranked among the top priorities in business schools (Gardner & Korth, 1998).

Portfolio is an assessment method used to document the learning of the individual student. Portfolio assessment is widely documented and used (Anderson, 1993; Banta, 2003; Beishuizen *et al.*, 2006; Knight *et al.*, 2008; Mullin, 1998; Speck, 1998).It became popular in the 1990s, providing feedback about student performance to improve curricula and pedagogy as well as determining the individual student's learning outcome (Ewell, 2002). Palomba (2002) argued that portfolios changed the students' role in assessment, as they became active participants in documenting their own learning process. Using portfolio as assessment method needs some extra effort to plan, evaluate, and store. But the results may be worth the effort. I found from experience that a combination of teamwork and portfolios help students to improve learning outcomes and therefore in this chapter I describe my experiences.

My journey

One of my responsibilities is teaching a management course for first year undergraduate students. A typical semester requires 12 weeks of teaching. Once a week a professor teaches the core component of the course (theory), and I follow up (once a week) with exercises and case studies (*frontistirio in Greek*). Ideally, exercises and case studies help students develop the following learning outcomes: discussion skills, problem-solving skills, broadened awareness, communication skills, changed attitudes, teamwork skills. Furthermore it enables them to understand relevant and practical application of the course requirements by encouraging critical and analytical thinking. Class sizes in our department are very large - typically more than 370 students- so the question is, "How much can one do with a class that size?"

Reflecting on previous student class attendance and levels of participation after my first year of teaching in 2004, I reconsidered my teaching approach. A multiple-choice exam in the fall of 2004 showed an average grade of 6 (on a scale from 5-10). While talking with the professor before the 2005 fall semester, I expressed an interest in introducing portfolio assessments to the students as a pilot project. I had experienced portfolio assessments during my studies in the US and I was familiar with portfolios, teamwork, and the virtual learning environment named Blackboard. My inspiration for using portfolios was Banta's (2003) book and general work. In addition, my ideas stemmed from the literature, conference participation, and from discussions with colleagues from abroad.

Thus, I first introduced portfolios as a pilot project in the fall semester of 2005. In the first experiment, the student enrolment was 483, but many students neither attended class nor participated in the final exam. Then I graded 177 portfolios. The number of students who sat for the final exam was 410. Only 293 passed the course, while 119 failed. The average grade rose from 6 to 7. During that first year the professor and I did not perform any evaluation; however, personal communication with some students sporadically showed that they were very satisfied with the new approach of using portfolios. I used mostly individual work in the classroom and a few times I divided students into groups and handed out a case for group discussion (teamwork).

In 2005 I used a similar approach now with more teamwork assignments in the classroom. Continuing with the same process in 2006, I felt confident because it worked. Most of the students took on active roles and during class most saw themselves as managers ready for action!

The fall semester of 2007 was the third time that teamwork and portfolio was used for the management course. It was followed by an evaluation survey in January 2008 with 40 questions for both theory and *frontistirio* and 5 open-ended questions. In a class of 240 students, 128 students answered the questionnaire (53%). 107 (84%) stated that they participated in the portfolio assessment process. 79% perceived that teamwork assignments were the most favorable part of the course. 65% perceived that participation in this type of portfolio (individual and teamwork assignments) was valuable because it enabled them to connect practice with theory. All 107 students who participated in portfolio assessment process commented that they would highly recommend it to other students.

Teamwork and portfolios appeared to be a tool that motivated students to participate in the course and improved their learning outcomes. I need to clarify that the student's participation in the course is voluntary. Teamwork and individual assignments included in portfolios and provided a tangible reward in the form of points added as extra credit in students' final exam. From the student feedback, I discovered that they were more interested in working as teams while in the classroom. In one of our questions, we asked students if they wished to make any suggestions/changes to the course. Out of the 53% who answered the question, 29% said that they wanted more teamwork assignments during the class sessions. I got the message: more teamwork next year. Judging from students' feedback, there is an increase in team spirit and they said it helped them understand the course in more depth.

Designing and implementing teamwork and portfolios

In this section I describe the ways in which I design and implement teamwork and portfolio assessment. As mentioned above, the course curriculum includes a theory lecture on the first day of each week followed once a week by exercises and case. My teaching takes place in a large lecture hall (amphitheatre). The overarching pedagogical method I use is portfolio assessment, which includes both teamwork assignments and individual assignments. The portfolio assessment is designed in such a way that each student who participate will work on eight dedicated assignments during the semester (3 teamwork assignments and 5 individual assignments). Once the semester is over they hand in their personal portfolio, which I then grade. A typical example of the portfolio-requirements is shown in Table 1.

Teamwork assignments
1. Six to eight cases/exercises per semester in the classroom.
2. Students were asked to transform a family business company to a modern company. Students had the freedom to choose any type of business always following ethical guidelines.
3. Analysis of the Greek economic/legal, political, technological, global, and socio-cultural environment. As future managers, students needed to understand their environment. In cases where students were from abroad, I asked them to analyze their home country environment and in such a case the assignment was in the English language.
Individual assignments
4. Create a list with books, journals and newspapers related to management. This assignment was perceived as important for students' further development and research techniques. In order to prepare this assignment students were obliged to visit the department library and internet.
5. Present the profile of a management Guru.
6. Present the CSR practices by business or public organizations- including universities.
7. Identification of the mission and vision of any Greek/foreign university and to develop the organization chart of the same university. Mission, vision, and organization charts were part of the management theory. Students had to be knowledgeable about the mission and the vision of the university.
8. The final assignment consisted of an essay of 4-6 pages. Students were asked to find an article which related as much as possible to the theoretical part of the course. I directed them to summarize an appropriate article either from a journal or from a newspaper and to discuss it in relation to the theoretical background. It was necessary before their analysis to check the appropriateness of the articles, if students did not find an article I provided them with an appropriate one.

Table 1: Typical example of portfolio-requirements

As a teacher I taught case studies directly connected to the theory lectures. Students were divided into teams of 4-6 persons and were given similar case studies. They had to demonstrate understanding of the examples presented in order to find a solution and link their answer to theory. I asked students to bring their course textbook with them to each class session and asked them to look at a particular case. I also often provided them with other case handouts. In order to maintain their attention, I asked the students to read the case by themselves. Sometimes, when a case involved several people (managers, employees, etc), I asked students to practice role play, one reading the manager's side, another reading the employee's side making it look like a mini-drama. In a big class with at least 70 students, one needs student involvement to maintain their attention and the case parts seemed to capture their interest. At other times, I asked them to read paragraph by paragraph and keep notes; both strategies seemed to attract more attention from the students. I also used this strategy as an icebreaker technique in order to encourage them to speak to each other. The first year students were usually more reserved and they did not express their ideas openly. I can report that the students thoroughly enjoyed this technique and some of the international students took active roles unless their spoken Greek was poor. In that case, I asked students to take notes and we discussed the cases later. I listened to their opinions, their thoughts, and what they planned to do in cases that involved managers etc. My intention was to remind them that they must learn to think as managers because this course was an introductory course. Although they were first year students with limited managerial knowledge, they needed to remember what the professor taught in the theory lecture and I encouraged them to read their notes and textbook in order to use appropriate terminology. Additionally, I asked them to read newspapers and articles that were related to managerial issues and many students perceived it as a simulation game.

During the teamwork, I moved around the big amphitheatre, in order to maximize interpersonal involvement and be knowledgeable about each team's learning procedures. I wanted to know what my students thought and how they reacted to each team's case assignment. In addition, I wanted to allow time for each student to express individual ideas personally and in their team discussions. I used to be a basketball coach and that experience reflected in my exercises. As a coach, I had dealt with many players and without assistants because of lack of budget, so I employed a quality management principle *do more with less*. For players, it is extremely boring and disappointing to wait in a line doing nothing, especially during practices. Therefore, coaches need to find solutions and strategies to keep all their players active and enthusiastic. By including a running approach in my classroom, I was able to get a picture of my students' abilities, interests, expectations, and habits. Students were free to choose and work in their same groups during the semester and it made it easier for them to express their ideas to me in a friendly small group environment rather than in an audience of 120 students. I sought direct interaction with them and discovered that it was easier for them to speak as a team. Sometimes I invited former students to present their teamwork assignments that they had completed during their previous year's participation including portfolios in order to motivate current students to take on a more active role.

Because of the large number of students (which varied between 70 and 120) I divided the class into two large groups. Not all students present in the classroom decided to participate in the portfolio assessment. However, all students were required to participate in teamwork assignments, as this was my new teaching and learning approach. Depending on the number of students participating, I changed the style of my teaching as well as the teamwork assignments. Students had the opportunity to present their work to the class for 3-5 minutes and they were particularly motivated to do so. A few times, I asked the teams to evaluate the work of other teams. Students compared their performance with others. I collected students' classroom teamwork assignments and each team received the same points in their portfolio for the teamwork assignment. I developed data which included all students registered for the course and I tallied teamwork points for each student and it was only at the end of the semester that I was finally able to know how many of those students benefited from the extra points (teamwork and individual assignments).

The criteria for the portfolio evaluation consisted of three stages: 1) class participation and teamwork assignments; 2) focus on the central meaning of each essay, good organization throughout, use of appropriate language, and good grammar (for both teamwork an individual assignments); 3) focus on the overall portfolio presentation. A student who passed the final course examination with an excellent portfolio was able to gain an extra 20%.

Integrate new technologies into teamwork

As a teacher, I was aware of my students learning outcomes in relation to new technologies integrated in teamwork. Therefore, besides teamwork, I encourage students to submit their teamwork and individual assignments to me by e-mail. This was the first step before introducing the full version of e-portfolio as I plan to do next year. E-portfolio needs time for adoption and available software. One of the advantages for instructors is that the e-portfolio provides a quick, electronically accessible means of assessment. I particularly like this approach, because it gives me the ability to detect and verify plagiarism quicly, either from failure to cite sources properly or from copying other students' work within groups. Between the software capabilities of modern word processors and high powered internet search engines, it makes my work of monitoring student assignments less time consuming and allows me to concentrate on higher order thinking in the student papers as well. It also allows me time to give them more effective feedback if needed. For instance, in one semester, I received 557 e-mails and I responded to 417 of them (75%). Although it might still be possible some students do not own a computer or have not learned effective computer skills, the campus library allows students access to university-owned computers and students can also use the designated computer laboratory. The use of computers and the campus Blackboard became an integral tool to introduce new tasks - i.e. announcements, assignment, and on-line submission on my version of e-portfolio. All of my previous classes, in the fall of 2005, 2006 and 2007, were instructed on their first day of class to make use of e-mail and Blackboard. This set the tone for the new term.

As noted, the teamwork assignments are included as part of students' portfolios. I kept the same format - teamwork and individual assignments - except that I had to help my students with the new technologies. PowerPoint presentations from theory and some cases were posted on-line through the Blackboard platform and through a course webpage in Greek language. I also used the Blackboard to place announcements and to provide directions for specific assignments, to post due dates, etc.

In order to help students with on-line submission and with my hope to use the e-portfolio for the next year I had to help them individually with the new technologies. I started to teach in the computer lab itself. I received some help from our librarians who were responsible for operation of the Blackboard. In this demo course in our computer lab, my students worked in teams of three or four students at each work station. With 27 stations it was possible for some 90 students to receive additional help. At the outset the librarians gave a short introduction to Blackboard and at the same time I uploaded exercises on Blackboard in real time. Thus I was able to check students' weaknesses in using Blackboard and new technologies. Since I had more than 200 students who participated in the course, I had to know as much as possible about their strengths and weaknesses. With the big class size and other technical requirements, it was impossible for the new students to submit their assignment via Blackboard; therefore, I adopted e-submission via e-mails. During this demo course, students submitted their work as a team. I received their teamwork assignments and I encouraged them to e-mail copies to the rest of their team members. I had the opportunity to teach them computer competencies besides the case-studies in a teamwork environment. Although some students were advanced, others were only beginners when it came to computer skills. I had to encourage beginners not to become disappointed by their lack of computer skills and at the same time I had to reward advanced students for their performance. I encouraged students to use our computer lab, whose staff was happy to help. In addition, I asked students who were more knowledgeable in internet skills to help their team member achieve faster performance. Students then understood that teachers cared for them and in my opinion that is an important factor for improving students' learning outcomes.

I also encouraged students to choose different team members so that they would meet other students in the class and build friendships and meet others whom they did not already know. Typically Greek students whose parents live near the university still live with their parents, while those who come from other cities rent local apartments. There are only a few dormitories. These factors tend to limit the number of students who can meet with each other outside of class hours. Therefore, I also encourage international students to mix as a team with Greeks.

I also recognize that it can be difficult to work in teams. During the class hours, teamwork is easier but it can be very challenging to work on a team project outside the classroom. I recognized that if I required on-line assignment submissions only, then I risked missing students. Therefore, in order to have the best available results for the team project, I had to build their skills. It helps students to perform better on their projects and it is also helpful for the instructor to communicate with one team member rather than with the entire team. I experienced that in the US when I was the only international student among New Yorkers. The truth is that I did not want to work in a team project; but the Americans love it and it was a requirement. Ultimately, those team members became some of my best friends.

I had hoped that the year of 2008-2009 would allow for on-line essay submission. Finally, the combined electronic and teamwork approach encouraged my students to work together with a new enthusiasm for learning, which could be assessed. It also cultivated a renewed atmosphere of team involvement and flourishing creativity. The riots in Greece in December 2008 hit my department, which meant that access to the university access was extremely limited. Even under adverse circumstances it seemed that students and teachers were able to cope by shifting from crisis management to fact-based management. In retrospect, what the management course taught in theory became, by the end of the fall 2008 semester, a practical situation where students learned the reality of how to act as managers, as a leader of their teams, and how to perform as a team. The resilience of the students and faculty illustrated a Greek saying, "*In stormy weather the captain needs to perform well*".

During December 2008, two assignments were left incomplete. These related to Greek or other countries' environment (teamwork assignment) and the final individual assignment. I posted specific information regarding those two assignments on Blackboard and I sent e-mails to teams that had already formed. Students responded immediately. As the time was limited for the students to present their teamwork assignments in the classroom I asked them to present their work just before their exam as a poster session in our amphitheater. I posted instructions regarding poster development on Blackboard. In addition, I developed an area with questions from students and my answers and explanations which were available for all students. Finally, 95 students participated in the final teamwork assignment by presenting 23 team projects in the final poster session. The quality and student/teamwork creativity from these teams was very high. The professor and I had not expected that only with instructions via Blackboard and especially during the period when the access to the university was limited, these teams of students could successfully provide us with their projects. During that final day, I met more than 130 students including non-participants in teamwork assignments, because the course was voluntary, as previously noted. The team members were happy and proud about their teamwork assignment (projects). I asked them to vote and select the first 5 best posters and the results were also announced on-line. Regarding final portfolios for the academic year of 2008-2009, I received 130 paper made portfolios. During the poster presentation and the exam, we also administered a course evaluation survey (not yet analyzed).

A quick review of the Blackboard statistics indicated that during the semester, the course had 6079 hits; 900 of those were from me. During December and January, I accounted for 3053 hits, while the system recorded students' visits to the course's announcements almost every day including on New Years Eve. These encouraging results provide hope for 2009-2010 to fully engage the use of Blackboard in teamwork and individual assignment as an e-portfolio during our management course.

Lessons learned

Data indicates that both teamwork and portfolios have become popular with our students because our survey indicated that the majority would recommend it to other students. In addition, several students asked if this approach took place in other courses. However, a number of fundamental and strategic questions beg for answers in order to define a practice as being more effective and efficient.

One of the most challenging topics in education is the challenge of improving students learning outcomes. The argument favoring teamwork and individual assessment of student projects through portfolios appears to advance educational practice through improved "student motivation in course participation", promoting "teamwork," and facilitating "student-faculty interactions" substantiated by the results of this process. Furthermore, in order to characterise this process as more or less effective, we need to take into consideration parameters such as characteristics of higher education systems, student population characteristics, trends, habits, and most importantly, the circumstances in which the teaching and learning approach took place.

The combination of using teamwork and individual assignment in portfolios for the management course is generally accepted. In my experience, this process seems to yield a maximum benefit if each student actively participates in theory and in *frontistirio*.

It is challenging as a teacher to confirm whether the desired leaning has occurred and meets the required objectives, which are clearly defined in measurable terms. This may require more rigor in methods of investigation along with the usual ways of grading. SLOs in the management course are outlined in their syllabus. However, it is difficult to provide evidence of the extent to which students that pass this course and participate in teamwork and portfolios have actually met these objectives. Although I did not measure the exact effect of teamwork and portfolios on students' learning outcomes, I observed their participation in class as well as in their written assignments. This revealed which students worked on their portfolios, because they became more confident and argued with more theoretical weight. It is my belief that when they were writing their portfolios they had to argue for their personal understanding of the academic content and, as such, were forced to construct arguments, defend them in front of others, and reflect upon their conclusions. The literature strongly supports the approach to read, discuss, argue, re-read, discuss, and write. It involves different learning styles and engages learners at multiple levels of cognitive learning. Jonassen *et al.* (1999:56) noted that: *"Traditional instruction insists on providing all of the concepts and theory prior to applying it by solving problems, while constructivism argues that learning information in the context of meaningful activity makes it better understood and more resistant to forgetting".*

The literature on portfolios addresses the benefits of portfolios for students. Mullin (1998:80) listed several benefits for using portfolios that faculty, who represent a variety of disciplines, have identified. Among those listed, portfolios demonstrated both the process of learning over time as well as products of learning; portfolios encourage students to reflect on their own progress as learners and participate in the evaluation process; portfolios develop collaborative capabilities among students; portfolios emphasize the development of student's self-esteem and problem solving abilities. Thus, one could perceive that similar benefits would accrue in my teaching approach included the teamwork assignments.

During the process of developing their portfolios, students had the opportunity to reflect on their learning and apply their creativity as Mullin's list suggested. Additionally, the portfolios were organized around the specific goals as stated in their course syllabus. Therefore, valid assessment criteria were provided because each item in their portfolio provided evidence to demonstrate each learning outcome of the course had been accomplished. In addition, students commented that they identified the benefits of using teamwork and portfolios and they emphasized that the teamwork and individual assignments included in their portfolios helped them to better understand the theoretical part of the course. Whereas I did not make a thorough semantic analysis of the discourse of the students' portfolios, my experience indicated that the students who did write a personal portfolio improved their understanding of the theoretical and empirical content of the course. The "dialogue" in their teamwork and portfolios was on a higher level than the dialogue usually presented by students not participating in teamwork and doing portfolios. The students who submitted portfolios not only referred to theory, they argued for their analysis and they made synthesis between different parts of the theoretical and empirical content.

It is important to realise that this type of process teamwork and portfolio was both a useful process and helped students to learn how to communicate better and to respond well under difficult and unexpected circumstances because they produced excellence projects and worked as teams. On the basis of student participation in teamwork and individual assignments (and from the survey results), the teamwork and portfolios provided evidence of a technique that improved their learning experience. It also offers ways to further develop specific student learning outcomes, in particular, working as an effective team member – one of the aims of management courses.

Conclusions

This chapter has demonstrated that the use of teamwork and portfolios may serve as important tools for improving SLOs. As mentioned above, the new trend for on-line submission is a way to achieve improved teaching and learning. Coincidentally, as a user-friendly technique, the utilization of electronic files changes students' learning and it can be observed and documented as students participate in a large class.

After four years of using teamwork and portfolios, while taking into account students' perceptions about this process, the professor and I evaluated it as crucial for the students and decided to continue using it the next year. In my case, the impact of this teaching approach improved student/teacher interaction, facilitated better student communication and helped students to express their ideas more efficiently. For example, after introducing the topic of social responsibility for universities, students suggested and implemented a battery-recycling program which was then adopted by our department. During the 2005 course, student participation was very active and peaked at 65%. I was able to ascertain that students, though well versed in theory, were initially unable to apply critical and analytical thinking skills. But students' final grades showed that their ability and knowledge had increased.

To start with, this process does not require extra resources, but it is time consuming for the teacher and requires some class management techniques. It involves a shift in beliefs and attitudes about what is possible in education. I perceive that the success factors for improving SLOs resulted from my motivation and desire to work with students like a team. As a former basketball coach, I saw my class as a team, which needed to win greater understanding and critical thinking to succeed.

The main objective of our management course is to provide students with an overview of the principles and the basic concepts of management and organizations. Emphasis is given to planning, organizing, leading, and controlling. Other elements in the course objective are for them to understand the meaning of management; what it means to be a manager, and how working as a team is very effective.

For any teacher who teaches management theory or/and practices, it is a challenge to bring managerial skills into the classroom, while providing relevance and yet performing that role well. The most important consideration during the management course is how to teach without violating the objective of the course.

Data from student comments, grades, participation levels, and teamwork and portfolios provide me with sufficient evidence that my methodology and process directly relates to improvements in student learning outcomes. During this process our students learn the reality of how to perform as members in a team, because via teamwork, they learn the basics of applied management. Future research is needed into the question of how SLOs are used to frame teamwork and portfolios, which include feedback from students and the teacher, and what is its long-term impact on student learning. I plan to perform a follow-up study in May 2010 on our senior students who took part in the teamwork and portfolio process. It may then be possible to shed more light on these questions.

Although many questions remain, the current application of technology, teamwork and portfolios provide a new teaching paradigm for Greek higher education. However the issues surrounding huge class sizes may complicate broad adoption by faculty and staff since it might increase their workload. Perhaps such an adoption could be limited to no more than one course per semester for huge classes. Faculty rewards and graduate student assistants might become a means to motivate faculty to adopt new teaching approaches.

Helping students learn is the core idea of teaching and there is always room for improvement. My personal experience suggests that teachers need to innovate their teaching process and think about how to provide students with opportunities for active learning. More importantly, how we can help students identify knowledge and skills beyond the semester while we reinforce SLOs, and help them understand the short-term and long-term benefits, including the importance of turning learning outcomes into life skills.

About the author

Antigoni Papadimitriou is a research teaching staff member in Department of Economics at Aristotle University, Thessaloniki, Greece. She can be contacted at this e-mail: antigoni@econ.auth.gr

CHAPTER 13

Using Assessment Centre Approaches to Improve Student Learning

Arti Kumar

Introduction

The need to develop students' generic employability skills and link them with specific learning outcomes has prompted the University of Bedfordshire in the UK to explore employers' recruitment practices and to innovate an Assessment Centre (AC) project. ACs are widely and increasingly used by graduate recruiters, usually after candidates have been pre-screened through applications and interviews in order to observe, assess and select suitable candidates for job roles. Contrary to what the term implies, an AC is not actually a centre or a place but a series of tasks designed to elicit the behaviours required for success in a job role. Trained assessors can then more objectively observe and assess a candidate's performance in these tasks against pre-defined criteria (AGR, 2008a).

While employers typically use ACs for recruitment, they are also sometimes used to promote and provide developmental feedback for existing staff (Byham, 1971; Gatewood & Field, 1994). It is this use of ACs that is potentially more relevant for educators as it can develop competencies and not simply test them. As the AC project has evolved, in parallel with the implementation of the University's revised curriculum, some academic staff have turned AC approaches into practical, collaborative activities for students, aligned with self-assessment, peer observation and formative feedback to improve their skills. Different ways of conceptualizing skills, learner development, assessment and feedback have opened up. I believe the AC concepts and practical examples presented here are a unique application in their scope and purpose, although a few other educators in the USA use ACs with college students (e.g. see Kottke & Shultz, 1997; Aguirre *et al.*, 1995; Hakel, 1993).

This chapter is divided into four sections. First I outline the background and ethos of the University of Bedfordshire as the context in which I am currently implementing the AC project. Secondly I explore employers' use of ACs and show how these were translated from workplace to academia. Third, I describe specific case examples of AC-type activity and evaluate the learning outcomes from different disciplines to indicate how such activities may be integrated at various levels of a study programme. Lastly I suggest future possibilities for spreading, embedding and enhancing the use of AC approaches.

The learning outcomes in this chapter relate to the development of 'behavioural competencies' which integrate the skills, attributes and attitudes that students essentially need for effective study, work and life in today's world, but which they do not learn through traditional teaching methods in higher education. For example, the intellectual skills of critical thinking, problem solving, research, analysis and written communication are highly valued in academia, but how do these transfer and apply in the workplace? What do they look like to others as behaviours and actions? What else is needed? This chapter shows how ACs make key competencies visible and comprehensible. Moreover the broader competencies that employers seek in an ideal employee are similar to those that educators seek in an effective learner. When staff perceive them as two sides of the same coin they also see the relevance, importance and possibility of integrating them within curricula. As educators we know that assessment drives and focuses student learning and it also helps students to understand and recognise what they have learnt (Gibbs & Simpson, 2004). Therefore, if we value a skills-rich curriculum which actively supports the development of wider attributes, we need to find a way of assessing skills. ACs are one such way. They provide the means as well as the criteria for students to undertake self-assessment in order to identify their personal possession and unique mix of competencies. The same criteria can be used for peer observation and for assessments and feedback by peers and tutors.

Empirical evaluation indicates that AC methods can motivate students to engage actively in an enriched experience of formative, holistic development – *if* they are effectively informed and facilitated as part of their personal and career development. They encourage students to develop the knowledge, attributes and personal agency needed to become good professionals. By extension students can also develop habits of reflection and realistic self-assessment against frames of reference formulated to take account of tutors' and employers' requirements. Such attributes and abilities to learn from multiple contexts and identities are useful in study, life and work in a complex, hi-tech, global economy. The chapter invites readers to consider how:

- AC approaches can raise awareness of the attributes that employers (and tutors) seek and that candidates need for success in learning as well as in competitive 'graduate careers';
- ACs make key competencies visible as effective behaviours and therefore make them more accessible for students to observe, assess and develop, through exercises that are subjected to self-assessment, observation and feedback from peers, tutors and employers;
- AC-related concepts and exercises may be contextualized in curriculum design and delivery, and facilitated as part of a supported and structured process of learner development;

The examples and resources referred to here may be adopted or adapted for use in different contexts with different cohorts of students.

Background, context and rationale

The University of Bedfordshire was formed in August 2006 by the merger of the University of Luton with the Bedford faculty of De Montfort University. Both institutions had a history and ethos of vocational education and skills-rich curricula; the University of Luton had won substantial funding through competitive bidding in 2005 to establish a Centre for Excellence in Teaching and Learning (CETL), based on its distinctive curriculum that included personal, professional and academic development for all students. CETL funding was provided to enhance such approaches. Functioning within the new merged institution, one of the CETL's initial actions in 2006 was to invite key staff to 'begin with the end in mind' and develop a clear vision of an 'ideal graduate for the 21st Century'. The resulting agreed vision was that of: "*...a graduate who is knowledgeable, critical and creative; who understands who they are and what they want to achieve; who can communicate effectively, evidence attainments and function in context, and who has the skills, self-confidence and self-regulatory abilities to manage their own development. Such a graduate is eminently employable, capable of working with and learning from others, of adding significantly to their local community and prepared for life in an ever-changing environment*" (Atlay *et al.*, 2008:238).

Working towards this end-goal, the vision was further developed through Curriculum Revision for implementation in 2008. This came to be known as CRe8 – or, when spoken, 'create' – and colloquially, *CRe8ing CRe8* (see Atlay *et al.* (2008) and the website: www.beds.ac.uk/aboutus/tandl/cre8). The CETL has worked with staff across the University to re-focus 'teaching' as 'stimulating learning', around five strands, namely personalised learning, curriculum design, realistic learning, employability and assessment. In all subject fields and in support areas, staff have been invited to define more specifically the learning experience, subject understanding, skills and wider attributes of the 'ideal graduate' as envisioned above.

Within CRe8 there is implicit recognition that it is not enough to simply embed skills in subject curricula. Ideally, graduates should leave with expertise in their subject *and also* a critical appreciation of their unique possession of skills, attributes, values, interests and personal styles. They need to have analysed (and preferably also experienced) the extent to which their strengths and priorities might fit with different options and with the demands of their chosen occupation, in the context of a changing world. In other words, graduate attributes are insufficient without career development learning.

Drawing on my experience of facilitating career development learning, and my involvement in 'Cre8ing CRe8', I authored an integrated student-centred process of development within a *SOARing to success* framework (see Kumar, 2007) which is now integral within CRe8. SOAR, standing for self, opportunity, aspirations and results, presents ways of animating the dynamic inter-relationships between these four elements. The SOARing process generates the learning outcomes that individuals need for lifelong career management. Since the AC approaches are framed by SOAR, I will return below to show how the concepts and practical examples work together. I initiated the AC project along these lines and in this context so that its approaches are fully aligned with the University's evolving emphasis on the personalised, active and meaningful learning of the individual, linked with formative assessment methods leading to employability. Before I describe some case examples it will be helpful to provide some background on the way in which employers use ACs

Employers' use of ACs

Since ACs were first used for selection in military applications (in 1942 in the UK, 1948 in the USA), their popularity has steadily grown until they are currently widely used by graduate recruiters in almost every occupational and industry sector. The AGR Graduate Recruitment Survey of 2006 found that 91% of respondents used final round ACs or selection events. These are designed to simulate critical aspects of a job role across a variety of standardized assessments in order to gather behavioural evidence of a candidate's existing capabilities and potential success in job performance (AGR, 2008a).ACs typically last for one or two days.

Typical AC activities	What employers are looking for
Individual introductions Candidates are asked to say something briefly about themselves in a (semi)formal setting.	Positive and professional self-presentation: friendly, respectful, intelligent and motivated individuals who have integrity and good self-esteem.
(Second) Interviews AC interviews usually follow an initial pre-screening interview. These may be technical or general interviews but are usually competency-based and provide an opportunity to discuss the candidate's performance at other AC activities.	Extended evidence of strategic self-awareness of job-fit and company-fit, communicating relevant strengths, interests, priorities and development needs. Willingness to continue learning and improving.
Small group discussions Usually 4 to 6 candidates discussing cooperatively or debating competitively a given topic within a timeframe. The topic may be general or pertinent to the job, and usually involves some complex issues. Groups may be leaderless with a common brief, or have assigned roles, with each member being given different information.	Effective communication and cooperation with others to analyse information, deal with ambiguity, solve problems, make sensible decisions or plans and achieve results – possibly looking for managerial or leadership potential. Critical, creative / constructive thinking. Time and task management in group-work.
Individual presentation - may be a separate component or a follow-up to the group discussion, requiring personal views and recommendations arising from the discussion topic. Usually timed 5-10 minutes.	Ability to structure a presentation and communicate its key points and message clearly, convincingly and confidently to an audience within the allocated time, justifying one's views under cross-examination.
Psychometric ability tests Job-specific (e.g. IT) or generic tests are used, either for pre-screening or at an AC. May be computer or paper-based.	Technical expertise or job-specific abilities such as spatial judgment or abstract reasoning; or generic abilities, e.g. verbal and numerical reasoning.
Personality questionnaires / Interest inventories Questionnaires that elicit personal preferences and styles.	A certain profile that is aligned with the position, the existing team, the company's culture and values.
In-tray or e-tray exercises Simulations of job-specific or managerial tasks, requiring reactions to 'a day in the life of...' Candidates are instructed to read and react to a pile of reports, letters, messages, etc.	Common sense solutions in judging relevance, urgency and importance of everyday tasks; values in managing time, workload and pressure, prioritising and planning. Performance under pressure.

Table 1: Typical AC activities and competencies sought

They may be held on employers' premises, or at a hotel or conference centre. Best practice in ACs dictates that the environment should be structured and formal but friendly and welcoming, allowing all candidates an equal chance to perform at their best on multiple dimensions. They are not competing against each other, so several candidates can be observed together to see if any - or none - of them measure up against the job-related criteria. Despite the considerable costs, time and effort involved, employers find - and research shows - that an AC significantly reduces the risk of a selection mistake (AGR 2008b; Hunter & Hunter, 1984).

Assessors are trained to observe performance behaviours objectively against agreed criteria, and to record what candidates do and say. In a final 'wash-up' meeting the panel of assessors integrates and discusses the data they have gathered, and award total scores for each candidate. These multiple judgments by trained assessors elicit a more rounded, richer picture than it is possible to achieve through CVs, applications, biographical interviews and degree results alone. Information about candidates obtained across a range of scenarios gives a more accurate, unbiased and balanced assessment of suitability – matching the candidate's profile to the demands of the role.

The most common 'tests' used in graduate ACs are interviews, group discussions and ability tests. According to AGR's Graduate Assessment Centre Usage Survey 2006, 77% of graduate recruiters use group discussion exercises, and these have remained consistently the most popular AC exercise since their initial survey in 1993. Also popular are in-tray/e-tray and written exercises, business case studies, group and/or individual presentations, role-plays and questionnaires (e.g. on personality, motivation or values). Table 1 summarises AC activities and the competencies sought.

Transferring AC concepts from workplace to academia

The performance behaviours that employers are looking for (see right-hand column of Table 1) are those that students need to develop and graduate applicants need to possess. Note that these are not only needed for entry to employment but also for success in general. For educators this column implicitly contains a variety of competencies that can be promoted to students as desirable learning goals. However employability is often perceived in academia as a complex and problematic concept as its components are difficult to define, measure, assess and transfer – due to the different perspectives of multiple stake-holders in multiple contexts. On the basis that curriculum change is only possible with a prior change in teachers' beliefs and attitudes, it was crucial to show that AC approaches can be supportive of learning and not inimical to academic practice. To help make these connections I asked staff at a workshop to define what students need to do and be like, for success in learning and improving. I collated their responses onto flipchart paper.

After a brief introduction to ACs I used *The Assessment Centres video* (AGCAS, 2000) to raise awareness of the competencies employers seek. The video is now in DVD format; it shows graduate recruiters briefing, observing and assessing a range of typical AC activities, to select suitable applicants for general management positions that are open to graduates from any discipline. This viewing is therefore relevant for a whole range of different subject areas and for creating shared understanding around the generic aspects of employability. The criteria employers use becomes comprehensible as their discussions about the candidates bring to life the professional behaviours they are looking for through typical AC testing techniques such as group discussion, presentations, interviews and social situations.

The viewing of course needs some critical questioning to encourage deeper engagement. I asked staff to draw out answers to the following questions while viewing the DVD:

1) What AC activities do you see being observed and assessed?
2) What skills (behavioural competencies) do recruiters look for? De-scribe these as explicitly as you can. (A summary of the activities and competencies shown in the DVD was drawn up in collabora-tion with staff at this point, as represented in Table 1).
3) How do employers assess these? What criteria do they use?
4) Which of these behavioural competencies
    a. are similar to those needed for effective learning?
    b. are important and relevant for students to develop?
    c. are already being developed in the curriculum?
    d. need to be enhanced because there is a shortfall?

The DVD was thus used as a trigger for discussions, and I punctuated these with topical information from employer surveys. For example,

- 86% of employers consider good communication skills to be im-portant, yet many employers are dissatisfied that graduates can ex-press themselves effectively.

- 'Soft' skills such as team working are also vital and even more important than most 'hard' skills, although numeracy and literacy skills are considered essential by 70% of employers (Archer & Davison, 2008).
- Recent research (CBI & UUK, 2009; UKCES, 2009) reveals that – no matter which occupation, job level, industry sector or country is under scrutiny – there are more similarities than differences in the skills that employers want (e.g. AGR, 2008).

Through every such exercise it is interesting to note that the success factors identified for good learning outcomes in HE are not far different from those that employers seek and those needed for success in life-careers generally. Basically educators need to produce well-rounded, self-aware, confident and motivated individuals with ability to communicate in a professional manner, build effective relationships with others, retrieve, use and analyse relevant information to make decisions and solve problems, maintain motivation to learn and achieve results. Educators begin to see that fostering these generically effective attributes should help to improve knowledge gains *and* to address a key challenge and need: to develop mature and professional conduct in students, and to move them gradually from student to graduate to professional identity. ACs can therefore provide a major focus and integrated rationale for both educational and employability gains in the curriculum.

A curriculum designed for this dual purpose is seen to be beneficial but ACs can do more than this – the methods can help educators to link *how* they teach with *what* they teach. So at a follow-up session with staff, a Computing lecturer and I set up a mock AC-type group discussion as a taster for participants to experience the methods. They were given a general proposition to discuss for 15 minutes, and asked to generate five statements to support it. Replicating AC methods, the groups were observed and given constructive feedback – not so much on the cognitive outcomes or content of their statements, but also on how well they had managed the dynamics and process of the task. However the significant learning outcomes for staff from this exercise were achieved in the discussion that ensued about the possibilities and implications of transferring AC-type activity into classroom practices.

The value but also the difficulty of replicating AC tasks and methods in normal classrooms was discussed. It was clear that staff could not be expected to have the expertise, inclination, time and resources to directly replicate employers' recruitment methods as high-stakes assessed activities in order to test students. It was also felt that testing students' attributes without having set them up for success first was unfair. Academic staff commented that the attributes in question were slow to develop and should be introduced early in any programme as low-stakes formative activities, and re-visited in a coherent manner throughout. Students' courses should be punctuated by employability messages, practical experiences, opportunities to identify their strengths and personal qualities, and reflect on the implications of their self-beliefs and motivations. Throughout this process of development the competencies assessed at ACs are particularly useful as behavioural frames of reference or end-goals.

Questions were raised about how to run AC-related activities for learning and improving, rather than simply as preparation for recruitment: how to create a motivating and challenging environment, but one that stretches learners out of their comfort zone into a safe-risk, supportive zone; how to teach students themselves to take ownership of skills-development; how to train them to give and receive specific – and even critical - feedback while still enhancing each individual's confidence and self-efficacy beliefs.

Some staff have since addressed these issues (see examples below). Others felt some of their existing practice allowed for AC approaches to be tied in quite easily. At our University we are currently attempting to audit and map CRe8 practices at a whole-course level, to ensure students are receiving the full range of intended benefits and progressing from one level to the next. Tutors are currently being asked: *What learning, teaching and assessment opportunities and resources do you provide that enable students to develop graduate attributes and key employability competencies? How do you know what effect these opportunities are having on students?*

Skills may not have exactly the same meaning in education and employment, but it is essential for the relationships and overlap between different skill-sets to be explicitly articulated, so that synergy can be created through congruent and complementary approaches in curriculum design and delivery. My experience in careers education and guidance tells me that students develop many skills within and outside their curriculum, but do not adequately recognize and promote them. Articulating the transferability of skills clearly and convincingly is a complex ability that few people naturally possess but can learn. In this respect behavioural descriptors (that are such an important hallmark of ACs) can provide a lexicon and create shared understanding between staff and students, clarify skills expectations and outcomes, and provide criteria for behavioural observation, feedback and outcomes assessment.

The AC project has therefore attempted to take some marginal employment-related concepts and move them more centre-stage into academic practice. They are now explicit expectations expressed in the University's Education Strategy and related policies as part of the development of a 'rounder graduate'. The examples provided below will show how ACs can take students from initial awareness-raising through a clear line of sight to the practical activities and benefits associated with them.

Case examples of AC-type activity with students

Example 1: Setting key competencies as learning goals
In the first session of some first-year Personal, Professional and Academic Development modules, competencies were brought to life in an engaging and visual way by showing clips from the same ACs DVD mentioned above. To make skills outcomes, standards of behaviour and expected results visible as end-goals, and as an explicit focus of the module, students were asked to find answers through the DVD viewing to the following questions:

- *What are employers testing through each AC activity?*
- *Describe the skills and knowledge applicants need to achieve success in these activities.*
- *Discuss what you would need to do and develop in order to cope effectively with an AC.*

Then students and tutors together generated a written summary of activities and competencies (as in Table 1). Students were asked to write individual plans for self-development, thus encouraging them to take responsibility and set a direction of travel towards the competencies they needed to develop. They themselves perceived and articulated the relevance and importance of achieving the learning outcomes tutors had planned for them anyway, and tutors could then offer these as stepping stones towards students' self-selected goals.

This exercise is consistent with the first two of Covey's Seven Habits of Highly Effective People – *"Be proactive"* and *"Begin with the end in mind"* (Covey, 1989). In the words of a Computing student, taken from his reflective blog: *"This helped us get a good insight into the actual skills requested by employers when looking for suitable candidates for roles. It was interesting to see how many different skills are expected of potential employees and that employers are looking for more rounded individuals instead of just those with only technical ability. I learnt about performance and mastery goals/skills which are both needed to become a rounded, multi-talented individual. I see myself more as a performance goal person so I am looking to develop and set myself more mastery goals".*

Perhaps 'beginning with the end in mind' may not represent an improved learning outcome in itself, but a raised awareness of requisite skills and personalised goal-setting towards achieving them is both a valuable learning goal *and* a learning outcome from this exercise. Having set a direction of travel, tutors and students could constructively align their shared perception of learning outcomes with objectives for each contact session, and develop skills incrementally through AC-related learning, teaching and assessment methods. Tutors on these modules designed a coherent, structured, supported sequence of experiential, interactive learning opportunities, discussions, self-reflective and psychometric audits related to the requisite competencies. Each session's methods were agreed with students and presented as learning objectives constructively aligned with outcomes that are relevant for real-life learning and work.

AC protocols implicitly correspond with many existing notions of best practice in HE. For example the educational principle of 'constructive alignment' (Biggs, 1996) stipulates that course design should start with identifying intended learning outcomes and then develop learning objectives and activities, teaching methods, assessment protocols and criteria that all fit together. This reflects the constructive alignment or close 'fit' between all aspects of ACs, which is a fundamental principle of their design. In HE such alignment is rare in relation to the assessment, development and verification of students' wider attributes. In this respect lessons learned from AC approaches can be applied to improving and evaluating students' skills outcomes through criteria aligned with formative, challenging developmental feedback *and* final summative assessments.

Central to my concept of learning outcomes in this chapter is the idea of engaging students in their own self-managed learning journeys, for which they take progressive responsibility. For example, 'SOAR-ing to success' conceptualises 'self as hero' in a lifelong learning journey, in which key competencies and personal agency are emphasised. To navigate through the journey students build self-MAPs: they identify strengths and development needs which arise from their MAP

(Motivation, Ability and Personality); they engage appropriately with opportunities and with others; generate, clarify, test and implement realistic aspirations; achieve, demonstrate and evaluate their results. The framework is informed by a variety of learning theories, such as constructivism (Vygotsky, 1978) and career theories (e.g. Watts *et al.*, 1996). The practical exercises that flow from these concepts help students to recognise the value and diversity of learning for a variety of relevant purposes.

Self-awareness and realistic self-assessment is a central tenet in the SOARing approaches, where results refer in one sense to the effective behaviours that students may be expected to develop and practise, in relation to AC requirements and other external frames of reference. The SOAR model is comprehensively described in my book (Kumar, 2007), which contains a set of self-audits based on employability and expressed as behaviours. Indicative examples of these are also downloadable from the book's companion website at: www.routledge.com/professional/978041542360-1/aboutbook.asp

For the AC project I created an audit for students to rate their effectiveness in AC-related interactions, particularly in group interactions and presentations (see Table 2 below). To maximize learning gains from such tools it is important to use them as part of a process of development and within a mix of strategies. It is good practice to involve students in building up these perceptions of effective behaviours, and to discuss how they might be applied in different contexts – e.g. *How are they effective in learning and/or in work? Why are the skills involved in group-work so important in today's global economy? What are the consequences of not demonstrating these skills?* They can be used as the basis for a learning contract, a springboard for reflection, self-assessment, peer-assessment, discussion and action planning.

Each statement represents an ideal end-goal, and therefore implies a learning outcome, but students should be advised that it would be unrealistic to expect perfect behaviours all the time, in every situation! The purpose for students is not simply to come up with a score. They should identify their strengths and limitations; low ratings should be taken simply as raw material for self-development. Based on this, a personal action plan that identifies relevant opportunities and support can help to drive change towards improving their ratings.

Initially you might administer a self-audit for students to use as a diagnostic tool (time 1), and return after a period of time to use it as an evaluative tool (time 2) – to see if any changes in outcomes have occurred between initial diagnosis and subsequent evaluation.

Instructions to students:

Each of the following statements represents an effective or ideal way of coping with various aspects of the Assessment Centre (AC) session, as a developmental experience for you. This involves several skills and personal attributes that are key requirements for success in both your current studies, entry to employment and job performance. They are therefore of high value in your current student role as well as in positioning yourself for any future work role. They can be enhanced once you understand what is expected of you.

1. Approach this exercise with an honest desire and positive attitude to see what these competencies and attributes look like as behaviours and actions.

2. Use it to think honestly about your current behaviours and remember the aim is not to say you are excellent in everything (nobody is!) but to identify weak areas to work on.

3. Once you have done this we will discuss the implications of your high and low ratings, any further action you may want to take, etc.

4. Please now assess the extent to which you feel you participate and perform effectively in the AC exercises, by allocating ratings to each statement along a 4-point scale, where 1 = never, 2 = rarely, 3 = frequently, and 4 = very frequently.

To what extent do you cope effectively with the general aspects of Assessment Centre (AC) exercises ?	Ratings 1 - 4
I appreciate and can explain what professional competencies employers are looking for (and the criteria they use) at ACs	
I can use the same criteria to observe and assess others in AC activities	
I make a positive impression through appropriate: - posture (upright and alert but relaxed); - facial expressions (friendly, interested, etc.); - hand gestures (under control, apt in context); - eye contact (conveying engagement with others); - attire, accessories and grooming	
I discern effective behaviors from those that impact negatively	
I give constructive feedback to others to help them improve	
I can evaluate my own performance objectively	
I use feedback suggestions that will help me improve	
My strengths are reflected in the contributions I make to AC activities	

In group discussions and problem solving exercises...	Ratings 1 - 4
I express myself confidently and assertively	
I contribute ideas and suggestions relevant to the topic or task	
I take on a specific role when required	
I listen respectfully to others	
I support others' positive contributions	
I focus (or re-focus) the group on its tasks and goals	
I help the group to achieve its goals within a given timeframe	

When making presentations...	Ratings 1 - 4
I identify the main purpose of my presentation	
I make essential and relevant points convincingly	
I can adapt to the needs and interests of my audience	
I back up my points with credible examples, experience and/or evidence	
I speak at an appropriate pace – neither too fast nor too slow	
I use positive body language and self-presentation	
I make confident, clear and comprehensible speeches	
My tone is appropriate to the context	
I keep to the allocated time	

Table 2: Student self-audit - success at assessment centre activities

If you ask the same student cohort to hand in copies of their self-ratings at both time 1 and time 2, this can be one way of collecting quantitative data to explore patterns of change and exactly which ratings (learning outcomes) have improved over that time period. This data does need to be interpreted qualitatively too, within a mixed-methods approach to evaluating outcomes, because students' ratings are simply claims unless they are substantiated by convincing real-life evidence. It is important to debrief and discuss the tool and the process in plenary. Have students challenge each other in pairs with the type of questions they might encounter in interviews, e.g. in this case: *Where are you most (or least) effective in coping with AC activities? Tell me about your worst AC experience. What made it so bad? What did you do? What would you do differently now?*

Example 2: Designing skill-development opportunities
In another similar module example, second year Business and Marketing students were briefed to view the ACs DVD, but in this case mainly to generate ideas for designing their own skills-development opportunities. Their assignment required them to design and run activities for each other that would enable them to:

- develop the competencies they had viewed on the DVD;
- observe and give useful feedback to develop each others' skills.

They were asked to record their reflections in e-portfolio assignments, based on the following prompts set by tutors:

- *How I would apply what I've learned to real-life situations: e.g. what I would do more/less of; what should I start/stop doing.*
- *The tips I would give to my peers.*
- *Questions or concerns I have about achieving the success factors.*
- *Opportunities I intend to use to develop my employability.*

From discussion and students' blogs it appeared that they developed a variety of skills through working with others in small groups, creative thinking in order to design activities, the communication skills involved in giving and receiving feedback constructively in order to improve. Other outcomes that were mentioned included the ability to discern effective behaviours from those that were unproductive, e.g. in areas such as time-management and collaborative learning.

218

Students were surprised to discover the extent to which 'opportunity' is differentially available to each of them due to their varying assets and constraints, and that each displayed individual differences in reacting to real-life opportunities. They also realised they could – and indeed *should* - be proactive in creating personal development experiences – *when opportunity doesn't knock you have to build a door*, as one student put it. There were many hidden variables that influenced their capacity and capability to take advantage of opportunities that might be realistically available to them, but each could develop coping strategies given the right type of support. They discovered their own capability to support and mentor each other. A student peer mentoring project is to be created, partly as a result of this experience.

Example 3) Creating a mock AC experience for final year students
Psychology tutors have worked with Careers staff to design and deliver an AC Day for final year students. They are currently evaluating this intervention through an action research process. The students are briefed and taken through a series of AC activities similar to those that they view on the AC DVD. They are helped to introduce themselves with impact (given the importance of making a positive first impression). The main aim of the AC Day, however, is to set up AC-type group work to improve team effectiveness. The ability to work effectively with others is high on the wish-list of almost every employer, and some form of group discussion or task is the most frequently assessed activity at ACs. Related to team effectiveness, communication skills are highly prized but often mentioned as a skill in which graduates fall short of expectation.

This demand from employers chimes well with the fact that assessed group projects are increasingly being included in HE curricula. At the same time too much group work is unstructured and unfocused. There is much anecdotal evidence to suggest that students experience group work as dysfunctional, problematic or irrelevant. There is clearly a need to engage students in group work that will improve communication and team skills, both for immediate and future success in working with others.

Accordingly the main activity for Psychology students on the AC Day is a group task. They are given a complex unseen topic that requires them to discuss and retrieve relevant information in groups of four, and come to a consensus decision in 20 minutes. Then they have 20 minutes to prepare a group presentation with individual verbal contributions. They are briefed to present a clear, concise, convincing case to support and justify their decision(s).

Table 2 is administered as a self-audit, which students complete before they discuss their AC experience. This form can be adapted and used not only for self-assessment but also for observing, diagnosing, evaluating, giving feedback and improving competencies used in interviews, group discussions and presentations. It indicates the type of body language, interpersonal interactions and contributions that employers typically look for in candidates during AC activities. Staff use the same competency criteria against which to observe and assess these activities, and again as frames of reference when providing both group and individual feedback on the performance of students. After lunch students have an individual interview with a panel consisting of tutors and employers. Here they can discuss their own perceptions and ratings on the self-audit.

Since tutors cannot be present in sufficient numbers to observe and assess each individual or group, students can learn to give specific, constructive feedback with sensitivity and consideration to help their peers improve. On the other hand, feedback should be received in the spirit that 'it is better to be saved by criticism than ruined by praise.' They should involve the recipient in feedback: *What do you think went well? What didn't? What did the participant do best? What one thing should he or she improve?* These are valuable learning outcomes in themselves.

All aspects of such an exercise - participating, observing, recording, assessing and giving feedback – develop valuable higher order competencies and professional attitudes. There have been insightful comments from participants in evaluating the benefits of such experiences. At the end of the day students are asked:

- *What have you learned today?*
- *How will you use/apply the knowledge and skills you have gained?*

The following are comments taken from a focus group transcription:

- *"I became aware of how to enter and become part of a new group more intentionally, instead of leaving it to chance."*
- *"Seeing the difference between group process, group dynamics and task content has been immensely helpful. I am good at managing the group process - keeping others on track with the time and task!"*

- *"If I am not knowledgeable about the topic I can still invite others' views and listen to the discussion with an open mind. Maybe next time I will suggest doing a SWOT analysis and offer to write things up..."*
- *"I was surprised to discover that others thought I hadn't said a word! I should try to contribute more and not get lost in my own thoughts."*

Psychology students on the AC Day were also asked: *If you are given the opportunity to run an assessment centre day for other Psychology students would you do the same or differently?*

Typical answers to this question were:

- *"I would like to do the same. It was very useful, my first time and the feedback was excellent."*
- *"I think all Psychology students would greatly benefit from this experience. The opportunity to get feedback is invaluable. I think it was well run and managed. Thank you."*

It is clear from this type of student evaluation that even the short, sharp exposure to AC tasks on a single day can have considerable benefits.

Some reflections and future possibilities

Lessons have also been learned on the importance of creating the right psychological and physical environment for skills-development. Any worthwhile development requires participants to be brave in tackling challenging new tasks, as indicated from students' comments:

- *"All activities although scary were relevant and good."*
- *"Presentations/interviews always push outside the comfort zones."*
- *"I am still extremely nervous and lack confidence – but the experience will help me manage my nerves for the future."*

Tutors acknowledge students' fears, and foster positive attitudes in a learning environment where nobody is expected to be good at the tasks, so falling and failing is simply raw material for collaborating and supporting each other. Striving to achieve better outcomes each time is a matter of pride in itself. The strategy seems to have worked, as the vast majority of students reported enhanced confidence and motivation for self-development – even those who had not achieved good results.

For AC-type group activities, the physical layout of the room needs to support the requirements for objective observation and providing confidential feedback, etc. Good practice in interviewing also calls for suitable rooms. Employers seem to protect the brand of their company and strive to make a good impression on all candidates – including the ones they reject - and educators need to do the same with all students.

As the AC project has progressed it has become apparent that ACs can be used in different ways - from awareness-raising in the first year to real practice for development and recruitment purposes. Doing this changes - or rather diversifies - the role of a tutor and requires considerable management of the methodology and process, especially prior to the actual event. The point is that AC-related competencies and methods can add variety to - and enhance - an assessment regime in almost any curriculum, in the ways outlined in this chapter.

Students may be required to develop such attributes and record their achievements in (e)-portfolios in any component of study at any level, but AC approaches are of greatest advantage to students as part of a coherent, structured and supported process of integrated personal, professional and academic development, as in *SOARing to success*. The ideal would be to leverage students' skills-development outcomes at every programme level, enhancing not only subject knowledge and learning power, but key qualities and personal agency needed for graduate employability in its broadest sense.

ACs activities may then provide a means for students to develop competencies throughout their programme, and feel that they are set up for success when they demonstrate these attributes for final summative accreditation, assessment and certification. One possibility to consider is to stop teaching for a week and run a dedicated 'ACs week' for final year students in order to value, capture and verify that richer picture of students' achievements that is recommended by the Burgess Group (2007). A matrix listing the main competencies can be used to record and build up that picture incrementally, Unit by Unit and level by level - until it is finally used as a summative document to score and sign off a student's final level of attainment.

The idea of recording and verifying, using a matrix, reflects the type of evaluative assessment that is built up at an AC and finally scored through multiple assessors pooling their judgments on each candidate at a data integration meeting. The equivalent of this in academia would be the final Scheme or Exam Board meeting, where currently each student's grades are signed off by tutors, and the degree award is decided. In addition, a collated assessment of skills outcomes would give a much richer and more diversified input to the final award decision.

Conclusion

Ideally students need to be given plenty of opportunity to discover and develop their unique possession and combination of strengths - which arise not only from formal academic study but also from their aptitudes, interests, priorities and personal qualities. They need to understand and articulate how they express these in real life, how they are perceived by others and how they might promote their strengths to suit the requirements of different situations. AC approaches can help to achieve this by:

- making key competencies visible as effective behaviours and actions, learning goals or outcomes;
- providing criteria that students can use to 'measure' and develop their own effectiveness, and also to support peers;
- opening up broader perspectives and frames of reference for assessment and feedback that include self, peer, tutor and employer assessment for formative purposes;
- helping participants to discover their limitations and development needs, and target for development those that they need in their chosen option or occupation.

Staff who have been introduced to these approaches find them interesting and useful too, but are sometimes constrained by the practicalities and demands of implementation: the time and resources required, the change in their roles from 'teacher' to 'facilitator and guide', getting to grips with the different methods of setting up activities and engaging students. Those staff who have used AC approaches are enthused by their potential to release the motivation and learning power of students. However there is plenty of scope to evaluate such interventions through robust action research, in the way that Psychology tutors are currently doing. If anyone reading this is implementing AC approaches, further discussion, evaluation, action research and comparison can improve our understanding of the effects such interventions might have in different contexts with different cohorts of students. We would welcome collaboration!

Acknowledgements

I would like to thank the students who have given me permission to quote their comments from blogs, written evaluations and focus groups. Staff who have participated in AC approaches include Rob Manton (Computing), Rosemary Burnley (Business), Eileen Scott (Careers), Pat Roberts and Isabella McMurray (Psychology).

About the author

Arti Kumar is Associate Director of the Bridges CETL at the University of Bedfordshire, Park Square, Luton, UK. She can be contacted at this email address: arti.kumar@beds.ac.uk

CHAPTER 14

Learning with the Masters – Using Art in a Research Methodology Class

Widya Suryadini

Introduction

This chapter is about my experimental project of using a different approach to create an unusual learning environment in a research methodology course for students of a planning school in Indonesia. I introduced masterpieces in paintings and sculptures, and related them with important terms and issues in science and research methodology. Although most of the students had never been properly introduced to fine art, the masterpieces definitely changed the atmosphere in the class, assisting the process of learning in a unique way, and eventually resulted in a significant improvement in learning outcomes.

We teachers of today do not only teach or 'transfer' our knowledge to our students. Our responsibility now is to create a powerful, stimulating, and rewarding learning environment. In creating such an environment, we design learning experiences that are meaningful to students and encourage them to be active learners. We also monitor our students' achievement to see if they were gloriously satisfactory or dangerously falling behind. Whatever the result, there will always be the question: how to improve our students' learning outcome? In addressing that question we continually try to improve our design, our method, and our professionalism.

In the real world, we are so accustomed to the old ways of teaching, and our students with their way of studying, that creating such environment becomes a big problem. We are in need of a transitional process that will enable us to become experienced learning designers. We need to innovate our teaching approach so we can shift swiftly from being a sage on the stage to be guide on the side. Moreover, this innovation should also improve the way our students learn, which in turn will develop the desired learning outcomes.

With that in mind I decided to develop a new and original approach to teaching my students of urban and regional planning in a research methodology class. I took them on a tour through 'virtual galleries' of paintings and sculptures and show them how those works of art can reveal so much about research and research methodology. I encouraged them to speak up and discuss how a particular object relates to the topic covered at the moment. The form of the class itself is still semi-classical, as I am not yet ready to give up all the stage.

So, this chapter is a story of a project that will give you a glimpse of what it is like to do something different in class, challenges I had to face, obstacles I had to overcome and adjustments I had to make, in order to make the experiment yield the intended results. This chapter will also show the learning outcomes resulting from the experiment, and compare them with those from previous traditional classes, as well as with the objectives of the course itself.

My inspiration

It came as an accident. In 2004 I was obliged to ask one of my colleagues to cover for me for the first two or three weeks of my class. He has a very keen interest in art and history and he used images about events in history to explain some of the materials in that class. He also possesses quite an unusual way of describing each image he had chosen. His students confessed that listening to what he was saying was like entering a previously unknown world. Although some students seemed to be puzzled by his peculiar way of teaching, as most of them had never been properly introduced to appreciating art, some others seemed to grow a particular interest and began to use the images as visual cues - something to remember the topics by. By the end of the semester, when I asked the students which parts of the course they found most interesting, the answers were unanimous: the images.

At that time, I read Robert Magee's book, 'The Story of Philosophy' (1998) and it caught my full attention. This was a very serious book about the history of philosophy, yet it was so full of beautiful illustrations of artistic objects, ranging from ancient images on terracotta, to mural, to paintings, to sculptures, to photographs of various objects of scientific and non-scientific interest. Professor Magee made those objects "speak" about various topics in philosophy in such an exciting tone that I believe readers in general can easily Understand his philosophy. And I can say that he was very successful in making philosophy become something human. Later I read the Winter 2003 edition of WSAC newsletter which stated that:

"The arts are languages *that all people speak—that cut across racial, cultural, social, educational, and economic barriers. They are symbol systems as important as letters and numbers. They integrate mind, body, and spirit and provide opportunities for self expression, making it possible for abstractions to become more understandable as they take concrete form in the visual arts, music, dance, and drama."* (WSAC, 2003:2)

So it seems that art possesses a unique power, so powerful that it can alter the way we look at things. It helps us to see things clearly, to help us understand the world around us much better, and to enable us to see the intangible aspect that lie behind. Arts take us far beyond words, making words redundant. And more importantly, it seemed to catch the attention of my students. And that was how I got the inspiration to start the project.

My earlier class

Before the project, the class was just an ordinary research methodology class, and I was the assistant to the lecturer. By 'ordinary' I mean that it was a class with the traditional approach of teacher-centered learning with no fancy images to show during lectures except for diagrams about research process and the standard textbook materials about research. The class was usually held in the afternoon, when the heat and humidity caused most of the students to struggle to keep their eyes open, despite some serious efforts by the lecturer to keep the class lively.

As assistant to the lecturer, I was responsible for assigning students to do their own research. But I found that the students did not think that it related directly to the topics covered in class. Both the students and assistants ended up being more frustrated than enriched by the experience. It was not a surprise that most of the students had a difficult time trying to make a connection between this course and other courses about urban planning. For them, this course about research methodology only became useful for their final project because, in their mind, that is the only real research they had to do. They failed to see that this course was designed to give them very important skills which will enable them to survive in the real word. It never occurred to them that this course was not rote memorization about research method or its tools, but about learning to think and act scientifically.

On the other hand, lecturers also had their complaints. They complained that although the students had taken the course on research methodology, they demonstrated no significant knowledge, let alone attitude, toward scientific principle. It seemed that students simply abandoned the concepts of scientific inquiry once they had passed the course. Those who passed soon forgot anything they had learnt from the course. And the students who failed the course and had to take it for the second time on the next year also displayed similar memory loss, as if they had never taken the course. So we knew we had serious problem.

Several factors were causing the problem. Students were failing to retain important concepts and identify relationships between concepts. There was also a serious shortcoming in their critical and creative thinking ability because they were often baffled when confronted with multiple possible solutions, or where a response with good reasoning would be better than one memorized textbook-style answer.

My project

In the first two years of teaching this course, i copied what the previous lecturer did, thinking this was the easiest and safest way. Then inspiration struck, I put the bet on the table, and started the project in 2005. I am still using the method but this chapter is about the project between 2005 and 2008. This part contains the description characteristics of the course and the students in general, the design of the project itself, how the project was implemented, as well as challenges, obstacles, and adjustments in implementing the project.

The course

This research methodology course was compulsory for second-year students in their fourth semester. The main objective of the course is to develop a scientific mind and stimulate the habit of critical thinking. This course sets out to equip students with the basic principles of research methods and tools in research, as well as knowledge about basic concepts of ethics in research and scientific writing. This was done, mainly through old-fashioned lectures once every week. But since this course also offered the students hands-on experience in doing research, we also designed practical side activities such as a closely-guided process of research designing, data collection, data processing, and data analysis. The students will finish up with a scientific paper of 3000 words which summarizes their project, and concludes their research experience.

The project was implemented as a variation to the traditional lecture format. And those side activities constituted our laboratory where we collected evidence of the effectiveness of the method through observation and interviews. Two teaching assistants were involved in every semester, and we all acted as the principal researchers for the students' projects. 30 to 35 students signed up for the course in each semester and we divided them into groups of 5 to 7 students.

The course itself is not declared as compulsory in the core curriculum of the Indonesian Planning School Association but we included it in our school's curriculum for one very strong reason. This scientific-inquiry mode of thinking and doing is what we believe to be the core competence of our graduates which will enable them to compete, and win, in the real world. In the shorter term, everything the students learned in this course should be able to serve as valuable aids to completion of their fourth-year final project. To take them there, we consistently sought to ask the students to demonstrate their competence throughout their studies. In other words, we required the students to exercise continuously the habit of scientific and critical thinking in order to progress to the desired graduate attributes.

The project design

The objective of the project was to stress to students the importance of living the concepts of scientific inquiries in academic life. The project was also seen as an innovative way to attack the problems mentioned earlier. It was our first attempt and we believed that something of the sort has rarely been done in non-art higher education institution. The basic idea of the project is to include artistic provocation in every topic throughout the semester. These artistic objects act as visual cues, thought-provoking stimuli, central ideas for debates or discussions, or sometimes only as merrymakings in creating a relaxed atmosphere in class. The artistic objects were displayed as digital images using PowerPoint™ slides, and were randomly chosen from masterpieces of painting and sculpture from a very wide range of styles.

In the first year of the project, I began to allow time for myself to adjust to the change, and also to see how the students reacted to my method. The classes were rather conventional, but with different objects to talk about and to relate to. Students were introduced to the work of art, the artists, the title, and the style. I displayed only two to three artistic objects for each topic, and did most of the talking. I interpreted the objects and described how each object was relevant to the topics covered at that particular day. I then went on to talk specifically about the topics of the day. At the end of the semester, I used a feedback sheet to seek their comments about the course: topics they like best, topics they hated most, the atmosphere of the class, and if they had suggestions about anything that might improve the course.

In the second and third year of the project, I slightly changed the method as I had gained more confidence in the method and was more comfortable in using it. I displayed more objects for each topic, and did less of the talking. Upon each display, instead of giving out information about it and giving my opinion, I asked the students to do the thinking themselves and share his/her thoughts with the class. I encouraged them to speak up, even if they thought they had the most ridiculous idea about that piece of art. Whenever appropriate, I asked them to relate one of their thoughts with the topic of the day. At the end of the semesters, in addition to their comments in writing, I also interviewed some of them informally to learn more about their experience. In the third year, I held a re-assessment exactly one year after they completed the course to gauge the students' recollection of the art works used and the concept that each related to.

Challenges I had to face

From the very start, I understood that the method was quite innovative and provocative - especially in Indonesia. At first I thought I was ready to take up any challenge that came, but I should have known better. I had ventured where no teacher I know had gone before and the project became a three-year roller coaster ride of ups and downs.

The first challenge I had to face was the fact that most of the students had never been properly introduced to fine art. Our system of formal education put art simply as one subject to be taught. The point of teaching art was to introduce students to the concept of art, which was usually abstract and detached from real life. Students in Indonesia study the history of art, but in the most unimaginative way because they have to memorize everything. They also study the right skills and techniques to create some form of art, but the emphasis is on the word "right" instead of the word "create". In short, they study everything about art but the true meaning of art itself. They had neither been taken to enjoy and appreciate art, nor to appreciate any work of art they had created themselves. This resulted in students became apprehensive when asked simply to enjoy a work of art, as if there was a right or wrong way to do it, and to be reluctant to give away their opinion about it.

This is a classic case of excluding art from any other aspects of human life in education. As Dickinson (1993) argues, art provide opportunities for self-expression and also exercise and develop higher order thinking skill including analysis, synthesis, evaluation, and "problem-finding". Without art, we get the opposite of all of the above, and several important social skills remain undeveloped - such as self-confidence, self-control, conflict resolution, collaboration, empathy, and social tolerance (Ruppert, 2006). As this characterised many of the students in my class it seemed that I had bigger challenge than I had anticipated.

The second challenge came when I tried to find reports and literature concerning the use of art in any non-art department in higher education. I sought insights on how to carry it out in order to secure a successful result, or to avoid any potential pitfall. Deasy (2002) provides a compendium of 62 studies about the effects on academic and social skills of learning in the arts. However, most of the cases were about primary or secondary schools for children in the US. But it was encouraging nonetheless and gave me a firm foundation.

The final challenge was be the demographic of the class itself, in terms of academic performances. The structure was unusual, with one fifth of the class being high achievers and, three fifths being low to very low performers. This abnormal type of distribution required more attention in case some assumption was not met. Arguably, this pattern of distribution in students' academic performance might be caused by diversity in learning styles, approaches to learning, and intellectual development level (Felder & Brent, 2005). Each of these three factors had important implications for teaching and learning and the three challenges I faced.

Obstacles I had to address

The biggest obstacle I expected was the students' resistance or reluctance to participate in the method. The first time I displayed art images in class, students exchanged looks and expressed confusion, and even a hint of fear. They were shocked; the first step people usually go through when confronted with a traumatic experience (Woods, 1994, in Felder, 1995). The class just went into a complete silence when I asked questions about the display, and students seemed trying really hard to melt into their chairs and become invisible. Discouraged, I went on to explain everything about the object in question, all by myself. This went on for a couple of weeks, but gradually students seemed to be more and more interested in the stories behind the images. Perhaps it was not because I was becoming more proficient but because they had surrendered and accepted the fact that they stuck with me and my game (Felder, 1995).

The next obstacle would be their lack of effort and willingness to learn. This happened to some of the students who failed to pass Wood's fourth step of resistance and withdrawal (Felder, 1995). Some saw this method as a dumb game and refuse to take part in it. When, at last, other students raised their hands to ask questions or make comments, they just stared blankly into the screen, mumbled their answer, and tried to get away with that. But then someone challenged and questioned the method itself, saying that it only distracted them from their main duty, which was to study research method. I strongly believed that the thought was shared among wider audiences, but this mutineer was the only one to speak his mind.

Adjustments I had to make

To meet these challenges and obstacles I had to make several minor and major adjustments while not completely changing the experimental method. News of my method must have carried because the second and third year students seemed well-prepared to sit in the class and abide by the rules of the game. But instead of telling them stories about the images, I asked them to tell the stories themselves. By doing that, I thought I might raise their confidence and enhance their communication skills. I might even develop their higher order thinking skill as well. This was risky, but I believed it was a necessary step forward, or a giant leap, and it would be worth it.

There were also setbacks. Time devoted to the basic concept of research methods was reduced because more time was being spent on appreciating art. So I had to persuade the students to spend more time learning about research on their own. This posed a problem because students usually only studied immediately before their exams. They were not ready to take the responsibility of learning by themselves, finding their own materials, or doing their part actively without a teacher's involvement. I had to take care in case students claimed that they had learnt nothing from my course, and put me under scrutiny from my colleagues. Reluctantly, I decided to hand out my lecture notes in advance to the students. Those notes became a key resource for them and they were happy with that. But I wished my students had read Leamnson (2002) and appreciated their role in making this project successful.

The findings

In general, the experiment was satisfactory in terms of students' performances and the learning atmosphere. By the end of each semester, some of my students' feedback was positive, and some was critical. This part will discuss the results of the experimentation, and compare them with students' performances from the earlier class of the same course which was conducted on traditional lines. I also analyze why the project worked the way it worked, and how it helped in improving students' learning outcomes and smoothed the transformation from teacher- to student-centered learning.

How the students took it

Despite a slow and reluctant acceptance in the beginning, it turned out that most students welcomed the method I used in this project. For three consecutive years, students found the images amusing and challenging, inspirational and thought-provoking. They also recognized the way the images helped them to understand some of the concepts. Some used them as visual cues although some also confessed that they had difficulties in making connections between images and concepts. Of course, not all students were happy with the way the class worked. They complained that they did not get it, they were bored, and thought that talking about art instead of studying real scientific method was a waste of time. One student asserted that he got nothing from my class – but passed the exam.

It required almost half a semester to get the students to cooperate and volunteer their participation to the class. It took even longer in the first year project because I had to fine tune the method more often and the students were more resistant than those in the next two years. Students in the first year project seemed to sense my uneasiness, and one student suggested that I should come to class more prepared and less anxious. On the other hand, students in the second and third year project seemed to sense my confidence and comfort in doing what I did. They expressed support and gained self-confidence from that. Either way, their feedback was always welcomed.

Contrasts with the way it used to be

In an effort to observe the effect of this project to the students' performances in general, I compared the grade distribution from three consecutive years during project implementation, plus one result from one year before the project. The result from the first year was discouraging, as it was worse than the previous year, which can be seen from the decrease in the number of A-grade students and a steep increase in the number of failed students (D and E). However, the second and third year results showed that the project yielded positive effects, as the grade distribution now tend to skew to A and B grades. Table 1 shows the complete grade distribution in four consecutive years.

Academic year	Grade A #	Grade A %	Grade B #	Grade B %	Grade C #	Grade C %	Grade D #	Grade D %	Grade E #	Grade E %
2004/2005	8	18	9	20	17	38	6	13	5	11
2005/2006*	5	9	10	18	21	37	6	11	15	26
2006/2007	4	11	10	30	12	33	5	15	5	15
2007/2008	5	12	15	37	14	34	3	7	4	10

*project commencement

Table 1: Grade distribution of the course during the project

But grade itself cannot be used as the only measure for students' learning outcome. It will require some more years to see the real impact of using art provocatively in a non-art field of study because the use of art develops not only tangible skills, but the intangible as well. Dickinson (1993:12) argued that:

> "...arts create a seamless connection between motivation, instruction, assessment, and practical application--leading to deep understanding ... merging the learning of process and content ... improving academic achievement - enhancing test scores, attitudes, social skills, critical and creative thinking."

The effect from all of the goodness in art would not be observable and measurable in one semester only, no matter how good our tool was. To examine the long term effect from this project, we prepared a close observation for our current fourth year students who were involved in the art project during their own real research for their final assignment.

Students' feedback had already explained the positive change of learning atmosphere in the class, which might relate to the improvement of students' academic achievement. In addition to that, I conducted a simple re-assessment one year after the third year project, to see if students still retained simple information about selected images and their association to certain concepts in research. Students were shown several images they should have seen during the course the previous year, and then choose the answer from the selection of multiple answers provided in the answer sheet. The results were stunning. On the average, students made 14 correct choices out of 20 questions. Statistical tests reveal no significant correlation between numbers of correct answer with gender, so we had to discard the possibility that male and female students store and use images differently. But the test also revealed that there was no correlation between the number of correct answers to the test and their examination grade. Since the form of mid-semester and final exams was of open questions or essay, one possible explanation could be that students understand the concept but have difficulty expressing their ideas in writing. Perhaps further assessment should be made based upon the type of learning, approaches to learning, and intellectual development level, as suggested by Felder & Brent (2005).

Why it worked the way it worked

I will draw on published research, especially in the US and Europe, to establish the benefit of learning in and through arts to inform the following review of the findings from my own experiment. Although several interesting findings emerged during the project, it is a limited study in its depth and scope, so I will position my case as a speculative finding worth further investigation.

The concept of transfer in neuro-cognitive science might explain why the project yielded some interesting results. As shown by Catterall (2002), transfer is a condition where learning in one context assists learning in different context. In this project, learning to appreciate visual arts became the context to learn another context of a completely different concept of research and its scientific methodology. Root-Bernstein (1989) sees many similarities between science and art. For him, science is a process of discovery, whereas creative thought, or transformational thinking, is the ability to conceive an object or idea interchangeably or concurrently in visual, verbal, mathematical, kinesthetic, or musical ways. He suggests that we use what he terms "tools of thought" to give meaning to facts and to facilitate creative or transformational thinking. These tools, most of which are embodied in the arts, include analogizing, pattern forming and recognition, visual and kinesthetic thinking, modeling, playacting, manual manipulation, and aesthetics. In effect, he believes that the mind and senses alike must be trained equally and in tandem to perceive and to imagine.

Eisner (2000) gives us ten lessons – all of which are keys to the success of improving my students' learning outcomes. According to Eisner, art teaches students to pay attention to qualitative relationships, and that problems can have more than one solution and that questions can have more than one answer. He says that art also celebrates multiple perspectives, and shows that there are many ways to see and interpret the world. The arts can open students' minds in a way that is unique and special. Arts change the way the students see the world because arts teach that small differences can have large effects. The arts traffic in subtleties. Paying attention to subtleties is not typically a dominant mode of perception in the ordinary course of our lives. We typically see in order to recognize rather than to explore the nuances of a visual field. Closing his lessons, Eisner concluded that the arts contribute to the growth of mind, meaning, and experience. Science has become an important part of our academic life and draws together our analytic, perceptive, and emotional capacities to deepen our understanding, building the only true and lasting foundation for rational life.

My reflection

In this last part, I will describe my own learning from this project. It might not be a big project but I know it has made a big difference to me and for my students. But there are still some unanswered questions. Frankly, I failed to develop a reliable means to assess the effect of using art in developing their thinking skill or their motivation to study further. There are some areas that are still unclear and hazy. Was this method really helpful in improving the students' learning outcome? If yes, then how exactly does it work? Was this method really smoothing our way in switching our learning orientation from the teacher to the student? I could ask further questions but will now reflect upon everything I have gone through in the last three years.

What I had learned

First, being a teacher means that you can never stop innovating. There are always new ways of managing the class, in upgrading the quality of your teaching, in creating a perfect learning atmosphere. It can be risky but one of the most rewarding aspects in being a teacher is the dynamics of teaching. You can never teach the same class because there is no such thing as the same class. You do the same thing differently every time you do it.

Second, there is no instant result in education. The challenges, obstacles, and setbacks I faced during the project followed my 12 years of education. Everything we learned in primary and secondary education, the good and the bad, became something we had to work with and sort out in higher education. Everything our students learn from us will also be revealed in a distant future, not necessarily in our lifetime. I expect the result of my project will show someday, but I cannot imagine how and in what way it would reveal itself. Being a teacher could mean that we change someone's life forever.

Lastly, when students come to class, motivated or not, they give us an opportunity. We might give them the experience of a lifetime, or we might lose their attention. It is our choice, and we give it to them. Education should give the opportunity to people to develop themselves and to re-create, as the artists recreate the world around them in their chosen medium. We should never give up on our students, nor give them false hope. Be true to your students, as the artists are to their works.

Concluding thoughts

As I considered my project of artistic provocation quite successful in improving my students' learning outcomes, I do not, however, recommend it to others if they are not into the world of art. As Baum (2002) notes, teachers should adopt a style that is natural for them, enables them to enjoy being in the classroom, and to be comfortable to do whatever they have to do. When we teachers enjoy our place in our class, we will be enthusiastic about it, and as popularly believed, enthusiasm is contagious. I am comfortable in using art as the main attraction in my class because art comes as natural for me. This interest in art is not something I commonly share with most people in my country, thus it creates a unique atmosphere for my classroom, and has become my professional signature.

Another lesson I have learned from this project is that being a teacher means taking the road less travelled, and everything that comes with it. If we do not facilitate the process of learning to achieve the desired results, we should never blame the students when the desired results were not achieved. Felder (1992) argues that it is exactly the process of education that creates the very students we are so dissatisfied with nowadays. The title of his paper, "There's Nothing Wrong with the Raw Material", reminds me never to complain about the student I have to teach. If I seek to be a good teacher I should be able to turn a frog into a prince or princess, no matter how ugly the frog was or how murky the water that the frog came from.

About the author

Widya Suryadini is a lecturer in the department of Urban & Regional Planning at the Institut Teknologi Nasional, Bandung, Indonesia. She can be contacted at this email: wsuryadini@gmail.com

CHAPTER 15

Learning Outside the Classroom: Environments for Experiential Enrichment

Sue Waite, Roger Cutting, Robert Cook, John Burnett & Miles Opie

Introduction

Graduates in the 21st century need to be able to work with other people and engage in critical thinking in order to perform successfully in working lives likely to be characterised by change and new challenges (Green *et al.*, 2009; Barnett, 2000). Narrow transmitted knowledge of subject disciplines is insufficient in a competitive job market to give students an edge in achieving economic wellbeing (DfES, 2005b) or to deal with global problems such as sustainable living (Lugg, 2006). Despite the above, much higher education teaching remains abstracted and separate from its application in the real world. Biggs & Tang (1998) distinguished between 'objectivism', where knowledge is decontextualised and understood as something which already exists and simply requires transmission; and 'constructivism', where meaning is created by the learner through individual and social activity and builds on the learner's motives and prior knowledge. Lave & Wenger (1991) propose a model of *situated learning* where participation in structured communities of practice provides the context for the social engagement that underpins effective learning. In this chapter, we present three case studies sct in learning environments outside the conventional classroom where experiences enable the acquisition of knowledge to be practical, applied and relevant to the world beyond the academy (Wilson & Fowler, 2005).

The first case study examines peer support through group work with Global Positioning Systems locating fiction in the 'real world'. We then consider Steiner Waldorf student volunteers' learning while creating community environmental awareness. Finally, groups of students experience sustainability first-hand, thereby stimulating critical en-

gagement with environmental issues. We explore pedagogical principles of authentic experience, collaborative working and aspects of social constructivist learning which underpin these activities, and illustrate how taking student learning outside the classroom provides
unique teaching and learning possibilities that transcend purely cognitive learning outcomes and contribute to the wider graduate skills
agenda for higher education.

This wider skills agenda poses a number of questions for those
working in the higher education sector? What sorts of learning outcomes are important in today's society and for the future that awaits
our students? We argue that graduate attributes necessary to respond to
the demands of a knowledge economy and global challenges include
interpersonal skills, creativity and environmental awareness. It is these
learning outcomes we address principally in this chapter. How do we
ensure that students' learning can be applied and prove useful in their
future life? Experiences which elicit positive feelings appear to render
learning more accessible to use in everyday lives (Waite, 2007).
Higher education's traditional emphasis on cognitive achievement and
skills has, over decades, begun to include the idea that affective learning is an important aspect of a successful programme. Bloom *et al.*'s
(1956) three learning domains: cognitive; affective and psychomotor
established a broader perspective in which emotions, values, integrity
and spiritual depth can all be recognised as factors informing the development of the whole person. The more recent work of Gardner
(1993) and Goleman (2004) has introduced the idea of multiple intelligences, significantly extending the landscape from which notions of
effective teaching, learning and assessment can be viewed. Alias &
Alias (in this volume) define affective learning outcomes as 'behaviours manifesting beliefs, feelings and attitudes'. When positive, these
behaviours result in 'attitudes of awareness, interest, attention, concern
and responsibility, ability to listen and respond in interaction with others'. How then can we engage students and enrich their learning? Sociocultural perspectives imply that cognitive growth is dependent on a
process of collaboration within communities of learners (Wenger,
1998). Moreover, the motivation to learn comes not just from an internal drive, but is also derived from interactions the individual has with
others in meaningful activities (Waite & Davis, 2006a). The authors
advocate immersion in the school environment as a strategy for enhancing affective learning outcomes for the student teachers they work
with. In this way, they have the opportunity to engage with the educational milieu in ways which are authentic; they can self-assess their

developing skills and reflect on the disparity which can be experienced between perceptions and the day-to-day realities of classroom work.

In the Faculty of Education at the University of Plymouth, England, we develop motivation and graduate skills through experiential and social constructivist pedagogy that integrates content with process (De la Harpe *et al.*, 2000). Our Research Group on Outdoor and Experiential Learning provides a focal point for practice and research about how including teaching and learning outside the classroom can enrich and extend learning outcomes for our undergraduates and the children they will teach. In acknowledging graduate attributes as proper outcomes of higher education alongside discipline content knowledge, an 'interesting pedagogical space' (James *et al.*, 2004: 176) is created drawing attention to how such outcomes can be facilitated. Different types of learning are stimulated by different contexts (Illeris, 2009). Action learning courses such as those described in this chapter are predicated on social constructivist notions of learning. Action learning has been found to engage deeper processing strategies in students who typically adopted surface strategies for learning (Wilson & Fowler, 2005) with concomitant benefits for their learning. We therefore suggest that attention to this process will illuminate appropriate pedagogies, including self-directed, reflective and authentic tasks in support of these graduate skill outcomes.

In the following pages, we offer three case studies to exemplify the benefits we see accruing from adopting increasingly wide perspectives on 'environments' and 'communities' for learning. These benefits are qualitative and as much to do with attitudinal and affective transformation as with quantitatively measurable learning. They are tentative, provisional and intuitive; arising through process rather than as a direct consequence of structured teaching and learning objectives. It would be useful to formally recognise and assess such learning outcomes, but current university assessment processes do not standardly measure them and we have yet to develop an appropriate methodology to do so. This represents important future work in order to validate and value these 'other' outcomes.

We begin with a case study that uses small group work as a context for sharing expertise. Small group work and formative assessment have been demonstrated to develop graduate attributes (Kift, 2002). Students bring different skills to the groups, which enable them to benefit from strengths in storytelling, literacy, geography and technology to their mutual benefit. Locating expertise within peer groups helps to break down usual power relationships between teacher and taught. As Waite & Davis (2006b) reported, developing a learning community with tutors as fellow learners helps to interrupt the common designation of the 'tutor as expert' (Brew, 2001). We show how task authenticity and skill mix enrich the learning experience and contribute to creative learning outcomes through teamwork.

Case study 1: Small group work and GPS Technology with primary student teachers

Traditionally, the use of Information and Communication Technology (ICT) has been an indoor, passive activity, but this is starting to change. At home, games consoles requires more active interaction, such as the games developed for the Nintendo Wii, where infra-red technology enables the player to reference aspects of their game within spatial environments. More generally, improvements in portability have led to technology becoming part of outdoor experiences. At university, students now work outdoors with laptops, Personal Digital Assistants (PDAs), digital cameras and camcorders, data logging equipment and, more recently, mobile phones and Global Positioning Satellite (GPS) technology. GPS in education has focused on Geographic Information System (GIS) applications, using GPS devices in conjunction with digital mapping software or using the devices as a virtual compass, involving simple treasure hunting. Futurelab (2006) has studied GPS embedded in PDAs running Create-a-Scape software. As the mobile device is moved into a location, the GPS triggers relevant information to appear on the screen. Interactivity allows the learner to add information to the existing pages in the form of a photograph, video, sound recording or simple text entry, supporting creative uses.

A further recent development is an application called Wherigo. Wherigo's aim is to take the adventure game away from a virtual world into real world locations. The activity is presented in the form of text and images on the screen of the device. As the user moves to a set location, the location-sensitive GPS signal triggers a set of information to appear on the screen. This provides an excellent teaching and learning opportunity, where stories can be brought alive by linking them to real locations. Technology thus offers the opportunity to create exciting new media to support learning. Stories can move from the printed page to an experiential participatory experience where the reader interacts with real locations. Imagine not simply reading how Sherlock Holmes solved the mystery of the Hound of the Baskervilles, but moving around key locations on Dartmoor, picking up elements of the story *en route*. Using this application, students can create locationally dependent stories, which either follow traditional linear pathways or increase interactivity with the 'reader' by embedding greater choice into the story. The mystery genre works particularly well; although the principal strength lies in bringing authenticity to the printed word. Having created their own stories, the student teachers are enabled to support pupils in school to use this medium in their own storytelling. It is likely to have particular value for students seeking ways to engage more reluctant readers and writers by providing a meaningful context and structure to these activities, not only in South West England but in the global world embraced by the world-wide web. Alias & Alias (in this volume) cite internet technology and its capacity for creating virtual environments as a potential tool for instigating immersive learning programmes for trainee teachers.

Principles of pedagogy

The Primary National Curriculum in England is currently under review. The publication of the Independent Review of the Primary Curriculum: Interim Report (Rose, 2008) proposes a series of changes. ICT will play an increasingly prominent role with English and Mathematics but cross-curricular studies will be given greater weight. With ICT continuing to evolve rapidly and providing new and exciting opportunities for education, the project using Wherigo is being developed to provide student teachers with a cross-curricular approach to teaching and learning which will prepare them for the new shape of the National Curriculum for England in 2011.

The aim of the project described above is to allow the student teachers to use ICT as a tool both to empower both their own learning and to provide a range of teaching opportunities for children within the classroom. The student teachers work on this project in small groups which mirror the pedagogical practices encouraged in school classrooms, and allow the student to experience what they may ask of their pupils. The student teachers have to draw upon knowledge across the curriculum; literacy, geography, history and ICT. As the students have different strengths, the use of group work in developing the interactive stories is particularly beneficial as they can utilise each others' expertise, learning from and teaching their peers (Vygotsky, 1962), increasing their sense of autonomy in learning (Waite & Davis, 2006a) and developing the skill of working together (Kift, 2002).The introduction of these innovative new technologies and the skills required in their use as tools for teaching and learning, is likely to challenge traditional modes of assessment

Throughout the project the student teachers develop a range of skills. Initially these are subject-based as they gain knowledge of the geography and history of their chosen area. Their early study is supported by both traditional and ICT based fieldwork, collecting a range of data that will allow the student teachers to map story events to the real locations, accurately by using satellite images, digital mapping and GPS data. In fieldwork using this technology, learners have the opportunity to develop their knowledge and skills in ways that impact on their everyday experiences in the classroom. There can be a positive impact on long-term memory through the linking of information to a particular location. A key finding has been the reinforcement of affective and cognitive learning modes, which can lead to higher order learning (Rickinson *et al.*, 2004; Waite & Davis, 2006b).

Having completed the fieldwork element, the focus then moves towards literacy. The narrative develops from storyboarding, through scripting to its merger; via the Wherigo application to the final GPS enabled hardware. Whilst there is a clear outcome, creating the Wherigo cartridge as the fruit of the students' interactions with the technology and the environment, the *process* is equally important for the students' learning as the achievement of a final product. Throughout this social constructive experiential process of learning, the students experience, reflect, plan, and act iteratively (Kolb & Kolb, 2005) in a collaborative group. The conclusion of the project involves testing the Wherigo cartridges in situ, so that the participating student teachers are actively involved in peer review and reflect on the processes and learning involved, their implications and application in the context of future primary school teaching.

Learning outcomes

The process of creating these narratives, shared through Wherigo cartridges, allows the student teachers to consider creative opportunities for teaching and learning in the Primary phase, for example, supporting initiatives such as 'Improving Boys' Writing: Visual Texts' (DfES, 2005a) and the Gifted and Talented Programme (DfES, 2006).

The student teachers gain insights into how technology can provide the opportunity for a literacy project to take its inspiration and its application outside the classroom and how curriculum subjects can be combined and refreshed in real-life contexts - important insights in view of the Rose (2008). The project aims to build a learning community of student teachers immersed in the outdoor environment from initial research through the creation of the cartridge to its end-user. Fol-

244

lowing the story-line as it unfolds in a real location provides motivation through active learning, continuity and authenticity. Its success relies on the sharing of creative skills, both literary and technological, of the authors. In the process, students have the opportunity to learn much about distributed expertise, valuing their own and others' contributions, teamwork and project management - all skills which stand to serve them well in their future lives.

This case study illustrates how group work can provide a skill mix to underpin peer support and the development of independent learning (Waite & Davis, 2006b). Its strength also lies in the experiential nature of the project whereby the student teachers go through the stages of development that they will ask children to engage in and in so doing gain a fuller awareness of the proposed task. This first case study concerns a learning community squarely situated within the assessment framework of a university module. As such, it will be subject to programme review in terms of its programme relevance, the quality of its assessment and formative feedback from student participants. The next case study, however, exemplifies a different kind of motivational pull in that the participants are voluntary members of a 'learning community' arising from impulses for wider social community contributions. It clearly demonstrates the motivational power of authentic experiences where there are actual problems to be solved (Waite & Davis, 2006a). It also shows how graduate skills of working with others, creativity and citizenship may be readily developed in real life contexts by engaging students' wider motivations for education (Karns, 2005) beyond instrumental assessment criteria.

Case study 2: The Trebullom project

The Trebullom Farm Project was launched in September 2006 by tutors and students from the University of Plymouth. Its aim was to develop a low-cost rural teaching and learning centre where the arts, crafts and land-skills could be regularly taught and researched for university students and academics whose day-to-day experience was in a predominately urban setting. The idea was originally inspired by the experiences of a group of final year students who attended a free week-long environmental course at Schumacher College, a small residential centre offering programmes on a range of environmental and holistic education themes. The college runs an MSc programme under the auspices of the University of Plymouth and is located in the grounds of Dartington College in Devon.

The residential involved not only participation in lectures but also regular involvement in house-keeping, preparation of food, composting and the general cultural life of the college. The positive effect on the student group of this social-participatory approach to learning was marked, corroborating the conclusions of SEER (2000) and Eaton (2000) regarding the effectiveness of outdoor learning experiences in comparison with narrow classroom-based learning. It became clear that the semi-rural character of Schumacher and its secluded setting was a significant element in the continuing motivation and engagement of students throughout the rest of their residential course (Sterling, 2001). The high cost of Schumacher programmes prevented continuation of this, so we developed the idea of founding a learning community with similar aims and values but accessible to students and others in the community with limited financial means.

The site identified for the project was Trebullom, a beautiful, early nineteenth century farmhouse with nearly 12 acres of overgrown fields and gardens, situated in rural North Cornwall about an hour's drive from the University. Over the past twenty years, Trebullom had been little used, despite being relatively well-equipped with basic accommodation for up to 25 people and excellent resources for outdoor education linked to gardening and rural crafts. Its potential as a teaching and learning centre was recognised by Bowhill Educational Trust who offered to work with the Peredur Educational Trust in piloting some student-run residential courses. These courses, focused around voluntary contributions from University lecturers and craft specialists, were conceived as preparatory training for a large scale public event which would generate awareness of environmental issues and celebrate the range of activities possible in a rural setting. Catering, the running of workshops and the management of the event would be provided by student volunteers. This was run as a pilot project which could lead to Trebullom becoming a centre promoting education for sustainability.

The public event called LEAF'07 (Local Environmental Activities Fayre), was run in June 2007 and offered educational activities for local schools and the general public, attracting over three hundred people from the South-West. It was staffed by forty-seven student volunteers from all over the University, providing a range of activities including: tree-planting, greenwood turning, whole-food cafes, Slow Food, woodland crafts, produce stalls, circus skills, story-telling, music, a ceilidh with country dancing and music performed in the local pub in the evening. Feedback from those attending the event was overwhelmingly positive with enthusiasm for the event becoming an annual event within the region.

Since LEAF'07, there have been continuing initiatives regarding the development of Trebullom. A series of *Green Fingers* residentials has been launched, introducing university students to gardening methods and land culture. These have proved very successful with requests for a continuation programme to further develop the link that students have with the local rural community and to foster a positive contribution to social awareness and cohesion among all concerned.

Student and staff involvement in the Trebullom Project has been voluntary with financial resourcing for training workshops in practical skills coming from a range of sources external to the University: *ES-Calate* (Advancing Teaching and Learning in Education); *Awards for All* (National Lottery) and *Aim Higher* (Widening Participation) have all contributed funds out of a recognition that the project aims to enhance the quality of community life whilst encouraging student involvement in social renewal activity.

Pedagogical principles

While preparing for the LEAF '07 festival, staff and students, had to take responsibility for managing budgets, health and safety issues, publicity and liaising with the public. They also had to acquire practical land and craft skills to be shared with and taught to children and adult visitors to the festival. If deadlines were missed or health and safety requirements inadequately dealt with, consequences could be serious, jeopardizing the running of the event. The team constituted a different form of learning community with real life problems to be solved; how to function as a team, take minutes at meetings, chair meetings, enact collective decisions, deal with occasional emotional clashes and cope with the stress of realizing pressing deadlines for a community event. The students learnt experientially and in a meaningful context the value of Kolb's experiential learning cycle of plan, do and review (Kolb & Kolb, 2005). Although the context of the project was the promotion of environmental awareness, the learning outcomes were as much to do with business management and organisational skills. When LEAF '07 was reviewed, students spoke enthusiastically about the range of practical life-skills they had acquired and the deep satisfaction they experienced in learning to work as a team committed to promoting environmental awareness. As in the previous case study, hierarchical roles were broken down and re-established in new forms based on trust, interdependence and exchange of skills expertise

(Waite & Davis, 2006a). Lecturers and students shared responsibility for preparing meals, house-keeping and waste-disposal, thereby enhancing intellectual discourse and dialogue and weaving a new social fabric (Sterling, 2001). Furthermore, during a course offered on *Eco-Philosophy* at Trebullom, staff and students were able to explore first-hand such principles and to experience the actual practice of a sustainable learning community (Hargreaves & Fisk 2003), leading to deeper and more informed critical reflection (Waite & Davis, 2006a).

The particular pedagogical model of a community of learners (Wenger, 1998) as developed at Trebullom has precedents. Hatcher & Bringle (1997:153) use the term *community-based learning* to describe: *"...the type of experiential education in which students participate in service in the community and reflect on their involvement in such a way as to gain further understanding of course content and of the discipline and its relationship to social needs and an enhanced sense of civic responsibility"*.

Commenting on the rising popularity of community-based learning programmes, Mooney & Edwards (2001) note a certain conceptual imprecision in the design and evaluation of such projects. Open-ended approaches to teaching and learning are likely to foster creativity, autonomy and social-orientation but tensions between this and formally-assessed learning linked to vocational pathways in credit-bearing programmes are also likely to exist (Gibbs, 2006). As the project was, essentially, a volunteer activity, tensions related to assessment did not surface in the initial phases of the Trebullom project. However, it is proposed henceforth to use action research to monitor the developing project.

Hargreaves' & Fink's (2003) work on sustainable learning communities has had a significant influence on the work of the project team, particularly their *Seven Principles of Sustainable Leadership* which:

- *create and preserve sustaining learning;*
- *secure success over time;*
- *sustain the leadership of the other;*
- *address issues of social justice;*
- *develop rather than deplete human and material resources;*
- *develop environmental diversity and capacity;*
- *undertake activist engagement with the environment.*

The above principles fitted well with the pedagogical ideals of the founders of Trebullom who had, themselves, been inspired by the work of Rudolf Steiner in meeting the educational and social needs of children and adults with learning difficulties. Steiner introduced, amongst other principles, the idea of schools and similar learning communities working together collegially as 'republican academies' (Gladstone, 1997) where administrative responsibilities were shared, non-hierarchically, and where the spiritual life of the community would be continually refreshed through a culture of shared action research.

Learning outcomes

Defining learning outcomes from a project is a complex process when students' involvement is voluntary, where 'leadership' is shared between student and tutor and where learning is 'emergent'. In such circumstances *"...the interrelation of teaching, learning and assessment is not a set of procedures that can be unilaterally invoked by teachers, but a social interaction."* (Torrance & Prior, 2003:168).

Following LEAF '07, two public dissemination events, related to the LEAF '07 event, were held on the University campus where the project team, together with student and staff volunteers, presented their work and spoke about their experiences and the learning they had acquired. Detailed minutes of management meetings, including action plans and evaluations, had been routinely posted on the University's student intranet and the volunteers were able to share in some detail with sponsors what had been for them an extended, immersive experience, culminating in a four day, on-site preparatory residential where all practical arrangements had to be put in place and checked against health & safety, legal and financial requirements. Volunteers received certificates marking their involvement and achievements.

The most significant aspect was the consistent affirmation by students that the teamwork, project management and creative problem solving they had learned through the project were life-skills which they would continue to develop after graduation. The festival was held in early June, close to final submission dates for assignments. Retrospectively, students commented that the festival had taken far more time than they had anticipated and strongly advised future organizers to fix future events for a time in the year which did not clash with assessment time in the University. At the same time, no one complained that their academic success had been compromised by the pressures. This is in stark contrast to Gibbs' picture of students who, 'pressed for time' and 'conservative' are *"...instinctively wary of approaches with which they are not familiar or that might be more demanding"* (Gibbs, 2006:20). For the volunteer students, their learning had been rooted in real life problems they had elected to participate in solving. The learning outcomes therefore had personal meaning for them and would prove useful in the future. Their practical achievements and the learning attached to this provided valuable material for their Professional Development Profiles (PDPs) and their CV's. One student reported in a dissemination meeting that the learning he acquired through being involved in the project led to him being offered a job in an environmental social project. Continuing exchanges on social networking sites such as Facebook provide the basis for an informal learning community based on shared practical experience and ideals. As things stand, the learning derived from the project is informal and non-assessed but, for the participants and supporting tutors, it was powerful and authentic. Social networking and informal civil society projects (Perlas, 1999) are relatively new cultural phenomena, able to advance alternative social agendas in the political and economic spheres of society without losing their identities as cultural institutions. The immersive, non-formal character of the Trebullom Project has a civil society character and has clearly engaged the attention and goodwill of students, tutors and volunteer agencies across the University. As a project, it has been essentially experimental and its achievements are tentative and provisional. It does, however, offer a model of practice in which a whole community learns from each other in interaction with the material and social environment.

So, through this second case study, we begin to see that social constructivist learning experiences and graduate attribute learning outcomes may be enhanced when there is a personal meaning for students; the elective nature of the project naturally selected those with a keen interest. Furthermore, authenticity in problem solving is a matter of degree. In the first case, the task was set by the tutors and it was only the form that the product took that was created by the students. However, in the second case, the nature *and* shape of the learning journey is determined largely by the student participants themselves. Furthermore, in this second case study there were strong social justice and environmental impulses that added weight to the relevance or 'meaningfulness' of the problems for the self-selected group. Yet, this too had some utility in that the festival was a one–off occasion created by volunteer students and staff to increase environmental awareness in the public community. In the final case study, we explore learning from 'lived experience', spending time within communities that pre-exist the learning experience for students. We reflect on how such an aspiration for authenticity may impact on the sort of learners that emerge and how challenge and reflection may be valuable components of experiential learning and collaborative enquiry to further develop students' critical thinking (Karns, 2005).

Case study 3: Low impact communities

Quietly and surreptitiously a number of small, yet distinct, environmentally orientated communities have been set up across the southwest of England over the last few years. Their low profile is in part due to the restrictions imposed by local and national planning legislation, and yet these communities provide a unique insight into the reality of sustainable living. A common theme of three such communities is that they attempt to live at 'One World levels of consumption', that is their consumption of resources is equivalent to the resources available on the planet if multiplied by the earth's population. They are 'off grid'-meaning that they provide their own electricity, water and sewerage. Dwellings are 'self-builds' using predominantly local, biodegradable, and recycled materials. Permaculture principles direct their development, and power is provided by their own renewable resources. Thus self reliance is optimized but needs are also minimized. These woodland communities are not part of any overarching programme; they have not been promoted and neither have they received funding from any external organisations, they are entirely independent and spontaneous. These are groups of people building their own communities independently from political executive and indeed, on occasion, in opposition to it.

Such alternative communities are often portrayed as little more than land occupations, yet in many ways they stand at the forefront of sustainable living. Moreover, they provide significant scope to extend the student experience beyond the theoretical confines of sustainability and allow them to experience first hand the practical problems and issues of low consumption living. To evaluate the effectiveness of such experiential approaches in providing insight to students in Higher Education, a project was set up at the University of Plymouth whereby undergraduates and postgraduates could live and work at these sites.

The students were placed with these communities to help on identified projects and/or community volunteer work days. The students are asked to keep reflective diaries of their visits, focusing particularly on their initial expectations and on any insights or learning they gain by the experience of living at such minimal levels of environmental impact. The project is not evangelical in the sense that any 'conversion' to green living is an intended outcome, but rather it simply provides an exposure to a different way of living, one not based on consumption. The value of providing alternative perspectives in developing critical thinking has been previously noted (Waite & Davis, 2006a). Student experiences are explored further through interviews by researchers. This means of scaffolded reflection is a key part of experiential learning pedagogy, but also forms a part of our research which will help illuminate the process of learning in real life contexts. Furthermore, the project hopes to elucidate something of the experiential learning and motivations of the community members themselves. In this case, the students themselves move into a pre-existing learning community and it will afford an opportunity to examine processes of assimilation of practices. Though much is written and spoken about sustainability, here students have the opportunity to experience living at high levels of self reliance which, unusually, integrates and fulfils the economic, environmental and social functions of sustainable development.

Principles of pedagogy

The debate relating to the effectiveness of outdoor learning in promoting environmental awareness is reviewed by Lugg (2007) who concludes that all such studies imply that the nature of the experience provides the framework for the pedagogical strategies employed. Nicol (2004:14) points out that: *"...it is lack of sensory immersion that leads people not to be aware of their connection to landscape. This is why taking people outdoors is so important so that they can engage their senses and experience their connectedness to places"*.

Accordingly, the pedagogical approach to this project was to provide an immersive learning experience as Nicol (2004) describes, and to promote and enable a personal involvement with the practice of living at something approaching a 'one world' level of environmental demand. This allows students, through both observation and participation, the opportunity to explore and evaluate interdisciplinary, holistic experiential learning. Furthermore it addresses many of the issues relating to the perceived gap between rhetoric and reality in the development of Education for Sustainable Development (ESD) curricula in Higher Education (Wals & Jickling, 2002; Lugg, 2006).Through direct experience of these communities it addresses some of the issues relating to the identified barriers to the development and promotion of effective HE curricula and pedagogy relating to ESD, such as institutional restrictions (resources, staff expertise etc) and the perceived distance between formal 'academia' and the deep experience of 'nature and cultural landscapes' (Sterling, 2004; Domask, 2007). The students are also able to observe at close hand the responses of a 'Community of Practice' that is itself learning and making communal decisions about the process of living 'sustainably'. In this respect the communities are not so much exemplars of sustainability but rather a 'work in progress' as they strive for consensus and direction, experiencing both 'successes' and 'failures'. As they work, and converse, with the community members, many students are surprised by the relatively minor part that appropriate technology has in the struggle for sustainability in comparison to the vital importance process of social dynamics and consensus decision making. Furthermore, students see the contested nature both of sustainability and the question of what level of resource use is necessary or acceptable in attaining that 'ideal' (yet essentially subjective) balance between environmental demand and human comfort. The situated nature of this learning and their engagement in a particular 'community of practice' clearly owes much to the concepts of Wenger (1998). The communities in which this learning takes place are authentic contexts and may offer radically different views from the students' experiences to date. In addition, our students are currently involved in another form of pedagogic engagement with the communities through their use as a locus of individual student dissertation research, which will lend another layer of reflection and opportunities for learning. Their involvement will enable deep engagement with ethnographic methodological and ethical issues, as well as honing skills in negotiating a balance between objectivity and subjectivity in research.

Learning outcomes
In the third case example, personal insights into the relevance that the student experience has to sustainable development are explored through individual reflection as well as group discussions. This supports recognition of learning points from direct experience which may not be explicitly planned or determined. Involvement with the communities occurs through visits by students working in certain University degree programme modules. Such students provide an interesting contrast to the others in that they are not volunteers and may have no prior understanding of the activities of the communities. Initial results indicate nearly 90% of student visitors who were questioned considered the experience to have been either 'fairly important' or 'very important' to their understanding of ESD. Comments have included: "*It's so different from reading about it*"; "*Without having the chance to visit I would never have understood sustainable living*"; "*It shows you that you don't need everything*", and "*You can survive on very little*". Some

253

volunteers have a reasonably accurate impression of the nature of the communities before visiting and the experience tends to confirm their, usually positive, expectations. However these and other more negative expectations appear deeply modified by new found insights into the problems and difficulties encountered by the communities through experiential learning.

The learning experience reflects the approach of Schumacher College in cultivating 'emergent properties' rather than pre-specified learning outcomes. Part of the power of this pedagogy therefore derives from the students themselves determining these learning points through critical reflection, so contributing to autonomy in learning. Sustainable living becomes an authentic experience rather than merely a concept and thereby integrates subjective psycho-motor and affective domain responses along with cognitive understanding into the learning process; this is important for subsequent application of learning (Waite, 2007). The idea of 'living sustainably' thus moves in many students' minds from a process of self denial for the sake of the environment to a means of living more cheaply and simply but in a more deeply fulfilling way.

In this final case study therefore, we see how participation in the lived experience of a community creates opportunities for fundamental shifts in beliefs and understanding; a transformative form of learning (Illeris, 2009) which impacts on the learner's identity. It is beneficial both for volunteers who share common ideals and as a challenge to the thinking of students within a university module. Although there is no closed problem to solve within this final example, the students' exposure to both alternative views *and* lifestyles in an authentic context promotes their capacity to think critically. Their expectations are challenged which may support their engagement with 'bigger' problems like sustainable living, potentially changing fundamentally the way they live their lives. The popularity of the experience amongst students, the growing number of volunteers, the use of the communities for dissertation research, and the independent return of students to the communities in the summer months, all evince the success of the project in terms of engagement. However, outcomes of such experiences cannot be easily delineated or prescribed. While the initial results are extremely positive, the longevity of the influence of such experiences will be difficult to quantify without continued monitoring of students beyond their university careers. Whether the experience will act as a catalyst for profound lifestyle change and/or learning approaches, or simply represent an interesting and enjoyable break from the tasks of more 'serious' study, remains to be seen. Challenge, through disruption of established beliefs, appears to introduce the possibility of transcendent and transformative types of learning (Illeris, 2009)

Conclusion

Writing in a sister volume to this publication, Nygaard & Holtham (2008) make the case for higher education becoming more learning-centred, where teachers and learners work on achieving specific learning outcomes based on the learner's educational aims. This chapter has built on these ideas out of a conviction that students in coming decades will increasingly need to be able to work with one another in practical-social environments whilst engaging in critical thinking. Ability to learn in the affective domain will also be an increasingly important aspect of student development. Different aspects of knowledge, understanding and skills may be foregrounded by the intended cognitive learning outcomes of different programmes. But for all the students, collaborative working in the field will have helped develop their interpersonal skills and capacity for critical thinking through authentic exposure to alternative perspectives (Waite & Davis, 2006b). These wider benefits of learning in experiential environments have been highlighted within the case studies of this chapter in terms of enrichment or 'value-added' to knowledge acquisition. We have illustrated a progression in different kinds of learning community, although this does not necessarily represent an individual's pathway in a modular system. Learning outcomes are deepened from their exposure to alternative views; firstly, with peer support in skill development, then through collaborative development within a team and finally as a challenge to existing beliefs through participation in other communities of practice. A variety of contexts and levels of challenge, support and authenticity may help students to develop graduate attributes for their move into the wider world (Illeris, 2009).

Indications are that students also enjoy and positively evaluate these authentic experiences; this would suggest that the learning acquired may be enduring and accessible in other contexts (Waite, 2007; Fredrickson, 1998). Thus, such pedagogical practice offers greater opportunities for broader graduate skills such as collaborative team working, problem solving and critical thinking, than those provided within more traditional didactic approaches. Our Faculty continues to research the psychosocial and sociocultural affordances of alternative contexts and pedagogies within its Research Group on Outdoor and Experiential Learning and Centres of Excellence in Teaching and

Learning of Experiential Learning and Sustainable Futures and seek ways in which both outcomes in terms of graduate skills and the supporting process can be better monitored and assessed.

About the authors

John Burnett is a Lecturer in Steiner Waldorf Education at the Faculty of Education, University of Plymouth, Devon, UK. He can be contacted at this e-mail: jburnett@plymouth.ac.uk

Robert Cook is an Associate Lecturer in the Faculty of Education at the University of Plymouth, Devon, UK and is also a research fellow of the Centre for Sustainable Futures. He can be contacted at this e-mail: robert.cook@plymouth.ac.uk

Roger Cutting is a Lecturer in Environmental Education at the Faculty of Education and is a research fellow at the Centre for Sustainable Futures, University of Plymouth, Devon, UK. He can be contacted at this e-mail: roger.cutting@plymouth.ac.uk

Miles Opie is Academic Support Tutor for the BEd Programme at the the Faculty of Education, University of Plymouth, Devon, UK. He can be contacted at this e-mail: miles.opie@plymouth.ac.uk

Sue Waite is the Leader of the Outdoor and Experiential Learning Research Group in the Faculty of Education, University of Plymouth, Devon, UK. She can be contacted at this e-mail: sjwaite@plymouth.ac.uk

CHAPTER 16

Improving the Affective Learning Outcomes of Trainees in Teacher Education: An Immersive Learning Approach

Nor Aziah Alias & Nor Aiza Alias

Introduction

This chapter focuses on the improvement of teacher trainees' affective learning outcomes through an immersive learning approach. By affective learning outcomes, we mean demonstrated behaviours that indicate beliefs, feelings and attitudes of the teacher trainees. The affective domain is one of three learning domains defined by Bloom *et al.* (1956), these being: 1) the cognitive domain (knowledge), 2) the psychomotor domain (skills), and 3) the affective domain (attitudes). According to Picard *et al.* (2004) it is important to focus on the affective domain, because in order for learning to become truly rooted, the learner has to have a deep emotional attachment to what is learned.

By an immersive learning approach we mean an approach in which the learner experiences as closely as possible the details of the "real" environment. This may include engagement in terms of emotions or the physical nature of the real setting. To be immersed is basically to be a part of the environment rather than being in a detached mode.

The main thrust of this chapter is the improvement of teacher trainees' affective outcomes through an immersive learning approach. Outcome is a paramount consideration of learning-centred education. Nygaard & Holtham (2008) illustrate the need to develop a learning-centred higher education curriculum that is founded on the following: 1) people learn based on their experience and expectations, 2) learning is both an individual and social process, 3) learning is a contextual process that is tied to particular situation, and 4) learning is a process affected by the identity of the learner and the learner's social position. Learning-centred institutions focus on these aspects and place the learners at the centre of the education. This simply means focusing on who is learning and what he or she desires to learn. Rather than giving the learners a prescribed *carte du jour*, the instructor and the learners work on achieving specific learning outcomes based on the learners' educational aims. On their part, the learners take responsibility for their own learning process. The contexts from which the learner comes and is to function become the key considerations in designing the learning-centred environment (Alias *et al.*, 2008). Thus the exploration of new knowledge and its application takes place in situations that are relevant and meaningful to the learners.

We do not deny the importance of cognitive outcomes and skills but we seek to discuss affective outcomes which are less probed. Currently affective outcomes have been less scrutinised due to the long standing emphasis on cognitive outcomes, perplexing definitions of affective constructs and the underdeveloped affective assessments. Hence, our first task in this chapter is to examine this facet in relation to teacher education prior to putting forward an approach that will enhance these outcomes. We refer to teacher education programs as the four-year teacher education program conducted by HEIs in countries such as Malaysia and the United States where the curriculum is delivered via general education coursework and subjects related to teacher education program area. We refer to teacher trainees as those who are undergoing teacher education programs and have yet to graduate. In the subsequent sections, we present an approach to enhance affective outcomes of teacher trainees. In order to do so, a preliminary discussion on affective outcomes in teacher education is essential.

Outcomes in learning-centred teacher education

HEIs play the role of furnishing teacher trainees with educational theories and classroom models. In most Malaysian universities for instance, the scenarios of teaching in schools are imagined, visualized and simulated especially in the early phase of the program. Since the educational context of HEIs differ from the real life context in which teacher trainees are going to work following their graduation, we find it important to formulate an approach that will enable teacher trainees to seamlessly fit into their profession and new working environment. One of the challenges for teacher educators in the current information society is to ensure that teacher trainees emulate the best attributes of good teachers. This is best achieved by giving them the opportunity to experience what good teachers do. Teacher trainees need to have a heightened awareness of contemporary local and global educational scenarios. They also need to see the relevance of theories in authentic school settings and to be able to apply what has been professed in lecture and discussion sessions at HEIs. It is through tying what they are learning to current worth and future needs that the teacher trainees will be motivated and prepared to teach.

A teacher education program thus needs to be learning-centred, to be enquiry-based and related to real life teaching practices. As learning-centred education means looking at what the students need to know rather than what we want to teach, the learning outcomes must be formulated early and the learning environment designed to meet their learning needs. Dimmock (1999) suggested learning-centred education as encompassing mission and curriculum delivery that are focused on providing successful learning experiences and outcomes for all its students. He further stated: *"Learning experience and outcomes include knowledge, values, attitude and skills considered worthwhile and desirable across the spectrum of academic, social, spiritual, moral, aesthetic and physical domain."*, Dimmock (1999:1).

With respect to teacher education, Nelson & Holdren (1995) espouse outcome-based measures as future-oriented, dynamic and geared to provide a model of teacher preparation. They suggest that HEIs can no longer claim to have an adequate teacher education program if they just include a set of core courses, an area major and professional education courses linked with practice. As outlined by McClenney (2003), the characteristics of learning-centred education include: 1) clearly-defined outcomes for student learning, and 2) systematic assessment and documentation of student learning. Nonetheless, outcomes should not be a list of constructed statements or competencies but also development of value orientation through thoughtful consideration of educational issues and ethical decisions. The strategy to let the teacher trainees know their learning outcomes is the first step in student-centred assessment that should enhance their ability to know "what we want them to know" so they can become more motivated and cooperative partners in the teaching-learning process.

We concur with the spirit of outcome based education and that the employment of outcomes will bring about a host of benefits to the teaching and learning process. The attributes of the graduates will be the foundation upon which the whole educational program is built. The whole person is of interest. This involves students in a complete course of learning, from developing their skills in designing to completing a whole process. As stated by Spady (1995) [cited by Acharya (2003:6)], outcome-based education requires the students to understand the contents by *"...extending the meaning of competence far beyond that of nar-*

row skills and the ability to execute structured tasks in a particular sub-ject area and classroom". Students learn through a constructivist, learning-centred approach with the teachers as the facilitators. There will be an alignment between the outcomes, the content and the assessments.

What then are the outcomes for teacher education? What does a teacher education program seek to produce? In other words, what are the attributes of a teacher education graduate? Cochran-Smith (2000) argues that the outcomes question is a particularly complicated one in teacher education. There are differing sets of assumptions about what teachers and teacher candidates should know and be able to do. Generally, teacher trainees are expected to demonstrate the acquisition of content knowledge not only in the subject matter such as Science, Mathematics or History but also theories of learning, educational psychology, philosophy and sociology. They also need to have the knowledge on the generic process of teaching (pedagogical knowledge) and blending of content knowledge and pedagogy to teach a certain subject matter (pedagogical content knowledge). Of late, teachers are also expected to acquire technological knowledge and be competent in technological pedagogical content knowledge (TPACK) as well. As explained by Mishra & Koehler (2006), TPACK involves an understanding of the complexity of relationships among students, teachers, content, technologies, and practices. It is about the capability of the teacher to combine the content knowledge (subject matter that is to be taught), technological knowledge and pedagogical knowledge (theories, practices, processes, strategies, procedures, and methods of teaching and learning). We foresee TPACK to gain grounds in future teacher education discourse and research as technology continues to expand and transform the way students live and learn. The teacher trainee also undergoes a developmental process that challenges his or her existing views and beliefs about teaching and learning. Thus, a teacher education curriculum must render coherent and transformational experiences for the teacher trainees to develop the knowledge, skills, attitudes, and characteristics that they will need to become the teacher they aspire to be. Our focus is on the outcomes that will lead to the making of the individual who will be able to function in the society. Higher education institutions generally harp on the graduates' cognitive achievement and skills as a measure of the success of their programs but this is just one perspective; emotions, values, thoughts and feelings are also integral to the development of the whole person we seek to produce. So are integrity and spiritual depth. To achieve this, we seek to concentrate on the affective outcomes. Furthermore, there is a de-emphasis on affective outcomes and most teaching and assessment in higher education have been focusing on cognitive outcomes rather than on values, attitudes and behaviours (Shephard, 2008). The affective domains are generally subsumed under what we treat as hidden curriculum since affective characteristics are not easily expressed. They are also subjective, imprecise, developed slowly, personal, private and difficult to observe and measure. However, we do accept that affective outcomes can be demonstrated, evaluated and thus be built explicitly into the outcome based teacher education program. A discussion on the taxonomy and conceptual model of affective outcomes is hence, foreseeable before we propose the broad outcomes of teacher education.

Affective outcomes in teacher education
Ewell (1985) states that a distinction between cognitive and affective outcomes is a distinction between gains in knowledge and changes in attitudes or values. The affective domain (from the Latin *affectus*, meaning "feelings") includes a host of constructs, such as attitudes, values, beliefs, opinions, interests, and motivation (Koballa, 2007). The domain emphasizes a feeling tone, an emotion, or a degree of acceptance or rejection. In contemporary psychology, affect encompasses the broad range of experiences referred to as emotions and moods (Petty *et al.*, 2001) [cited by Leder & Forgasz (2006)]. In terms of outcomes, Landy & Conte (2004) define affective outcomes as attitudes and beliefs that predispose a person to behave in a certain way. Others discuss these outcomes as motivation and engagement (McMahon & Ojeda, 2008), empathy (Barber & Clifton, 1980; Davis, 2008), attitude (Martin, 2006; Dorman & Fraser, 2008) and self efficacy (Martocchio & Hertenstein, 2003). For the purpose of the discussion in this chapter, affective outcomes are defined as the behaviours manifesting beliefs, feelings and attitudes. These manifestations subsist in different realms and dimensions such as moral, social and spiritual that are pertinent to a teacher trainee's education. In order to outline the affective learning outcomes of teacher trainees, we will next discuss the affective domain taxonomy by Krathwold *et al.* (1964) and Martin & Reigeluth's (1999) dimensions of affective development.

Krathwohl *et al.*'s affective domain taxonomy is perhaps the best known of any of the affective taxonomies (Huitt, 2001). The taxonomy developed in 1964 is ordered according to the principle of internalization. It is an attempt to classify how information is internalized by the learner. This is a process where the learner's affect towards information passes from general awareness to an internalization. Being internalized, the information will affect the learners' future behaviour and attention. Outcomes of the five levels are explained below.

1. Receiving refers to the student's willingness to attend to particular phenomena of stimuli (classroom activities, textbook, music, etc.)
2. Responding refers to active participation on the part of the student. At this level he or she not only attends to a particular phenomenon but also reacts to it in some way.
3. Valuing is concerned with the worth or value a student attaches to a particular object, phenomenon, or behavior. This ranges in degree from the simpler acceptance of a value (desires to improve group skills) to the more complex level of commitment (assumes responsibility for the effective functioning of the group).
4. Organization is concerned with bringing together different values, resolving conflicts between them, and beginning the building of an internally consistent value system.
5. Characterization by a value or value set. The individual has a value system that has controlled his or her behavior for a sufficiently long time for him or her to develop a characteristic "life-style." Thus the behavior is pervasive, consistent, and predictable.

Affective level	Action verbs describing outcomes (the student will be able to...)
Characterization (adopt behaviour)	act, influence, practice, demonstrate, display, perform, embody, habituate, internalize, produce, represent, validate, verify.
Organization (organizes, adapts behaviour to value system)	adhere, arrange, compare, contrast, identify, modify, organize, relate, alter, combine, integrate, order, prepare, synthesize.
Valuing (understand, accepts worth)	accept, defend, differentiate, explain, follow, join, propose, recognize, select, appreciate, describe, discern, express concern, demonstrate, invite, justify, share.
Responding (react)	conform, enjoy, help, perform, present, read, report, search, tell ,write, discuss, label, question, select, respond, recite, volunteer, participate, initiate.
Receiving (awareness, willing to notice)	ask, engage, give ,identify, locate, observe, select, use, choose, describe, attend, listen, name, point to, reply , show willingness, realize.

Table 1: Sample action verbs to describe affective learning outcomes

Table 1 illustrates sample verbs that are used to describe student's outcomes at each level adapted from Isaac (1996), Chapman (2006) and Fulks & Puta (2003). Other than Krathwohl *et al.* (1964), Martin & Reigeluth (1999) put forward another conceptual model of the affective domain. They acknowledge the complexity of the affective domain and propose six dimensions of affective development as depicted in Table 2.

Term	Definition
Moral development	Building codes of behaviour and rationales and following them, including developing pro social attitudes, often in relation to caring, justice, equality etc.
Social Development	Building skills and attitudes for initiating and establishing interactions and maintaining relationship with others.
Spiritual development	Cultivating an awareness and appreciation of one's soul and its connection with other souls, with God and with all his creation
Emotional development	Understand one's own and others' feeling and affective evaluations, learning to manage those feelings, and wanting to do so.
Aesthetic development	Acquiring an appreciation for beauty and style, including the ability to recognize and create it, commonly linked to music and art, but also includes the aesthetics of ideas.
Motivational development	Cultivating interests and desire to cultivate interests, based on the joy or utility they provide, including both vocational and avocational pursuits.

Table 2: Definitions of the dimensions of affective development

We find this model relevant when deliberating on the development or progression of the teacher trainees. It provides the dimensions of affective outcomes that embody beliefs, feelings and attitudes. We build on the work of both Krathwohl *et al.* (1964) and Martin & Reigeluth (1999) when we synthesize the teacher education outcomes at the end of this section. We reiterate that affective outcomes are behavioural manifestations of beliefs, feelings and attitudes. This means achievements of affective learning outcomes are demonstrated by behaviours indicating attitudes of awareness, interest, attention, concern and responsibility, ability to listen and respond in interactions with others, and ability to demonstrate those attitudinal characteristics, disposition or values which are appropriate to the field of study. Affective outcomes may also encompass students' personal goals, aspirations or perceptions about learning.

It is a common practice among outcome based education providers to concentrate on generic skills such as communication skills and leadership and assume affective outcomes to fall within these skills. It is true that affective gains can be derived from leadership roles, interaction with peers and faculty and involvement in student organizations. However, these affective outcomes are generally not defined. Skills such as communication skills are given priority and assessed through a student's oral and written presentation using rubrics that illustrate specific demonstrated skills. What the student feels is hardly taken into consideration. A student pursuing teacher education at one of the Malaysian universities aptly described his frustration when giving the rationale for a foster school program he suggested:

> *"I am tired of making presentations (about what I have learned) semester in and semester out. What is the point of reiterating stuff to my peers who are studying the same thing but like me, has no inkling as to how we can use them in actual classrooms. I want to be in and learn from the actual school".*

The dimension of immediacy and relevance of knowledge in teacher education requires higher education institutions to rethink their approach to training teachers. Cochran-Smith (2000) proposes that the outcomes of teacher education should be associated with "what teachers can do with what they know". This is precisely what the aforementioned student meant. It is also in agreement with Lampert & Ball (1999) who suggest that knowing teaching means understanding in such a way that one is prepared to perform (or practise) in a given situation for which one cannot fully prepare in advance.

Domain	Dimensions	Components of each dimension
Cognitive Psychomotor (knowledge & skills)	Content knowledge Practical skills related to teaching	Subject matter/areas such as Physics, Biology etc., Educational theories, Pedagogical knowledge, Pedagogical content knowledge, Technological – ICT skills, Technological pedagogical content knowledge.
	Generic/ soft skills – skills that transverse	Scientific and Problem Solving, Information Management, Life Long Learning, Leadership, Communication, Teamwork.
Affective (feelings, beliefs, attitudes)	Interpersonal	Social skills, empathy, building interactions.
	Intrapersonal	Moral, spiritual, emotional and motivational.
	Perceptual/ insight	Consciousness and understanding the occupation of a teacher; awareness of current educational scenario and the multidimensionality of teaching.

Table 3: Outcomes of teacher education

They emphasize how teacher candidates should know what they need to know rather than focusing on simply what they need to know. We see this as a progression of awareness and responsiveness to the workplace or school and educational issues. In lieu of the multifaceted nature of teacher education, we seek to propose the broad outcomes of teacher education to encompass the components in Table 3. We acknowledge that each dimension does not absolutely stand on its own. The three domains (cognitive, psychomotor and affective) are not entirely separated and unrelated to one another. Cognitive and affective outcomes do tend to overlap as the brain does not naturally separate emotions from cognition (Caine & Caine, 1991). As stipulated by Smith & Ragan (1999), there is some affective component to any cognitive or psychomotor outcome. However, the practice of zooming on the cognitive learning alone may not efficiently elicit the desired affective outcomes. Without knowledge about clear patterns of affective attributes of the teacher, we cannot be sure that the affective domain is being addressed effectively by the materials and methods currently used in the classroom. We also acknowledge the complexity of dimensions and levels in achieving these outcomes. In relation to the affective outcomes, each component warrants further explications of the levels suggested by Krathwohl *et al.* (1964). Empathy, for instance, may be developed through the different levels as shown in Table 4. Even though other components are as essential, it is not within the scope of this chapter to detail out all of them. Our next task is to suggest guiding principles and an approach that can be taken to enhance affective outcomes in teacher education.

Outcome	Level	Indicator
Empathy	Receiving	The student listens and gains awareness of the matter or problem faced by others.
	Responding	The student asks questions and perceives the feelings of others regarding the matter.
	Valuing	The student accepts and values the significance of the matter to others.
	Organization	The student consolidates her/his feelings and understands the bigger picture of the matter.
	Characterization	The student feels what others feel – he/she projects compassion and comprehension of the matter.

Table 4: Levels and indicators of empathy

Improving affective outcomes in teacher education

We are of the opinion that affective outcomes can be both 'caught and taught'. An environment that is not very engaging may have limited or negative effects on enhancing affective outcomes. In the light of learning-centred education, we seek to design learning experiences in learning environments that digress from the structured, classroom-based learning with the aim of enhancing these outcomes. Affective learning outcome that involves beliefs, feelings and attitudes calls for realistic, relevant, and stimulating instruction that elicit purposeful emotional involvement (Simonson & Maushak, 2001). On this note, we put forward five guiding principles for enhancing teacher trainees' affective learning outcomes.

1. Knowledge of practice and practise of knowledge in real setting.
2. Early engagement in future workplace environment.
3. Corroboration and reflective collaboration with practitioners.
4. Learning in context; rich task in authentic environment.
5. Continuous interaction and progression of knowledge of the workplace/ school and school culture.

We strongly believe that good teaching requires the teachers to believe, feel and have the right attitude. In order to do this they must have first hand experience. Through experience, the teacher trainees develop consciousness and come to appreciate the nuances of the teaching profession. Based on this argument and the principles laid earlier, we are advocating learning through experiencing as one of the strategies for enhancing affective learning outcomes. This notion is supported by Waite *et al.* (this volume). For teacher education, this directs us to *immersion* in the school environment. Through immersion, the teacher trainees have the opportunity to practise what they learned in university lectures, engage themselves in an authentic work environment, self-assess their skills and compare their perceptions with reality and collaborate with practitioners. Early immersion means not waiting until the last stage of the program before sending them to schools. Then again, this does not necessarily mean that the teacher trainees will be physically stationed in schools. They need to be in touch with the schools, to interact with practitioners, to understand the current situations and to apply the theories in order for them to have an insight into the profession and to value what they learn in class. The avenues to do so have proliferated over the years due to technological advances. We will describe one such example in the later part of the chapter.

Immersive learning approach in teacher education
In education, the use of the term immersive learning has been rigorously associated with immersive simulations in virtual environments and language learning where the learner speaks only the intended lan-

guage to be learned. However, immersive learning can be discussed in a broader context. We are proposing immersive learning as a process where learning is promoted by the learner experiencing as closely as possible the details of the real environment. Learning within community settings is immersive. Learning by sharing thick, rich experience is also immersive. Reading a book can be immersive. So is a virtual class where learners engage with other learners, teachers and experts through the media-rich interface.

Affective compo-nents	Learning outcomes	Example of immersive activity or task	What can be achieved through immersive learning
Inter-personal	Empathy	Trainees read school teacher's reflection and ponder. Trainees watch videos of scenarios and events that take place in real classrooms. Trainees observe school counsellors in session.	Trainees raise their level of awareness and understanding of the school, students and current educational scenario.
	Social skills, building interactions	Trainees ask for input from school teachers on matters pertaining to lesson plans and classroom management. Trainees and school teachers co-identify researchable issues and conduct action research.	Trainees develop the necessary etiquette and attitude to address a fellow teacher. Trainees collaborate and teachers corroborate on matters pertaining to teaching and managing real classrooms.
Intra-personal	Moral and spiritual	Trainees work on an authentic disciplinary case. Trainees go for externship in multiracial and multicultural setting. Trainees work with underprivileged school children. Trainees pay visits to areas stricken with poverty.	Trainees judge and challenge their own values when faced with alternative ones. Trainees develop a heightened awareness of their functions in relation to others.
	Emotional and motivational	Trainees identify and provide service to a "foster school". Trainees set up weekend or online tutorial sessions to help school children. Trainees volunteer as "big sister/big brother" to school children.	Trainees feel the joy and become involved with school children. Trainees become keen and interested when rewarded with authentic experience.
Percep-tual/ insight	Understanding profession, awareness of current scenario and the multidimen-sionality of teaching	Trainees develop instructional materials based on needs analysis conducted in a school. Trainees shadow school teachers. Trainees teach in schools during teaching practicum.	Trainees understand the barriers and challenges in the profession they are venturing into. Trainees have a foresight of what is in store.

Table 5: Affective learning outcomes through immersive learning

Immersive learning may not be tied to complex technologies; simple, accessible technology could be adequate to aid such learning. Immersive experiences promote learning beyond the lectures and discussion in the classrooms. They allow students to collaborate on projects with instructors and communities outside their higher education institutions. How does immersive learning support affective outcomes? Immersion represents the goals of affective experience. Norman Jackson, the Director of Surrey Centre of Excellence in Professional Training and Education (SCEPTrE) regards immersion in a rich, challenging experience as particularly constructive for learning and the development of insight and dispositions for working with complexity.

By being immersed in a particular environment, the learner develops an understanding of its intricacies. The sense of "being there" elicits feelings and emotions and may challenge a person's perception and beliefs. Through immersive learning, teacher trainees are engaged in an active learning process that is connected to real life scenarios. By being engaged in their future school environment, immersive learning allows teacher trainees to know what is currently practised and to actually practise what they know in theory. They learn to collaborate with school teachers who will also corroborate what the trainees need to know when they start out in the teaching world. Learning becomes contextual as they perform rich tasks in authentic environments. Waite *et al.* (this volume) reported students enjoy and positively evaluate authentic experiences. Through these processes, their beliefs, feelings and attitudes towards school and the teaching profession will undergo the internalization process depicted in Table 1 earlier. An illustration of how affective learning outcomes can be achieved through immersive learning is in Table 5. We contend that the higher the degree of immersion, the higher the level of affective learning outcomes achieved.

For a teacher trainee, immersive learning is about experiencing, immersing in the real context of the multicultural and multifaceted nature of teaching, managing the classroom and interacting with pupils and parents. Several techniques and methods can be deployed for immersion. Common ones include field experience, service learning, technology based virtual worlds, internships and externships. Another case of immersion is through community service in schools. Internet technology is also an excellent tool to instigate immersive learning.

Immersive learning is not a "touch and go" process whereby immersion ends when the student leaves the course at the end of the semester. We propose immersion to be gradual to support progressive development and for reasons of practicality. Immersion is also done through a variety of methods such as those mentioned above. Immersive learning may start with simulations in a technology-based environment before full immersion should happen at the end of the teacher education program when the teacher trainees set out for their teaching practicum in schools. Immersive learning should also be facilitated rather than prescribed. Figure 1 illustrates an immersion process for a typical four-year teacher education program. The degree of immersion increases as the student progresses into the program. Semester break immersion is also suggested as an option for the teacher trainees. They may be given credit for their involvement in a school community though activities may not be pertaining to classroom teaching per se.

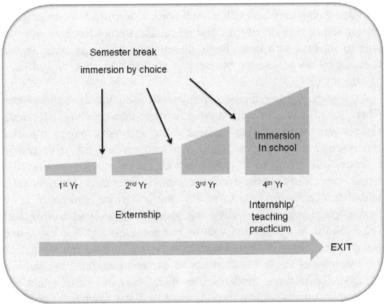

Figure 1: A gradual immersion process in teacher education

A Malaysian example

To further illustrate our point, we seek to describe an example from a Malaysian classroom. Malaysia's multi racial and multi cultural society lend to the complex and diverse nature of teacher education. Teacher trainees need to be aware of various school situations, teaching students of different races and religions and in localities that range from urban, industrialized areas to rural villages without basic amenities. Affective outcomes (beliefs, feelings and attitudes) in the three dimensions (interpersonal, intrapersonal and insights) are crucial for the trainees lest they become impervious to the reality of the teaching profession and suffer a considerable degree of "culture shock" when they land their first teaching assignment. Challenging work situations such as teaching indigenous people in the rural area warrants early immersion. Cultural immersion experiences, for example, contribute to enhancement of teaching culturally and demographically diverse students. A program where teacher trainees spend time among tribal communities in remote areas of Malaysia is one such case.

Capitalizing on three aspects which are: 1) the teacher trainees who need to learn, 2) the school teachers who want their voices heard, and 3) the trainees who are in schools for their internship/teaching practicum, we developed an immersive learning environment based on less complex technology accessible to all parties. We also took into consideration the constraints of time and place. The trainee teachers were unable to interact with the schools directly due to bureaucratic restrictions set by the Malaysian Ministry of Higher Education and Ministry of Education.

As a start, we conducted a pilot study utilizing an online forum where school teachers were invited to share their teaching experience and concerns while teacher trainees in the university logged in to read and respond to the issues raised. Six teachers and fifty five teacher trainees were involved in a four-month online sharing session. The trainees received first hand information without being in schools. The school teachers were able to portray the real world and describe authentic problems while letting out their concerns and having their voices heard. We permitted venting out emotions and display of both positive and negative thoughts. Secondly, we utilized the input from the teachers to allow the students to explore researchable issues on Malaysian education. Students identified areas of research and provided relevant research questions based on the teachers' narratives. Thirdly, we provided transcriptions of the teachers' reflections as data for an exercise in qualitative data analysis.

The practice is context driven, brings in cultural aspect, builds on the experience and knowledge brought to the sharing space by the contributors, exposes common misconceptions and creates connections between classroom learning and issues in the real world. The sharing process is collaborative and corroborative as well. Teacher trainees confirm their beliefs and concerns with the practitioners in schools. They have heightened awareness, reorganize their perceptions about teaching and displayed feelings of empathy. One such instance is when a teacher wrote:

On average, each class in my school has 44 students except Form Six classes. Believe it or not, our two Remove classes have enrolments of 60 and 61 respectively! How can a teacher be expected to teach effectively with so many students in class? Class control is obviously difficult, if not impossible, and students are easily distracted by their peers. ....A very enthusiastic teacher might try to memorize the names of his/ her students a.s.a.p., but I doubt that it can be accomplished within 2 months. With 5 or 6 classes to teach, a teacher actually has approximately 250 names to remember! As for me, I'm trying hard to cope but I do wish we have fewer students in each class so that I can concentrate on teaching and nurturing these young minds without leaving out any of them. Is that too much to ask?

Her post prompted 74 responses from the educational research class. We analysed the transcripts and discovered several themes including: 1) expression of feelings, 2) reflection on own experiences, 3) suggestion of ideas, and 4) confirmation and disconfirmation of views. We also categorized the responses from the teacher trainees based on Table 1 and found evidences of the different levels of affective learning outcomes. Below are some examples from each category.

Teacher trainees' responses	Action verb	Affective level
"...a class can accommodate up to 98 students.. Wow, I never knew that classes in Malaysian schools can be so big."	Realise	Receiving
"...to be honest, that is one of the reasons that make me sooo scared to be a teacher later on... having a big number of students... with different backgrounds??, and with different attitudes?? kids nowadays, u know."	Respond	Responding
"As a teacher wannabe, I am also afraid of facing this kind of problem."	Express concern	Valuing
"I must admit, that situation kind of gives me some uneasy feelings... Am I up to the challenge to teach and handle the students? I don't think I am ready... I wonder where teachers get the motivation and courage."	Recognise Express concern	Valuing

Table 6: Categories of teacher trainees' responses

There were limited discussions on theories initially. But by the end of two weeks, the teacher trainees were already discussing effective classroom management, the value of interactions in big classes, positive thinking and risk taking. Many proposed the use of technology. The school teacher read the trainees' responses and provided further elaboration and impetus for new discussion. Due to the limitations of this chapter, we only describe the consequences of a single post from a teacher even though there were countless responses to the other posts.

Despite the low degree of immersion, the online sharing space proves to be a valuable agent to enhance the trainees' affective outcomes. In the process of getting knowledge of current practice and practising their knowledge in authentic setting, they reflect on their own perceptions, values and on their future career. A student described her newly found awareness:

> *"It (the sharing of experience) gives us the idea of how it is actually to become a teacher... and somehow I think that the experience has provided us with the evidence that (the) teaching profession can no longer be the last resort. I now get annoyed with those who underestimated teachers... I agree with the kind of authentic exposure (we had)."*

The experience gave them a broader view of teaching in the Malaysian context and provoked the trainees to think about possibilities and constraints. What is most rewarding is the learning-centred process that they go through. They build upon and apply meanings to their existing knowledge and examine their own beliefs as well. The online platform is expected to be utilized by students in educational psychology, sociology, technology, philosophy and other classes such as classroom management as well. It is to be made available during their early years in the program when immersion is not expected to be in full swing. It is projected to become more than just a pedagogical resource; it is to enhance the affective outcomes of the students.

Conclusion

The main concern of this chapter has been the affective outcomes of teacher trainees. As defined at the beginning of the chapter, affective outcomes are demonstrated behaviours that indicate beliefs, feelings and attitudes. We have proposed a framework of affective outcomes for teacher trainees that encompass interpersonal, intrapersonal and perceptual dimensions. We have also advocated immersive learning as an approach to enhance these affective outcomes. A Malaysian case study involving the use of online technology to support immersive learning is presented. There are many more avenues for immersive learning. As mentioned in the chapter, new media and technologies are superb means for immersion. Plans to have add-ons to the basic online space such as uploading of lesson plans, placing video clips of classroom scenes and sharing journal entries of those undergoing teaching practicum in schools are under way. However, it is not the tools but the community sense and relationships which subsist in immersive learning that we are emphasizing on. In the words of Brown (2008:xii): *"Immersion comes from being surrounded by others interacting with us and is further facilitated by our deep desire to interact, be understood and express our needs. ...Nearly everyone with whom we interact is a teacher for us...".* We reiterate that teacher education program providers should make it a point to identify learning outcomes and teacher graduate attributes and then go beyond traditional teacher preparation to design learning experiences that support the attainment of the outcomes. Our approach to enhancing the affective outcomes has been less structured and more constructivistic. Tangible products such as journals and e-portfolios (Raiker, this volume) may be appropriate tools to measure the outcomes. This is in itself an intricate process that requires further discussion.

About the authors

Nor Aziah Alias is Associate Professor of Instructional Technology at the Faculty of Education, Universiti Teknologi MARA, Malaysia. She can be contacted at this e-mail: noraz112@salam.uitm.edu.my

Nor Aiza Alias is Senior English Teacher and an educational psychologist at Kepong Secondary School, Malaysia. She can be contacted at this e-mail: noraiza.alias@gmail.com

CHAPTER 17

The Effectiveness of Curriculum Maps of Alignment in Higher Education

Isabel Huet, José Manuel Oliveira, Nilza Costa & João Estima de Oliveira

Introduction

The intended Learning Outcomes (LOs) should drive the design of curricula in higher education (HE) - for example, teaching and learning strategies and activities, assessment, and allocation of European Credit Transfer System (ECTS). In practice, this goal is not so easy to achieve, as we can conclude from the report of the Portuguese 'Porto Bologna seminar' (Madill & de Azevedo, 2008). This chapter describes the use of Curriculum Maps of Alignment (CMA) as a tool to promote constructive alignment on the grass roots, thus allowing for better student LOs achievement, on the far run. Given the newness of using LOs in the Portuguese context, the authors also believe that the use of a simple tool (see Hinrichsen, this volume), such as the one discussed in this chapter, may be of great help in promoting alignment and an effective shift from the content-centered paradigm to the LO-centered paradigm. The tool we describe can therefore play an important role in the improvement of students' learning outcomes.

The authors present the experience of running staff development workshops on curriculum alignment and on the design of curriculum maps at four different Portuguese HE institutions. Subsequently, the staff members undertaking these workshops have been asked to fill in a questionnaire regarding the advantages of using CMA in their curricular units. The answers are qualitatively analysed to shed light on the usefulness of the tool in designing the alignment of the curriculum aiming to promote better student LOs.

Setting the scene

The effectiveness of the Bologna Process demands urgent curriculum reforms that take into consideration the characteristics of students now enrolling in HE, the competences required by the present society and by the HE institutions, in particular. The complexity of what is expected from a student today has an impact "...*in the way study programmes are designed, learning contexts are organized and students are assessed*" (Alarcão & Gil, 2004:202). In Portugal, one of the challenges consists on promoting curriculum design that aligns the LOs with the teaching, learning, and assessment activities (Huet *et al.*, 2008).

The re-design of the *curricula* based on LOs and on the student workload have been a motive for discussion within academia (Gallavara *et al.*, 2008; Kennedy, 2007). HE institutions across Europe are looking for strategies to overcome the gap between what still happens in practice and what research recommends. This gap is still more evident in Southern European countries where the predominant teaching model was, until very recently, centered on the teacher and on the scientific content of the courses. The final report of the Portuguese 'Porto Bologna Seminar' (Madill & de Azevedo, 2008) points out that there is still a long way to go in the design of courses based on LOs and to calculate the ECTS based on the student workload. The same report suggests the need to actively engage members of staff in Continuous Professional Development (CPD) courses, workshops or seminars allowing the possibility for academics to share and discuss the design and assessment of LOs: "*The shift to ECTS and learning outcomes requires a great deal of work and resource. For some it will represent a paradigm shift towards a more learner-centred approach to education, for others a development of what they already do. Support and training for staff in developing, writing and assessing Learning Outcomes is essential and this needs commitment at the highest level, including from heads of institutions and from ministers. Sharing of good practice should be a priority.*" (Madill & de Azavedo, 2008:4)

The authors of this chapter believe that an effective use of LOs requires background knowledge on the pedagogy of teaching and learning in HE and on the concept of constructive alignment. This concept refers to a very influential idea in higher education conveyed by Biggs (1999), whose fundamental premise is that learning activities and assessment tasks should be aligned with the intended LOs for any particular curricular unit. The whole idea translates into curricular consistency. Students are expected to construct their own learning (and thus the term 'constructive') and teachers (better referred to as facilitators, in this context) are responsible for the creation of an appropriate learning environment, one that is supportive of students in attaining the intended outcomes. Such an environment can only be achieved if the intended LOs are made clear for the students. By this recognition students can better share the responsibility for the learning process. Assessment is the final vertex of constructive alignment. One reason that supports this idea is that students tend to structure their learning activities around the usually proposed assessment tasks, which leads to the idea that we have to make sure that assessment does test the intend learning outcomes. Another reason is that assessment always leads to learning (Boud, 1995).

Although the authors come from the same institution, they have been separately involved in delivering a set of CPD programmes and workshops, in different institutions, to engage academics on redesigning their provisions based on LOs. A common theme of these activities, which triggered the writing of this text, was the use of curriculum maps of alignment as a tool to promote constructive alignment. The different contexts in which this tool was used will be described. In addition, a preliminary follow-up study was performed aiming to evaluate the impact of the competences developed after the workshops in the design and evaluation of LOs by the participants and on the elaboration of CMA. This follow-up study is essential for answering the next research questions: (i) how are participants aligning the LOs with teaching and learning activities, student workload and assessment?, and (ii) what are the advantages of using this tool in their practice?

Curriculum mapping of alignment

The concept of curriculum mapping is used more often for managing the curriculum and to demonstrate the links between its different components (Harden, 2001; Jacobs, 1997). In this case, the authors use the concept of 'curriculum mapping of alignment' to refer to the alignment of the teaching and learning process in the curriculum.

Curriculum maps of alignment were first introduced in 2000 at the University of Aveiro (Portugal) to the Higher Education Polytechnic School of Águeda's (ESTGA) staff by Professor John Cowan during a staff development workshop within the process of ESTGA's move towards a Project-Based Learning environment (Oliveira, 2006; Alarcão, 2006). The CMA were presented as a tool for checking constructive alignment at the course level, a tool that required teachers to think on the curriculum based on LOs (Cowan *et al.*, 2004). This task demanded explicit reflection on the necessary practices to help students achieve those outcomes. Curriculum maps of alignment have been regarded at ESTGA as a bottom-up tool in the sense that they have been used to describe alignment at the course level, and therefore express the view of staff members on the courses they are involved in. This view was expressed in terms of LOs, which represented an important shift, and a challenge to those involved, together with the requirement to reflect on the alignment of those outcomes with the proposed learning and assessment strategies. Once all maps of a particular programme become available, they constitute a snapshot of the programme, allowing for the identification of duplicated LOs and of unaddressed important aspects of higher-level outcomes. This is especially important in relation to transversal competences, which usually require the concurrence of several curricular units. In this perspective, CMAs also become an important top-down curriculum development tool. The whole process is clarified in Figure 1, in which CMA (expanded in Figure 3) are used together with the tables proposed by Felder & Brent (2003) (expanded in Figure 2), which allow for the verification of the translation of the higher-level objectives at the curricular unit level.

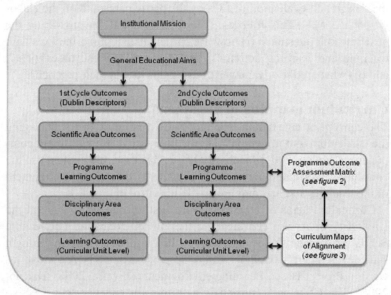

Figure 1: The place of the CMA at the ESTGA

Outcome indicators and courses	Outcome 1	Outcome 2	Outcome 3	Outcome 4	Outcome 5	Outcome 6	Outcome 7
Portfolio	3	3	3	3	3	2	3
FE Exam	3						
GPA	1						
GPA in CHE	2						
Design course: Project Report	2		3		3	1	2
Design course: Oral Presentations	2		3		3	2	2
Exit interviews with seniors	2	2	2	2	2	2	2
Alumni interviews	2	2	2	2	2	2	2
ENGR (Freshman engineering)				1	1	1	2
CS110		1					
ENGL 112 (Freshman composition)					1		
ENGL 365 (Technical writing)					3		
CHE 205	3				2	2	
CHE 311	3		1				
CHE 312	3		1				
CHE 315	3						
CHE 316	3						
CHE 330 (Engineering laboratory)	2	3			2	3	2
CHE 410 (Engineering & society)				3	2		2
CHE 446	3		1				
CHE 425	3		2				
CHE 450	3		2				
CHE 451 (Capstone design course)	3		3		3	3	2

Objective adresses outcome 1=slightly; 2=moderately; 3=substantially

Figure 2: Detail of the table proposed by Felder & Brent (2003)
Reproduced with the authors' permission. The listed Outcomes are also from the work by Felder & Brent (2003)

Outcome 1: Ability to apply mathematical, scientific, and engineering principles to the identification, formulation, and solution of engineering problems.

Outcome 2: Ability to design and conduct experiments & to analyze and interpret data using modern engineering tools and techniques.

Outcome 3: Ability to design engineering processes and products to meet desired needs.

Outcome 4: Ability to analyze important social and environmental problems and identify and discuss ways that engineers might contribute to solutions, including technological, economic, and ethical considerations in the analysis.

Outcome 5: Ability to communicate effectively in both writing and speaking in a variety of professional contexts.

Outcome 6: Ability to function effectively in both single-discipline and multidisci-plinary teams.

Outcome 7: Recognition of need for and ability to engage in lifelong learning.

The use of these latter tables can contribute to the curriculum coherence, which is another important goal of the developments taking place at ESTGA. As depicted in Figures 3 and 4 a CMA is a simple table in which, for each LO, the corresponding learning and assessment activities are registered, along with the expected student workload. The CMA serves two purposes: it can be used as a planning tool, demanding reflection FOR the delivery; and it can also be used afterwards, as a reflection tool ON the delivery, allowing for the identification of aspects in need of change or refinement. As in every learning process, this interactive process of reflection FOR the action and ON the action is bound to have a strong impact on the students' achievement of LOs, and in the adjustment of the intended LO for a particular curricular unit.

Learning outcomes	Assessment		How facilitated?	Work-load
	How?	On what basis?		
Use Diodes in their most common applications and analyse circuits containing them.	Analyse known applications (possibly unknown to students). Altering the initial conditions of a given circuit and ask for qualitative evaluation of the new situation. Project work usually provides application/analysis /synthesis situations.	Associated courses examinations. Project reports. Associated courses examinations. Final project discussion.	Active learning, in groups, around problem scenarios identical (in demand and scope) to the situations that will be used for assessment. Scaffolding in every possible situation provided by project work.	12h
Planning project activities.	Demanding regular planning of activities throughout the project work.	Project progress reports. Project Meetings.	Discussing and giving feedback on monthly revised planning of project activities.	2h

Figure 3: Part of a CMA developed at ESTGA

The use of CMA which, as previously stated, was first tried out during the move of ESTGA's technological programmes towards Project-Based Learning, was again the selected tool for the more recent curriculum development process involving all ESTGA's degrees, to comply with the Bologna Process. The process involved staff professional development that resulted, as a final product, in a CMA for each curricular unit. In the context of the Bologna Process, which involves the implementation of quality assurance procedures, CMA may assume another important role as tools for the systematic checking of the alignment in the field. In the context of a staff professional development workshop at the Polytechnic Institute of Viana do Castelo (IPVC), CMA have been introduced and tentatively used in the way depicted in Figure 1.

Curriculum maps of alignment have also raised interest in three other higher education institutions in Portugal. CMA were not used as systematic bottom-up tools as in the contexts previously mentioned above. Instead, they were used as a top-down curriculum development tool during staff professional development programmes at the University of Aveiro (Ramos *et al.*, 2006), the Polytechnic Institute of Leiria, and the Polytechnic Institute of Viseu. Participants were asked to reflect on the importance of aligning to competences, LOs, teaching, learning and assessment activities and students' workload. The activity of designing a CMA, either for a specific curricular unit (global matrix), or oriented in terms of a specific content (specific matrix) allowed the participants to rethink the curriculum based on the students' achievement of LOs. Following a model (Figure 4), the participants designed their own CMA.

Competencies	Learning outcomes	Teaching & learning activities	Students' workload (27h)	Assessment
To understand the implications of the Bologna Process on teaching and learning in HE.	1. Identify and discuss the generic guidelines, the implications and challenges of the Bologna Process.	Lecture: The Bologna Process in the European context.	4h lectures.	
	2. Explain the implications and challenges for teaching and learning at the University of Aveiro.	Discussion of the challenges and implications for the Portuguese context and for the University of Aveiro in particular.		Formative assessment of students' interactions in class.
			23h (individual or group work).	
To reflect on the students' and lecturers' role in HE.	3. Systematize the role of the lecturer and the student in HE.	Autonomous study: Research of papers in scientific journals. Writing and presenting a short assignment.		Summative assessment: Oral presentation of group work (40% of final mark) + written assignment (60%).

Figure 4: Model of a curriculum map of alignment

Staff members took into consideration five steps in developing their alignment process (in a way much similar to the ESTGA and IPVC's developments):

1. Defining the specific competences and intended LOs. The transversal competences were considered at the bottom-level;
2. Choosing teaching/learning activities likely to lead, help and encourage students to attain these LOs. These activities aimed at engaging students in the teaching and learning process;
3. Defining the intended students' workload (time spent in classes and outside classes) in order to calculate the ECTS;
4. Proposing techniques and activities for assessing students' LOs using suitable methods and including the giving of feedback in order to help students to improve their learning;
5. Including evaluation tools to find out the match between the intended and actually attained LOs.

From our experience we noticed that most participants did not feel confident to design a CMA without specifying the contents. Some of them still felt the need to include an extra column to list the contents to be covered in relation to the specified LOs. This need may reflect the difficulties in changing from a content-centered paradigm to a LO-centered paradigm. The content-based curriculum, as referred, is still very present in the four institutions mentioned. The activities involving CMA in the context of staff professional development programmes, in these four institutions, have been acting as seeds in promoting the paradigm shift and thus, hopefully, improving the attainment of the intended LOs by the students.

Results on the impact of using curriculum maps of alignment during and after staff development

In this section we present the results of the use of curriculum maps of alignment during the professional development workshops - the short-term impact - and to gauge the long term impact that such a tool may have in improving teaching and students' learning.

Short-term impact

As facilitators of the staff development workshops focusing on CMA between 2005 and 2009, the authors came to the next conclusions based on the observation of sessions and on the writing of field notes:

i. The first iteration of filling-in CMA proved to be a hard task, requiring difficult changes in the teaching paradigm and forcing participants to reflect on their intended practices, namely by addressing the question: *'what do we want students to be able to do as a result of learning'?* The CMA soon became a 'declaration of intentions' that could be shared and discussed among peers, thus assuming another important role in the curriculum development process - providing a basis for intra and interdisciplinary discussion on the overall curriculum;

ii. The design of CMA allowed the discussion on the definition of LOs, competences and objectives. For example, to clarify the distinction between learning outcomes and competences;

iii. As a consequence of i) and ii), the design of assessment activities was developed in terms of the LOs and not in terms of the contents. Formative assessment was considered to be the most effective method to assess students. Nevertheless, it was considered to be extremely challenging to assess students in terms of LOs;

iv. The biggest challenge that occurred during the discussions about students' autonomous work and the ECTS, lied on the management of time students spend outside the class in preparation of specific tasks and/or in independent study;

v. CMA have been generally regarded by participants as a useful tool to convey what is expected of learners and what they should expect from any given curricular unit.

Long-term impact

If change is to be effective, academic staff, students and other players need to be convinced about the purpose and benefits of such change. Therefore, a questionnaire was designed aiming to analyze how CMA are being used and the impact this tool is having on the change of their teaching practice. This questionnaire was delivered by mail in January 2009 to 150 participants that attended the workshops and the staff development programmes. The data analysis refers to 72 valid answers.

		Description of the Sample (N=72)
Institution	University of Aveiro	N=25
	Polytechnic of Leiria	N=28
	Other	N=19
Teaching experience in HE	<6	N=22
	6-10	N=30
	>10	N=16

Table 1: Institutions and teaching experience of the participants

The questionnaire was organized in three parts. The first part aimed to characterize the participants concerning the number of years of teaching experience in HE, the year of participation in the professional development workshops/programmes and the name of the institution. The second part had the purpose of evaluating the impact of the workshops: (i) in the design of the courses based on LOs, and (ii) in the use of CMA as a tool to maximize the alignment of LOs, teaching and learning strategies, student workload, and assessment. The third part consisted of an open question and had the objective of identifying positive and less positive aspects in the use of CMA.

Table 1 indicates that the majority of the respondents have up to 10 years of teaching experience in HE. These data emphasize the tendency of less experienced academic staff in looking for professional development workshops.

	1 Never	2 Some- times	3 Often	4 Always	Mode	Avg.	Stand. dev.
The workshop I attended, which included the use of CMA, helped me to clarify the notion of Learning Outcomes	0	4	51	17	3	3,2	0,51
The workshop I attended helped me to align LOs with Learning Activities and Assignment	0	13	47	12	3	3,0	0,60
I recognize the potential of the CMA in helping me change my teaching practice	1	10	41	20	3	3,1	0,69
I recognize the potential of the CMA in improving the student-centredness of my delivery	2	9	43	18	3	3,1	0,70
While planning for my classes, I specify the intended LOs	1	9	40	22	3	3,2	0,69
While planning for my classes, I specify learning activities for each of the intended LOs	0	9	43	19	3	3,1	0,62
While planning for my classes, I specify assessment tasks for each of the intended LOs	0	13	37	22	3	3,1	0,69
I use CMA in the curricular units I'm responsible for	5	21	29	17	3	2,8	0,88

Table 2: Data from part two of the questionnaire

From the gathered data (Table 2), the authors conclude the following:

(i)   The workshops had a reasonable impact on the clarification of what LOs are (average 3.2). Notably, before the workshops, few participants were able to define LOs and to design the curricular unit based on LOs;

(ii)   The workshops helped with the curriculum alignment and, more specifically, in articulating the LOs with teaching, learning, and assessment activities (average 3);

(iii)   A considerable number of participants claimed to specify the LOs (average 3.2) and to design the teaching and learning activities (average 3.1) and assessment (average 3.1) accordingly;

(iv)   Most participants recognized the potential of the CMA as a tool that helped in modifying their teaching practice towards a student-centered approach (average 3.1) but a lesser number admitted to use it in their curriculum units (average 2.8). This last result certainly needs further investigation.

In the open question of part 3 of the questionnaire, participants realized the importance of the workshops/programmes to exchange and discuss information with colleagues regarding students' learning outcomes and the design of CMA. This collaborative work was indeed one of the objectives of the workshops/programmes. As mentioned by one participant: *'we are so busy in our daily activities (teaching, research and management) that we don't realize how important it is to exchange and discuss ideas with colleagues from our or even other scientific areas. This process helps us to overcome some problems'*. The interaction with colleagues from different areas of knowledge seems to be very effective and start to join researchers from areas such as science, engineering and education in discussing transversal LOs that can be promoted in different curricular units.

Final considerations

At the stage of the curriculum development process, CMA served the very important purpose of recording constructive alignment on paper, making the ideas gain weight and form, become tangible and therefore manageable. CMA become, therefore, a useful curriculum implementation tool, helping to bridge the gap between conceptualization and actual practice, between higher-level competences and actual learning activities. A post-delivery analysis of the CMA may also prove to be very useful in reflecting on the teaching and learning process that has taken place, and in considering future adjustments, based on the outcomes. In this context, CMA become a fine-tuning tool, thus contributing to the improvement of student learning outcomes achievement.

The development of CMA was considered useful for the top-down curriculum development at the University of Aveiro and Polytechnic

Institute of Leiria, and as a powerful bottom-up tool at ESTGA. The authors believe that the convergence of these two movements (top-down and bottom-up), possibly after several iterations, could lead to substantiated curriculum development, ensuring constructive alignment and coherence across the curriculum. The attainment and improvement of students' LOs is only possible if intended LOs have been properly specified, learning activities have been coherently organized and assessment is clearly articulated with the intended LOs and the provided learning opportunities.

This chapter has argued that CMA contribute to the improvement of a curriculum based on LOs. On the other hand, our experience also shows that continuous professional development is important to engage academia in a different approach to teaching and learning.

As a final consideration, the authors believe that the overall process described in this chapter can lead to an improvement of students' LOs, as a result of the reflection process that CMA foster and of the effective alignment they promote. However, it is necessary to deepen this understanding by also taking students' views into account. This is the challenge we will now pursue.

However, and as reported in this book (see the chapter by Stuart *et al*) a coordinated strategy is needed if we want the overall process to be succeeded. Isolated initiatives are useful but can die very easily without the support of institutional strategies.

About the authors

Isabel Huet is a researcher on Higher Education and coordinator of the research line 'Laboratory for the Evaluation of Educational Quality in Higher Education' at the Research Centre for Didactics and Technology in Teacher Education at the University of Aveiro, Portugal. She can be contacted at this e-mail: huet@ua.pt

José Manuel Oliveira is Adjunct Professor of Electrical Engineering at the Higher Education Polytechnic School of Águeda, University of Aveiro. He has been deeply involved in the coordination of the move towards Project-Based Learning at his institution. He can be contacted at this e-mail: jmo@ua.pt.

Nilza Costa is a Full Professor of Education at the Department of Education, University of Aveiro, Portugal. She coordinates the 'Laboratory for the Evaluation of Educational Quality' at the Research Centre for Didactics and Technology in Teacher Education. She has been involved, together with Isabel Huet, in continuous professional training of higher education teachers. She can be contacted at this e-mail: nilzacosta@ua.pt

João Estima de Oliveira is a researcher at the Aveiro's Institute of Electronic Engineering and Telematics and the Director of the Higher Education Polytechnic School Águeda, University of Aveiro. He has been involved for several years in curricula development, namely as Pro-Vice-Chancellor, in the nineties, at the University of Aveiro. He can be contacted at this e-mail: jeo@ua.pt

Afterword

Clive Holtham

Back in mid 2007, Claus Nygaard at Copenhagen Business School had a dream that he wanted to turn into reality. His dream was to re-think the conventional academic conference. In many ways Claus wanted to return to the traditional academic form, which was small-scale and even intimate. The dream was holistic, people coming together without regard to boundaries, not in the modern way of being separated into narrower and narrower disciplinary groupings. It was also intended to be integrative, drawing these different perspectives together insofar as it made sense to do so.

Out would go bloated conferences with hundreds if not thousands of delegates. Out would go 15 minute presentations with desultory or even fractious questions and answers. As a result, out too went Power-Point™, and out went data projectors. A place at the conference would only be possible if delegates had submitted a book chapter a month ahead of the conference. This would be subject to peer review, but on an appreciative enquiry basis, emphasising the positive while still in-cluding critical review as necessary. In Claus's dream there were no presentations because all sessions were devoted intensively to the process of improving individual chapters, and then in the second half also integrating the chapters as a whole. So although there was no need for data projectors, what was essential for every delegate was a laptop. Delegates were caught at midnight on the hotel terrace still working on editing their chapter beneath the balmy Aegean moonlight.

To make the dream reality, Claus needed to work with others with complementary skills. He approached us at Cass Business School, City University, London. We signed up at once, because we could see that this was precisely the type of breakthrough that was long overdue. We were able to provide some logistical support and help in the facilitation and editing of the work, particularly latterly through my colleague from Cass, Dr Nigel Courtney.

The dream needed exactly the right location. Ideally it would be a place where the group could occupy a whole hotel or residence, in a pleasant location. A place that exactly fitted the bill was the Kavos Bay Hotel, on the island of Aegina, an hour's ferry journey south of

Athens. A theme was selected, and within just a few days of deciding to go ahead, Claus had produced a web site to launch the conference, to take place in June 2008. The call for papers had produced sufficient high quality chapters for the conference and so negotiations on the book contract could proceed.

The key element that Claus wanted in the book contract was that for content delivered to the publisher by the end of June, we would be guaranteed a book in the bookshops by the end of August. Even I, who had been relentlessly positive about Claus's dream, felt at this point that the dream might not be fully feasible. But Claus was persistent and eventually the Copenhagen Business School Press indicated that they would be able to meet the deadline.

The rest is history. The conference took place just as advertised. The book contract was negotiated with the Copenhagen Business School Press, and the book did come out by the seemingly impossible deadline of 31st August 2008.

A reprise
The second conference, LIHE 09, used the same format, at the same location, with a very similar call for papers. The major difference was that there was now a physical deliverable – the book – to show that the whole process actually did work. We had a dramatic increase in the number of abstracts that were submitted. Because of the usual limitations of a printed book, this meant that a good number of fine papers had to be rejected. This has caused us to think that in future years we should consider convening more than one conference per year.

Word of mouth also had a significant impact – several of the 2009 authors were strongly recommended by 2008 authors to submit abstract. Unfortunately abstracts from some of the very best contributors from 2008 did not get through the peer review process. Apart from the organising team, abstracts from two authors from 2008 were accepted and they were able to attend again in 2009, thus providing invaluable continuity.

The basic format of the conference did not need to be altered. But what was immediately clear to the organising team, right from the opening reception on the first evening, was that this year's group was distinctly different from the 2008 group. Not better, nor worse; just different. Of course, this is exactly the same as with groups of students. It is true with every other academic conference that runs from year to year. But the differences are much more visible and immediate with a group of 30 or so people. This is not something that organisers could or should do anything about. The participants are who they are, and the unique mix will develop its own momentum and chemistry.

What was clear was that almost all of the participants were passionate about education and learning. Many were also active researchers, but did not see research and teaching and learning in conflict. Several held awards for their good practice in teaching.

In this situation, organisers have to be willing to tear up their carefully worked over schedule in order to meet the aspirations of the audience. The group will be vocal if they are not happy with the process – for example, when at one point we gave groups and individuals too little time to distil their key messages.

As with the previous year, the participants were massively supportive of their co-authors. No matter how much they disagreed about particular things they put their critiques in a positive light. It helped enormously that written critiques were provided by peer groups prior to the symposium in Aegina. Then oral peer review at the confernec could amplify and clarify these.

Looking forward

Integrating the different chapters together had been a vital factor in the 2008 book and once again this took up a significant amount of time. This aspect is normally only carried out by book editors, so for the whole group of authors actively to contribute really makes for a much more authentically integrated piece of work.

For 2010 our theme will be based on creativity, and information will be accessible from the LIHE 10 website, or from the authors.

Special thanks

It only remains for me to thank all those who contributed to the success of the event. The Kavos Bay Hotel provided exceptional support and, in a remarkably generous gesture, donated an olive tree in recognition of the 2009 conference. The way in which conference participants actually dug the hole and planted the tree was an interesting example of iterative learning in an unfamiliar environment. Many of the 2008 participants volunteered to act as reviewers of the abstracts, a vital job especially with many good abstracts submitted. Nicola Jackson was a hyper-efficient administrator at the event, and Dr Nigel Courtney put tremendous expertise into editing and into the encouragement of the authors. So too did my colleague Claus Nygaard, whose dream, however impossible it seemed to some in 2007, was fully achieved in 2008. Even more important, it was possible to repeat it again in 2009 and I am in no doubt that, by now being so well established, it will go on from strength to strength.

There is a role for new types of academic conference, and for much faster publication of the results, and we all need to thank Claus for his vision and for enabling it to be realized both for authors and readers.

Bibliography

Acharya, C. (2003). Outcome–based education (OBE): A New Paradigm for Learning. *CTDLink Newsletter,* http://www.cdtl.nus.edu.sg/link/nov2003/obe.htm [Accessed 25 June 2009].

Adams, K. L. (2001). The Critical Incident Questionnaire: A Critical Reflective Teaching Tool. *The Online Journal of Teaching and Learning in the CSU.* http://www.exchangesjournal.org/classroom/ciq_pg1.html [Accessed 21 June 2009].

Adler, S. (1991). The Reflective Practitioner and the Curriculum of Teacher Education. *Journal of Education for Teaching,* Vol. 17, No. 2, pp. 139-151.

AGCAS (2000). *The Assessment Centres Video/DVD.* Sheffield: Association of Graduate Careers Advisory Services.

AGR (2008a). *Assessment Centres.* Briefing Paper Series. Warwick: The Association of Graduate Recruiters.

AGR (2008b). *The AGR Graduate Recruitment Survey 2008 Summer Review.* Warwick: The Association of Graduate Recruiters.

Aguirre, M.; B. Mayes & R. Riggio (1995). Assessment Center Methods Applied to Entering Business Students: Reliability and Convergence of Measures. In B. Mayes (coordinator). *Assessment Center Applications in Industry and Higher Education.* Symposium presented at the 36th Western Academy of Management Conference, San Diego, CA.

Alarcão I. (2006). Changing to Project–Based Learning. The Role of Institutional Leadership and Faculty Development. In E. Graaff & A. Kolmos (eds.) *Management of Change – Implementation of Problem–Based and Project–Based Learning in Engineering.* Rotterdam: Sense Publishers, pp. 69-82.

Alarcão, I. & V. M. S. Gil (2004). Teaching and Learning in Higher Education in Portugal: an Overview of Studies in ICHED. In I. Alarcão; V. M. S. Gil & H. Hooghoff (eds.) *Challenges in Teaching & Learning in Higher Education.* University of Aveiro, pp. 202-206.

Alexander, P. A. & F. Dochy (1995). Conceptions of Knowledge and Beliefs: A Comparison Across Varying Cultural and Educational

Communities. *American Educational Research Journal*, Vol. 32, No. 2, pp. 413-442.

Alias, N. A.; H. Wahab & H. Jamaludin (2008). A Context Driven Approach to Designing the Adult Learning Experience. In C. Nygaard & C. Holtham (eds.) *Understanding Learning–centred Higher Education*, Frederiksberg: CBS Press, pp. 211-229.

Alpert, F. & M. A. Kamins (2004). Doctoral Coursework is Needed in Australasia. *Australasian Marketing Journal,* Vol. 12, No. 1, pp. 66-72.

Anderson E. (ed.) (1993). *Campus Use of the Teaching Portfolio*: *Twenty–Five Profiles.* Washington, DC: AAHE.

Andresen, L. W. (2000). A Usable, Trans–disciplinary Conception of Scholarship. *Higher Education Research and Development*, Vol. 19, No. 2, pp. 137-153.

Angelo, T. A. (2006). *Developing the Scholarship of Assessment: Guidelines and Pathways.* Indianapolis: University of Indianapolis.

Archer, L. (2008). Younger Academics' Constructions of 'Authenticity', 'Success' and Professional Identity. *Studies in Higher Education,* Vol. 33, No. 4, pp. 385-403.

Archer, W. & J. Davison (2008). *Graduate Employability: What do Employers Think and Want?* Council for Industry and Higher Education.
http://www.health.heacademy.ac.uk/themes/employerengagement/whatemployerswant.pdf [Accessed 22 June 2009].

Ashworth, E. (2008). Medieval Theories of Analogy. In N. Zalta (ed.) *The Stanford Encyclopedia of Philosophy.* Fall 2008 Edition. Stanford University: http://plato.stanford.edu/archives/fall2008/entries/analogy-medieval/ [Accessed 22 June 2009].

Atherton, J. S. (2005a). *Learning and Teaching:Reflection and Reflective Practice.*
http://www.learningandteaching.info/learning/reflecti.htm [Accessed 21 June 2009].

Atherton, J. S. (2005b). *Learning and Teaching:Experiential Learning.*
http://www.learningandteaching.info/learning/experience.htm [Accessed 21 June 2009].

Atherton, J. S. (2005c). *What's Wrong with Surface Learning?*
http://www.doceo.co.uk/hetereodoxy/surface.htm [Accessed 22 June 2009].

Atkins, M. J.; J. Beattie & W. B. Dockrell (1993). *Assessment Issues in Higher Education.* Newcastle: University of Newcastle upon Tyne, School of Education.

Atlay, M. T.; A. Gaitan & A. Kumar (2008). Stimulating Learning: Creating CRe8. In C. Nygaard & C. Holtham (eds.) *Understanding Learner–Centred Higher Education*. Frederiksberg: CBS Press, pp. 231-250.

Australasian Qualifications Framework Advisory Board (1998). *Australasian Qualifications Framework Implementation Handbook*. Carlton, Victoria: Australasian Qualifications Framework Advisory Board.

Bailey, K. M. (1997). Reflective Teaching: Situating Our Stories. *Asian Journal of English Language Teaching,* Vol. 7, No. 1, pp. 1-19.

Banta, T. W. (1999). What's New in Assessment? *Assessment Update*, Vol. 11, No. 5, pp. 3-11.

Banta, T. W. (ed.) (2003). *Portfolio Assessment: Uses, Cases, Scoring, and Impact*. San Francisco, CA: Jossey–Bass.

Barber, C. E. & R. W. Richburg (1981). Emphasizing Affective Outcomes in an Introductory Gerontology Course. *Gerontology and Geriatrics Education*, Vol. 2, pp. 23-30.

Barnacle, R. (2005). Research Education Ontologies: Exploring Doctoral Becoming. *Higher Education Research and Development,* Vol. 24, No. 2, pp. 179-188.

Barnett, R (1994). *The Limits of Competence: Knowledge, Higher Education and Society*. Buckingham: SRHE & Open University Press.

Barnett, R. (1997). *Higher Education: A Critical Business*. Buckingham: SRHE & Open University Press.

Barnett, R. (2000). Supercomplexity and the Curriculum. *Studies in Higher Education,* Vol. 25, No. 3, pp. 255-265.

Barnett, R. (2000). University Knowledge in an Age of Supercomplexity. *Higher Education,* Vol. 40, No. 4, pp. 409-422.

Barr, R. B. & J. Tagg (1995). From Teaching To Learning – A New Paradigm For Undergraduate Education. *Change,* Vol. 27, No. 6, pp. 12-25.

Barron, D. & M. Zeegers (2006). Subjects of Western Education: Discursive Practices in Western Postgraduate Studies and the Construction of International Student Subjectivities. *The Australian Educational Researcher,* Vol. 33, No. 2, pp. 77-96.

Batchelor, D. & R. Di Napoli (2006). The Doctoral Journey: Perspectives. *Educate,* Vol. 6, No. 1, pp. 13-24.

Baum, L. (2002). Enthusiasm in Teaching. *PS: Political Science and Politics,* 35 (March), pp. 87-91

Baume, D. (2009). *Writing and Using Good Learning Outcomes.*
  Leeds: Leeds Metropolitan University.
Baxter Magolda, M. B. (1992). Students' Epistemologies and
  Academic Experiences: Implications for Pedagogy. *Review of
  Higher Education,* Vol. 15, No. 3, pp. 265-287.
Beaty, L., G. Gibbs & A. Morgan (2005). Learning Orientations and
  Study contracts. In F. Marton; D. Hounsell & N. Entwistle (eds.)
  *The Experience of Learning: Implications for Teaching and
  Studying in Higher Education.* Edinburgh: University of
  Edinburgh, Centre for Teaching, Learning and Assessment.
Becher, T. & P. R. Trowler (2001). *Academic Tribes and Territories.
  Intellectual Enquiries and the Culture of Disciplines.* Buckingham:
  Open University Press.
Beishuizen J.; P. Van Boxel; P. Banyard; A. Twiner; H. Ermeij & J.
  Underwood (2006). The Introduction of Portfolios in Higher
  Education: A Comparative Study in the UK and the Netherlands.
  European Journal of Education, Vol. 41, No. 3/4, pp. 491-508.
Bergquist, W. (1992). *The Four Cultures of the Academy.* San
  Francisco, CA: Jossey–Bass.
Berlin Communiqué (2003). *Realising the European Higher Education
  Area.* http://www.bologna-berlin2003.de/pdf/Communique1.pdf
  [Accessed 22 June 2009].
Biggs, J. & C. Tang (1998). Assessment by Portfolio: Constructing
  Learning and Designing Teaching. In P. Stimpson & P. Morris
  (eds.) *Curriculum Assessment for Hong Kong: Two Components,
  One System.* Hong Kong: Open University of Hong Kong Press,
  pp. 443-462.
Biggs, J. (1987). *Student Approaches to Learning and Studying.*
  Melbourne: Australian Council for Educational Research.
Biggs, J. (1990). Teaching Design for Learning. Paper presented at the
  Annual Conference of the *Higher Education Research and
  Development Society of Australia,* Brisbane: Griffith University,
  July, 1990.
Biggs, J. (1996). Enhancing Teaching Through Constructive
  Alignment. *Higher Education,* Vol. 32, No. 3, pp. 347-364.
Biggs, J. (1999). *Teaching for Quality Learning at University.*
  Buckingham: SRHE & Open University Press.
Biggs, J. (2001). Assessing for Quality in Learning. In Suskie, L. (ed.)
  *Assessment to Promote Deep Learning. Insight from AAHE's 2000
  and 1999 Assessment conferences.* USA: American Association for
  Higher Education.

Biggs, J. (2002). Aligning teaching and assessment to curriculum objectives. LTSN Imaginative Curriculum. http://www.ltsn.ac.uk/genericcentre [Accessed 02 March 2008]

Biggs, J. (2003) *Teaching for Quality Learning at University,* London: SRHE & Open University Press.

Biggs, J. (2003). *Aligning Teaching for Constructing Learning.* York: The Higher Education Academy. http://www.heacademy.ac.uk/assets/York/documents/resources/res ourcedatabase/id477_aligning_teaching_for_constructing_learning .pdf [Accessed 23 June 2009].

Biggs, J. (2008). *SOLO Taxonomy.* http://www.johnbiggs.com.au/solo_taxonomy.html [Accessed 22 June 2009].

Birmingham, C. (2004). Phronesis: a Model for Pedagogical Reflection. *Journal of Teacher Education,* Vol. 55, No. 4, pp. 313-324.

Black, C. (2005). Issues Regarding the Facilitation of Teacher Research. *Reflective Practice,* Vol. 6, No. 1, pp. 107-122.

Bloom, B.; M. Englehart; E. Furst; W. Hill & D. Krathwohl (1956). *Taxonomy of Educational Objectives: The Classification of Educational Goals, by a Committee of College and University Examiners. Handbooks 1 to 3: The Cognitive, Affective and Psychomotor Domain.* New York: Longmans Green.

Bologna Declaration (1999). *The Bologna Declaration of 19 June 1999.* http://www.bologna-berlin2003.de/pdf/bologna_declaration. pdf [Accessed 22 June 2009].

Borland, K. W. (2002). Towards a Culture of Assessment. In P. Schwarz & G. Webb (eds.) *Assessment Case Studies, Experience and Practice From Higher Education.* London: Kogan Page, pp. 97-104.

Boud, D. (1995). Assessment and Learning: Contradictory or Complementary? In P. Knight (ed.) *Assessment for Learning in Higher Education.* London: Kogan Page, pp. 35-48.

Boulton–Lewis, G. (1995). The SOLO Taxonomy as a Means of Shaping and Assessing Learning in Higher Education, *Higher Education Research and Development*, Vol. 14, No. 2, pp. 143-154.

Bourdieu, P. (1989). Towards a Reflexive Sociology: A Workshop with Pierre Bourdieu. *Sociological Theory,* Vol. 7, No. 2, pp. 26-36.

Bourdieu, P. (1991). *Language and Symbolic Power*. London: Polity Press.

Bourner, T.; R. Bowden & S. Laing (2001). Professional Doctorates in England. *Studies in Higher Education,* Vol. 26, No. 1, pp. 65-83.

Bowden, J. & F. Marton (1998). *The University of Learning: Beyond Quality and Competence in Higher Education.* London: Kogan Page.

Bowden, J. A. (1989). Curriculum Development for Conceptual Change Learning: A Phenomenographic Pedagogy. Paper presented *at the Sixth Annual Conference of the Hong Kong Educational Research Association, Hong Kong.*

Brew, A. (2001). *The Nature of Research. Inquiry into Academic Contexts.* London: Routledge.

Brookfield, S. (1995). *Becoming a Critically Reflective Teacher*. San Francisco, CA: Jossey–Bass.

Brown, D. & J. Clement (1987). *Overcoming Misconceptions in Mechanics: A Comparison of Two Example-Based Teaching Strategies*. Paper presented at the Annual Meeting of the American Educational Research Association.

Brown, D. & J. Clement (1989). Overcoming Misconceptions via Analogical Reasoning: Abstract Transfer versus Explanatory Model Construction. *Instructional Science*, Vol. 18, No. 4, pp. 237-261.

Brown, J. S. (2008). Creating a Culture of Learning (foreword). In T. Iiyoshi & M. S. V. Kumar (eds.). *Opening Up Education: The Collective Advancement of Education through Open Technology, Open Content, and Open Knowledge*, MIT Press, pp. viii-xiv.

Bruner, J. S. (1996). *The Culture of Education.* Cambridge, MA: Harvard University Press.

Brüssow, S. M. (2007). *A Learning Facilitation Framework to Enhance Academic Skills Development Among Underprepared Learners in South African Higher Education.* (Ph.d. Thesis.) Centre for Higher Education Studies, University of the Free State, Bloemfontein, South Africa.

Buelens, H.; M. Clement & G. Clarebout (2002). University assistants' conceptions of knowledge. *Learning and Instruction, Research in Education,* No. 67, pp. 44-57.

Burgess Group (2007). *Beyond the Honours Degree Classification.* London: Universities UK.

Burgess, R. (2007). *Measuring and Recording Student Achievement*: *report of the Scoping Group.* London: Universities UK & SCOP.

Byham, W. (1971). The Assessment Centre as an Aid to Management Development. *Training and Development Journal*, Vol. 25, No. 3, pp. 10-22.

Byrne, M.; B. Flood & P. Willis (2002). The Relationship between Learning Approaches and Learning Outcomes: a Study of Irish Accounting Students, *Accounting Education: an International Journal,* Vol. 11, No. 1, pp. 27-42.

Caine, R. N. & G. Caine (1991). *Making connections: Teaching and the human brain*. Alexandria, VA: Association for Supervision and Curriculum Development.

Cameron, K. S. & S. J. Freeman (1991). Cultural Congruence, Strength, and Type: Relationships to Effectiveness, *Research in Organizational Change and Development,* Vol. 5, pp. 23-58.

Campbell, S. P.; A. K. Fuller & D. A. G. Patrick (2005). Looking Beyond Research in Doctoral Education. *Frontiers in Ecology and the Environment,* Vol. 3, No. 3, pp. 153-160.

Cantwell, R. H. & J. J. Scevak (2004). Engaging University Learning: the Experiences of Students Entering University via Recognition of Prior Industrial Experience. *Higher Education Research & Development,* Vol. 23, No. 2, pp. 131-145.

Catrambone, R., & K. Holyoak (1989). Overcoming Contextual Limitations on Problem–Solving Transfer. *Journal of Experimental Psychology*, Vol. 15, No. 6, pp. 1147-1156.

Catterall, J. S. (2002). The Arts and the Transfer of Learning. In R. Deasy (ed.) *Critical Links: Learning in the Arts and Student Achievement and Social Development*, Washington, DC: AEP.

CBI & UUK (2009). *Future Fit – Preparing Graduates for the World of Work*. London: CBI & UUK.

Cerdan, R.; E. Vidal–Abarca; L. Martinez; R Gilabert & L. Gil (2009). Impact of Question–Answering Tasks on Search Processes and Reading Comprehension. *Learning and Instruction,* Vol. 19, No. 1, pp. 13-27.

Chapman K. & S. Van Auken (2001). Creating Positive Group Project Experiences: An Examination of the Role of Instructor on Student's Perceptions of Group Projects. *Journal of Marketing Education,*Vol. 23, No. 2, pp. 117-127.

Chapman, A. (2006). *Bloom's Taxonomy – Learning Domains.* http://www.businessballs.com/bloomstaxonomyoflearningdomains.htm#bloom's%20taxonomy%20overview [Accessed 25 June 2009].

Chehore, T. & Z. Scholtz (2008). Exploring a Pedagogy that Supports Problem–Based Learning in Higher Education. In C. Nygaard & C. Holtham (eds.) *Understanding Learner–Centred Higher Education*. Frederiksberg: CBS Press, pp. 145-160.

Chin, C. & D. E. Brown (2000). Learning in Science: a Comparison of Deep and Surface Approaches. *Journal of Research in Science Teaching*, Vol. 37, No. 2, pp. 109-138.

Christiansen, I. M. & L. Slammert (2006). A Multi–faceted Approach to Research Development (II): Supporting Communities of Practice. *South African Journal of Higher Education*, Vol. 20, No. 1, pp. 15-28.

Clegg, P. (2008). Creativity and Critical Thinking in the Globalised University. *Innovations in Education and Teaching International*, Vol. 45, No. 3, pp. 219-226.

Clement, J. (1987). Overcoming Students' Misconceptions in Physics: The Role of Anchoring and Analogical Validity. In J. Novak (ed.) *Proceedings of the Second International Seminar Misconceptions and Educational Strategies in Science and Mathematics*. Vol. 3. Ithaca, USA: Cornell University Press, pp. 84-97.

Clement, J. (1993). Using Bridging Analogies and Anchoring Intuitions to Deal with Students' Preconceptions in Physics. *Journal of Research in Science Teaching*, Vol. 30, No. 10, pp. 1241-1257.

Clutterbuck, D. (2003). *Learning Alliances – Tapping into Talent*. CIPD Publishing.

Cochran–Smith, M. (2000). *The Outcomes Question in Teacher Education*. AERA Vice Presidential Address for Division K (Teaching and Teacher Education), AERA Annual Meeting, April 2000. http://www2.bc.edu/~cochrans/default.html [Accessed 25 June 2009].

Colton, A. B. & G. M. Sparks–Langer (1993). A Conceptual Framework to Guide the Development of Teacher Reflection and Decision Making. *Journal of Teacher Education*, Vol. 44, No. 1, pp. 45-54.

Covey, S. (1989). *The Seven Habits of Highly Effective People* New York: Free Press.

Cowan, J.; J. George & A. Pinheiro–Torres (2004). Alignment of Developments in Higher Education. *Higher Education*. Vol. 48, No. 4, pp. 439-459.

Cranmer, S. (2006). Enhancing Graduate Employability: Best Intentions and Mixed Outcomes. *Studies in Higher Education*, Vol. 31, No. 2, pp. 169-184.

Crawford, K.; S. Gordon; J. Nichols & M. Prosser (1998). University Mathematics Students' Conceptions of Mathematics. *Studies in Higher Education*, Vol. 23, No. 1, pp. 87-94.

Crawford, M. (2001). Contextual teaching and learning: Strategies for creating constructivist classrooms. *Connections*, Vol. 11, No. 9, pp. 1-2. http://www.cord.org/uploadedfiles/Vol11No9.pdf [Accessed 25 June 2009].

Crick, R. D. (2006). *Learning Power in Practice*. London: Paul Chapman Publishing.

Crick, R. D. (2007). Effective Lifelong Learning Inventory– ELLI Online. http://www.ellionline.co.uk/ [Accessed 22 June 2009].

Cross K. P., (1998). What do we Know about Students' Learning and How do we Know it? *Research & Occasional Paper Series: CSHE.7.05*. AAHE National Conference on Higher Education.

Crossley, J.; G. Humphris & B. Jolley (2002). Assessing Health Professionals. *Medical Education,* Vol. 36, No. 9, pp. 800-804.

Crotty, M. (1998). *The Foundations of Social Research: Meaning and Perspective in the Research Process*. Thousand Oaks, CA: Sage Publications.

Curtis, R. & C. Reigeluth (1984). The Use of Analogies in Written Text. *Instructional Science*, Vol. 13, No. 2, pp. 99-117.

Dahlgren, L. & F. Marton (1978). Students' Conceptions of Subject Matter: an Aspect of Learning and Teaching in Higher Education. *Studies in Higher Education*, Vol. 3, No. 1, pp. 25-35.

Dahlgren, L. O. (1984). Outcomes of Learning. In F. Marton; D. Hounsell & N. Entwistle (eds.) *The Experience of Learning: Implications for Teaching and Studying in Higher Education*. Edinburgh: University of Edinburgh, Centre for Teaching, Learning and Assessment, pp. 19-35.

Dall'Alba, G. & R. Barnacle (2007). An Ontological Turn for Higher Education. *Studies in Higher Education,* Vol. 32, No. 6, pp. 679-691.

Dana, N. F. & D. Yendol–Hoppey (2009). *The Reflective Educator's Guide to Classroom Research. Learning to Teach and Teaching to Learn through Practitioner inquiry*. Thousand Oaks, CA: Corwin Press.

Davies, P. & J. Mangan (2007). Threshold Concepts and the Integration of Understanding in Economics. *Studies in Higher Education,* Vol. 32, No. 6, pp. 711-726.

Davis, M. (2008). Empathy. In J. Stets & J. Turner (eds.) *Handbook of Sociology of Emotions*, Springer.

De la Harpe, B.; A. Radloff & J. Wyber (2000). Quality and Generic (Professional) Skills. *Quality in Higher Education,* Vol. 6, No. 3, pp. 231-243.

De Long, J. & J. Whitehead (2006). *Researching Connections between the Systemic Influences of an Educational Leader and the Explanations of Teacher–Authors of their Educational Influences in Learning.* Paper presented at the annual conference of the Invisible College, Moscone Centre, San Francisco on April. http://www.jackwhitehead.com/aera06/jdcontinvisible06jointC.htm [Accessed 22 June 2009].

De Rosa, A. S. (2008). New Forms of International Cooperation in Doctoral Training: Internationalisation and the International Doctorate – One Goal, Two Distinct Models. *Higher Education in Europe,* Vol. 33, No. 1, pp. 3-25.

Dean, C. D., Dunaway, D., Ruble, S., & Gerhardt, C. (2002). *Implementing Problem–Based Learning in Education.* Birmingham, AL: Samford University Press.

Deasy, R. J. (ed.) (2002). *Critical Links: Learning in the Arts and Student Achievement and Social Development.* Washington, DC: AEP.

Deem, R. & K. J. Brehony (2000). Doctoral Students' Access to Research Cultures – are some more Unequal than Others? *Studies in Higher Education,* Vol. 25, No. 2, pp. 149-165.

DeFillipi, R. J. (2001). Introduction: Project–based Learning, Reflective Practices and Learning Outcomes. *Management Learning*, Vol. 32, No. 1, pp. 5-10.

Delany, D. & L. Boran (2008). *Advanced Learning and Adaptive Problem–solving Techniques: Practical Lessons from Cognitive Science.* Learning Innovations Network Conference, Athlone, Ireland, October 2008.

Dewey, J. (1909). *How We Think.* London: D. C. Heath & Company.

Dewey, J. (1938). *Experience and Education.* New York: Touchstone.

DfES (Department for Education and Skills) (2005a). *Improving Boys' Writing: Visual Texts.* http://nationalstrategies.standards.dcsf.gov.uk/downloader/219a3a 4eb84d0497d4a4b1e238fc2b05.pdf [Accessed 15 June 2009].

DfES (Department for Education and Skills) (2005b). *Skills for productivity*. Nottingham: DfES.

DfES (Department for Education and Skills) (2006). *Provision for Gifted and Talented Children in Primary Education*. http://www.standards.dfes.gov.uk/giftedandtalented/downloads/pdf /provision_g_and_t_primary.pdf [Accessed 15 June 2009].

Dickinson, D. (1993). *Why are the Arts Important?* New Horizons for Learning. http://www.newhorizons.org/strategies/arts/dickinson_why_arts.ht m [Accessed 10 June 2009].

Dimmock, C. (1999). *Designing the Learning Centered School: A cross cultural perspective*. Routledge Falmer.

Dirkx, J. M. (2006). Studying the Complicated Matter of What Works: Evidence–Based Research and the Problem of Practice. *Adult Education Quarterly,* Vol. 56, No. 4, pp. 273-290.

Domask, J. (2007). Achieving Goals in Higher Education: an Experiential Approach to Sustainability Studies. *International Journal of Sustainability in Higher Education*, Vol. 8, No. 1, pp. 53-68.

Dorman, J. P. & B. J. Fraser (2009). Psychosocial Environment and Affective Outcomes in Technology–Rich Classrooms: Testing a Causal Model. *Social Psychology of Education,* Vol.12. No. 2, pp. 77-99.

Dreisdtadt, R. (1969). The Use of Analogies and Incubation in Obtaining Insight in Creative Problem Solving. *The Journal of Psychology*, Vol. 71, March, pp. 159-175.

Driscoll, M. (2000). *Pscyhology of Learning for Instruction*. Massachusetts: Allyn & Bacon.

Driver, R.; H. Asoko; J. Leach; E. Mortimer & P. Scott (1994). Constructing Scientific Knowledge in the Classroom. *Educational Researcher,* Vol. 23, No. 7, pp. 5-12.

Duff, A. (1996). The Impact of Learning Strategies on Academic Performance in an Accounting Undergraduate Course. G. Gibbs (cd.) *Improving Student Learning: Using Research to Improve Student Learning*. Oxford: Oxford Centre for Staff Development, pp. 50-62.

Duit, R. (1991). On the Role of Analogies and Metaphors in Learning Science. *Science Education*, Vol. 75, No. 6, pp. 649-672.

Dunkin, M. J. & R. P. Precians (1992). Award–Winning University Teachers' Concepts of Teaching. *Higher Education*, Vol. 24, No. 4, pp. 483-502.

Dupin, J. & S. Joshua (1989). Analogies and "Modelling Strategies" in Teaching: Some Examples in Basic Electricity. *Science Education*, Vol. 73, No. 2, pp. 207-224.

Dweck, C. S. & E. L. Leggett (1988). A Social–Cognitive Approach to Motivation and Personality. *Psychological Review*, Vol. 95, No. 22, pp. 256-273.

Eaton, D. (2000). Cognitive and Affective Learning in Outdoor Education. *Dissertation Abstracts International – Section A: Humanities and Social Sciences,* Vol. 31, No. 10, A-3595.

Ecclestone, K. (1999). Empowering Or Ensnaring?: The Implications of Outcome–based Assessment In Higher Education. *The Higher Education Quarterly,* Vol. 53, No. 1, pp. 29-48.

Eisner, E. (2000). Ten Lessons the Arts Teach. In Spitz & Associate (eds.) *Learning and the Arts: Crossing Boundaries. Grantmakers in the Arts.* http://www.giarts.org/usr_doc/Learning.pdf [Accessed 25 June 2009]

Enders, J. & E. De Weert (2004). Science, Training and Career: Changing Modes of Knowledge Production and Labour Markets. *Higher Education Policy*, Vol. 17, No. 2, pp. 135-152.

Enders, J. (2005). Border Crossings: Research Training, Knowledge Dissemination and the Transformation of Academic Work. *Higher Education,* Vol. 49, No. 1-2, pp. 119-133.

English, L.; P. Luckett & R. Mladenovic, (2004) Encouraging a Deep Approach to Learning through Curriculum Design. *Accounting Education*, Vol. 13, No. 4, pp. 461-488.

Entwistle, N. J. & P. Ramsden (1983). *Understanding Student Learning.* London: Croom Helm.

Entwistle, N. J. & P. Walker (2000). Strategic Alertness and Expanded Awareness within Sophisticated Conceptions of Teaching. *Instructional Science*, Vol. 28, No. 5-6, pp. 335-361.

Entwistle, N. J. & Ramsden, P. (1983) *Understanding Student Learning.* London: Croom Helm.

Entwistle, N. J. (1997). Contrasting Perspectives on Learning. In F. Marton; D. Hounsell & N. Entwistle (eds.) *The Experience of Learning: Implications for Teaching and Studying in Higher Education.* Edinburgh: University of Edinburgh, Centre for Teaching, Learning and Assessment, pp. 3-22.

Entwistle, N. J. (2001). Promoting Deep Learning through Teaching and Assessment. In L. Suskie (ed.) *Assessment to Promote Deep Learning.* Insight from AAHE's 2000 and 1999 Assessment conferences USA, American Association for Higher Education.

Entwistle, N. J.; D. Skinner; D. Entwistle & S. Orr (2000). Conceptions and Beliefs About 'Good Teaching : An Integration of Contrasting Research Areas *Higher Education Research and Development*, Vol. 19, pp. 5-26.

Erskine, J. A.; M. R. Leenders; L. A. Mauffette–Leenders (1998). *Teaching with cases*. Ivey: Richard Ivey School of Business.

Ewell, P. T. (1985). Assessing Educational Outcomes. *New Directions for Institutional Research*. San Francisco, CA: Jossey–Bass.

Ewell, P. T. (2002). An Emerging Scholarship: A Brief History of Assessment. In T. W. Banta & Associates (eds.) *Building a Scholarship of Assessment*. San Francisco, CA: Jossey–Bass, pp. 3-25.

Falconer, A. S. & M. Pettigrew (2003). Developing Added Value Skills Within an Academic Programme through Work–Based Learning. *International Journal of Manpower*, Vol. 24, No. 1, pp. 48-59.

Falkhenhainer, B.; K. Forbus & D. Gentner (1989). The Structure–Mapping Engine: Algorithm and Examples. *Artificial Intelligence*, Vol. 41, Iss.1, pp. 1-63.

Felder, R. M. & R. Brent (2003). Designing and Teaching Courses to Satisfy the ABET Engineering Criteria. *Journal of Engineering Education,* Vol. 92, No 1, pp. 7-25.

Felder, R. M. & R. Brent. (2005). Understanding Student Differences. *Journal of Engineering Education*, Vol. 94, No. 1, pp. 57-72

Felder, R. M. (1992). There's Nothing Wrong With the Raw Material. *Chemical Engineering Education*, Vol. 26, No. 2, pp. 76-77.

Felder, R. M. (1995). We Never Said It would be Easy. *Chemical Engineering Education,* Vol. 29, No. 1, pp. 32-33.

Fendler, L. (2003). Teacher Reflection in a Hall of Mirrors: Historical Influences and Political Reverberations. *Educational Author,* Vol. 32. No. 3, pp. 16-25.

Ferraro, J.M. (2000). Reflective Practice and Professional Development. ERIC Digest. Clearinghouse on Teaching and Teacher Education. American Association of Colleges for Teacher Education. Washington DC. http://www.ericdigests.org/2001-3/reflective.htm [Accessed 25 June 2009].

Finkenthal, M. (2001). *Interdisciplinarity: Toward the Definition of a Metadiscipline?* New York, Peter Lang.

Fogarty, R. (ed.) (1998). *Problem–Based Learning*. Skylight Professional Development.

Foucault, M. (1972). *The Archaeology of Knowledge*. Tavistock Publications Ltd.

Fredrickson, B. L. (1998). What good are positive emotions? *Review of General Psychology,* Vol. 2, pp. 173-186.

Freeman, D. & J. C. Richards (1993). Conceptions of Teaching and the Education of Second Language Teachers. *TESOL Quarterly*, Vol. 27, No. 2, pp. 193-216.

Freire, P. (1985). *The Politics of Education*. Bergin & Gavey Publishers, Inc.

Friedman Ben–David, M. (2000). The Role of Assessment in Expanding Professional Horizons. *Medical Teacher* Vol. 22, No. 5, pp. 472-477.

Frye, R. (2007). Assessment, Accountability, and Student Learning Outcomes. Western Washington University, *Dialogue,* Issue 2. *http://www.ac.wwu.edu/~dialogue/#issue2*. [Accessed 9 June 2009].

Fulks, J. & J. Puta (2003). Learning Domains. http://research.ccc.cccd.edu/SLOs_Instruction/Writing_SLOS/Writing%20Student%20LearningOutcomes1rev.doc [Accessed 25 June 2009].

Futurelab (2006). *Mudlarking in Deptford*. Bristol, Futurelab.

Gabel, D. & K. Samuel (1986). High School Students' Ability to Solve Molarity Problems and their Analog Counterparts. *Journal of Research in Science Teaching*, Vol. 23, pp. 165-176.

Gallavara, G.; E. Hreinsson; M. Kajaste; E. Lindesjöö; C. Sølvhjelm; A. K. Sørskår & M. Sedigh Zadeh (2008). *Learning Outcomes: Common Framework – Different Approaches to Evaluating Learning Outcomes in the Nordic Countries*. European Association for Quality Assurance in Higher Education (ENQA), Occasional papers, 15.

Gardner B. & S. Korth (1998). A framework for learning to work in teams. *Journal for Education for Business*, Vol. 74, No. 1, pp. 28-33

Gardner, H. (1993). *Frames of Mind: The Theory of Multiple Intelligences*. London: Fontana.

Gatewood, R. & H. Field (1994). *Human Resource Selection*. Homewood, IL: Dryden Press.

Gentner, D. & A. Markman (1997). Structure–Mapping in Analogy and Similarity. *American Psychologist*, Vol. 52, No. 1, pp. 45-56.

Gentner, D. & D. Gentner (1983). Flowing Waters or Teeming Crowds: Mental Models of Electricity. In D. Gentner & A. Stevens

(eds.) *Mental Models*. Hillsdale, NJ: Lawrence Erlbaum
Associates.

Gentner, D. & J. Medina (1997). Comparison and the Development of
Cognition and Language. *Cognitive Studies: Bulletin of the
Japanese Cognitive Science Society*, Vol. 4, No. 1, pp. 112-149.

Gentner, D. & K. Holyoak (1997). Reasoning and Learning by
Analogy. *American Psychologist*, Vol. 52, No. 1, pp. 32-34.

Gentner, D. & R. Landers (1985). *Analogical Reminding: A Good
Match is Hard to Find*. Paper presented at the International
Conference on Systems, Man, and Cybernetics.

Gentner, D. (1977). Children's Performance on a Spatial Analogies
Task. *Child Development*, Vol. 48, pp. 1034-1039.

Gentner, D. (1980). *The Structure of Analogical Models in Science*.
Cambridge, USA: Bolt Baranek and Newman Incorporated, 1980.

Gentner, D. (1983). Structure–Mapping: A Theoretical Framework for
Analogy. *Cognitive Science*, Vol. 7, pp. 155-170.

Gibbons, M. (1998). *Higher Education Relevance in the Twenty–First
Century*. Washington DC: Education Human Development
Network World Bank.

Gibbs, G. & C. Simpson (2004). Conditions under which Assessment
Supports Students' Learning. *Learning and Teaching in Higher
Education*, Vol. 1, pp. 3-31.

Gibbs, G. (2006). Why Assessment is Changing. In C. Bryan & K.
Clegg (eds.) *Innovative Assessment in Higher Education*. p. 20.
London, Routledge.

Gick, M. & K. Holyoak (1983). Schema Introduction and Analogical
Transfer. *Cognitive Science*, Vol. 15, No. 1, pp. 1-38.

Gladstone, F. (1997). *Republican Academies*. Forest Row, Steiner
School Fellowship Publications.

Gladwell, M. (2000). *The Tipping Point*. Abacus.

Gladwell, M. (2008). *Outliers: The Story of Success,* London: Penguin
Books.

Glynn, S. (1989). The Teaching with Analogies Model: Explaining
Concepts in Expository Texts. In K. Muth (ed.) *Children's
Comprehension of Narrative and Expository Text: Research into
Practice*. Newark, USA: International Reading Association, pp.
185-204.

Glynn, S. (2004). Connect Concepts with Questions and Analogies. In
T. Koballa & D. Tippins (eds.) *Cases in Middle and Secondary
Science Education* 2nd edition. Upper Saddle River, USA: Pearson
Education, pp. 136-142.

Glynn, S. (2007). Methods and Strategies: The Teaching–With–Analogies Model. *Science and Children*, Vol. 44, No. 8, pp. 52-55.

Glynn, S.; B. Britton; M. Semrud–Clikeman & K. Muth (1989). Analogical Reasoning and Problem Solving in Science Textbooks. In J. Glover; R. Ronning & C. Reynolds (eds.) *A Handbook of Creativity: Assessment, Theory, and Research*. New York, USA: Plenum, pp. 383-398.

Glynn, S.; R. Duit & R. Thiele (1995). Teaching with Analogies: A Strategy for Constructing Knowledge. In S. Glynn & R. Duit (eds.) *Learning Science in the Schools: Research Reforming Practice*. Mahwah, USA: Erlbaum, pp. 247-273.

Goff, L.; A. Colton & G. M. Sparks–Langer (2000). Power of the Portfolio. *At Issue Teacher Quality*. National Staff Development Council JSD, pp. 44-48.

Goldstone, R. & J. Son (2005). The Transfer of Scientific Principles Using Concrete and Idealized Simulations. *The Journal of Learning Science*, Vol. 14, No. 1, pp. 69-110.

Goleman, D. (2004). *Emotional Intelligence and Working with Emotional Intelligence*. London, Bloomsbury.

Gow, L., Kember, D., & Sivan, A. (1992). Lecturers' views of their teaching practices: Implications for staff development needs. *Higher Education Research and Development,* No 11, pp. 135-149.

Graham, A. & J. Potter (2008). *Threshold Concepts: Enabling Open Dialogue on Teaching and Learning within and Across Traditional Boundaries?* NAIRTL conference, Waterford Institute of Technology, November 2008.

Graves, S. & M. Jones (2008). Enabling the journey from experienced practitioner to para–professional: using reflective dialogue in action learning triads. *Journal of Further and Higher Education,* Vol. 32, No. 4, pp. 309–319.

Gray, P. J. (2002). The Roots of Assessment Tensions, Solutions, and Research Directions. In T. W. Banta (ed.) *Buidling a Scholarship of Assessment,* San Francisco, CA: Jossey–Bass.

Green, K. (2006). No Novice Teacher Left Behind: Guiding Novice Teachers to Improve Decision–Making Through Structured Questioning. *Penn GSE Perspectives on Urban Education,* Vol. 4, No. 1, pp. 1-9.

Green, W., S. Hammer, & C. Star (2009). Facing up to the Challenge: Why is it so Hard to Develop Graduate Attributes? *Higher Education Research and Development,* Vol. 28, No. 1, pp. 17-29.

Gregan–Paxton, J.; J. Hibbard & F. Brunel (2002). So That's What That Is: Examining the Impact of Analogy on Consumer's Knowledge Development for Really New Products. *Psychology & Marketing*, Vol. 19, No. 6, pp. 533-547.

Gronn, P. (2002). Distributed Leadership. In K. Leithwood; P. Hallinger; K. Seashore–Louis; G. Furman Brown; P. Gronn; W. Mulford & K. Riled (eds.) *Second International Handbook of Educational Leadership and Administration*. Klüwer, pp. 653-696.

Gulikers, J. T. M.; L. Kester; P. A. Kirschner & T. J. Bastiaens (2006). The Effect of Practical Experience on Perceptions of Assessment Authenticity, Study Approach, and Learning Outcomes. *Learning and Instruction*, Vol. 18, No. 2, pp. 172-186.

Gunstone, R. F. (1991). Constructivism and Metacognition: Theoretical Issues and Classroom Studies. In R. Duit; F. Goldberg & H. Niedderer (eds.) *Research in Physics Learning: Theoretical Issues and Empirical Studies*. Bremen: IPN, pp. 129-40.

Haggis, T. (2003). Constructing Images of Ourselves? A Critical Investigation into 'Approaches to Learning' Research in Higher Education. *British Educational Research Journal*, Vol. 29, No. 1, pp. 89-104.

Hakel, M. (1993). *Beyond the Classroom: Implementing a Graduate Student Development Center*. Masters tutorial presented at the Eighth Annual Conference of the Society for Industrial and Organizational Psychology, San Francisco, CA.

Hall, D. L. (1987). Thinking Through Confucius. In R. Ames (ed.) *Confucius*. Albany, USA: SUNY Press.

Hall, M.; A. Ramsay & J. Raven (2004). Changing the Learning Environment to Promote Deep Learning Approaches in First–Year Accounting Students. *Accounting Education: An International Journal*, Vol.13, No. 4, pp. 489–505.

Harden, R. M. (2001). AMEE Guide No. 21: Curriculum Mapping: a Tool for Transparent and Authentic Teaching and Learning. *Medical Teacher*, Vol. 23, No. 2, pp. 123-137.

Hargreaves, A. & D. Fisk (2003). *The Seven Principles of Sustainable Leadership*. Available online at: http://www2.bc.edu/~hargrean/docs/seven_principles.pdf [Accessed 15 June 2009].

Harris, S. (2005). Rethinking Academic Identities in Neo–Liberal Times. *Teaching in Higher Education*, Vol. 10, No. 4, pp. 421-433.

Harvey, L & D. Green (1994). Employee Satisfaction Summary. Birmingham: Quality in Higher Education Project.

Harvey, L. & P. T. Knight (1996). *Transforming Higher Education.* Buckingham: SRHE, Open University Press.

Harvey, L.; S. Drew & M. Smith (2006). *The First–Year Experience: a Review of Literature for the Higher Education Academy.* http://www.heacademy.ac.uk/assets/York/documents/ourwork/rese arch/literature_reviews/first_year_experience_full_report.pdf [Accessed 22 June 2009].

Harvey, L; A. Burrows & D. Green (1992), *Someone who can Make an Impression: Report of the QHE Employers' Survey of Qualities of Higher Education Graduates.* Birmingham: QHE, The University of Central England in Birmingham.

Hatcher, J. A. & R. Bringle (1997). Reflection: Bridging the Gap between Service and Learning. *College Teaching*, Vol. 45, No. 4, pp. 153-158.

Hatton, N. & D. Smith (1994). *Reflection in Teacher Education: Towards Definition and Implementation.* School of Teaching and Curriculum Studies. The University of Sydney. http://alex.edfac.usyd.edu.au/LocalResource/originals/hattonart.rtf [Accessed 21 June 2009].

Hayes, D. & R. Tierney (1982). Developing Readers' Knowledge Through Analogy. *Reading Research Quarterly*, Vol. 17, No. 2, pp. 256-280.

Hayes, D. & R. Wynward (eds.) (2002). *The McDonaldization of Higher Education.* Santa Barbara, CA: Greenwood Press.

Hayes, J. R. & H. A. Simon (1977). Psychological Differences among Problem Isomorphs. In N. J. Casellan, Jr., D. B. Pisone & G. R. Potts (eds.) *Cognitive Theory,* pp. 21-41, Hillsdale, NJ: Lawrence Erlbaum Associates.

Hedberg, P. R. (2009). Learning through Reflective Classroom Practice. *Journal of Management Education*, Vol. 33, No. 1, pp. 10-36.

Heidegger, M. (1962). *Being and Time.* New York, Harper and Row.

Henkel, M. (2004). Current Science Policies and their Implications for the Formation and Maintenance of Academic Identity. *Higher Education Policy*, Vol. 17, pp. 167-182.

Henkel, M. (2005). Academic Identity and Autonomy in a Changing Policy Environment. *Higher Education,* Vol. 49, pp. 155-176.

Hernon P. & R. E. Dugan (2003). Student Learning Assessment: Options and Resources. Middle States Commission on Higher

Education. *Library and Information Science Research*, Vol. 25, No. 3, pp. 355-357.

Herrmann, F. (1989), *Physik, Unterrichtshilfen*. Teil 1, Auflage November 1989. Karlsruhe: Institut für Didaktik der Physik der Universität Karlsruhe, pp. 6-13 and pp. 54-58.

Hettich, P. (1997) Epistemological Approaches to Cognitive Development in College Students. In P. Sutherland (ed.) *Adult Learning: A Reader*. London: Kogan Page.

Hewson, P. W. (1996). Teaching for Conceptual Change. In D. F. Treagust; R. Duit & B. J. Fraser (eds.) *Improving Teaching and Learning in Science and Mathematics* New York: Teachers College Press, pp. 131–140.

Higher Education Academy (2009). Personal Development Planning. http://www.heacademy.ac.uk/ourwork/learning/pdp [Accessed 25 June 2009]

Ho, A. S. P. (1998). A Conceptual Change Staff Development Programme: Effects as Perceived by Participants. *International Journal for Academic Development,* Vol. 3, No. 1, pp. 24-38.

Ho, A., D. Watkins & Kelly (2001). The Conceptual Change Approach to Improving Teaching and Learning: An Evaluation of a Hong Kong Staff Development Programme. *Higher Education*, Vol. 42, pp. 143-169.

Hodgeson, V. (1997) Lectures and the Experience of Relevance. In F. Marton; D. Hounsell & N. Entwistle (eds.) *The Experience of Learning: Implications for Teaching and Studying in Higher Education*. Edinburgh: University of Edinburgh, Centre for Teaching, Learning and Assessment.

Hofer, B. K. & P. R. Pintrich (1997). The Development of Epistemological Theories: Beliefs about Knowledge and Knowing and their Relation to Learning. *Review of Educational Research*, Vol. 67, No. 1, pp. 88-140.

Hofer, B. K. (2001). Personal Epistemology Research: Implications for Learning and Teaching. *Journal of Educational Psychology Review*, Vol. 13, No. 4, pp. 353-382.

Hoffman–Kipp, P.; A. J. Artiles & L. López–Torres (2003). Beyond Reflection: Teacher Learning as Praxis. *Theory into Practice,* Vol. 42, No. 3, pp. 248-254.

Holtham, C. & N. Courtney (2008). Interlacing Teaching and Learning Strategy in Business Education. In C. Nygaard & C. Holtham (eds.) *Understanding Learning–Centred Higher Education*, Frederiksberg: CBS Press, pp. 301-324.

Holyoak, K. & K. Koh (1987). Surface and Structural Similarity in Analogical Transfer. *Memory & Cognition*, Vol. 15, No. 4, pp. 332-340.

Hounsell, D. (1997) Understanding Teaching and Teaching for Understanding. In F. Marton, D. Hounsell & N. Entwistle (eds.) *The Experience of Learning: Implications for Teaching and Studying in Higher Education.* Edinburgh: University of Edinburgh, Centre for Teaching, Learning and Assessment.

Huet, I.; J. M. Oliveira; C. Nilza; J. Estima de Oliveira (2008). *The Effectiveness of Alignment Matrices in Curriculum Design.* Paper presented at: Bologna Seminar on Development of a common understanding of Learning Outcomes and ECTS, Porto, Portugal.

Huitt, W. (2001). Krathwohl et al.'s Taxonomy of the Affective Domain. *Educational Psychology Interactive.* Valdosta, GA: Valdosta State University: http://chiron.valdosta.edu/whuitt/col/affsys/affdom.html [Accessed 25 June 2009].

Hunter, J. & R. Hunter (1984). Validity and Utility of Alternative Predictors of Job Performance. *Psychological Bulletin*, Vol. 96, No. 1, pp. 72-98.

Hussey, T. & P. Smith (2002). The Trouble with Learning Outcomes. *Active Learning in Higher Education,* Vol. 3, No. 3, pp. 220-223.

Hussey, T. & P. Smith (2003). The Uses of Learning Outcomes. *Teaching in Higher Education.* Vol. 8, No. 3, pp. 357-368.

Illeris, K. (2009). Transfer of Learning in the Learning Society: How can the Barriers between Different Learning Spaces be Surmounted, and How Can the Gap between Learning Inside and Outside Schools be Bridged? *International Journal of Lifelong Education*, Vol. 28, No. 2, pp. 137-148.

Isaac, G. (1996). Bloom's Taxonomy of Educational Objectives http://www.tedi.uq.edu.au/downloads/Bloom.pdf [Accessed 25 June 2009].

Jackling, B. (2005). Perceptions of the Learning Context and Learning Approaches: Implications for Quality Learning Outcomes in Accounting. *Accounting Education,* Vol. 14, No. 3 pp. 271-291

Jacobs, H. H. (1997). *Mapping the Big Picture: Integrating Curriculum and Assessment K–12.* Alexandria, VA: Association for Supervision and Curriculum Development.

James, B.; G. Lefoe & M. Hadi (2004). Working through Graduate Attributes: A Bottom–up Approach. In F. Sheehy & B. Stauble (eds.) *Transforming Knowledge into Wisdom: Holistic Approaches to Teaching and Learning.* Higher Education Research and Development Society of Australasia HERDSA Conference, Miri, Sarawak, pp. 174-184.

Jankowska, M. & M. T. Atlay (2008). Use of Creative Space in Enhancing Students' Engagement. *Innovations in Education and Teaching International,* Vol. 45, No. 3, pp. 271-279.

Jarvis, P.; J. Holford & C. Griffin (1998). *The Theory and Practice of Learning.* London: Kogan Page.

Jawitz, J. (2007). New Academics Negotiating Communities of Practice: Learning to Swim with the Big Fish. *Teaching in Higher Education,* Vol. 12, No. 2, pp. 185-197.

JISC (2008). *Effective Practice with e–Portfolios: Supporting 21st century learning.* University of Bristol, JISC.

Johnson D. & D. Johnson (1989). Social Skills for Successful Group Work. *Educational Leadership,* Vol. 47, No. 4, pp. 29-33.

Johnson, B. (2006). South African Academia in Crisis: The Spread of "Contrived Collegial Managerialism". *South African Journal of Higher Education,* Vol. 20, No. 1, pp. 56-69.

Jonassen, D.; T. Prevish; D. Christy & E. Stavrulaki (1999). Learning to Solve Problems on the Web: Aggregate Planning in a Business Management Course. *Distance Education,* Vol. 20, No. 1, pp. 49-63.

Jordan, A.; O. Carlile & A. Stack (2008). *Approaches to Learning: A Guide for Teachers.* London: Open University Press McGraw–Hill Education.

Kamler, B. (2008). Rethinking Doctoral Publication Practices: Writing from and Beyond the Thesis. *Studies in Higher Education,* Vol. 33, No. 3, pp. 283-294.

Kaper, W. & M. Goedhart (2003). *A Three–Phase Design for Productive Use of Analogy.* Amsterdam, Netherlands: AMSTEL Instituut.

Karns, G. (2005). An Update of Marketing Student Perceptions of Learning Activities: Structure, Preferences and Effectiveness. *Journal of Marketing Education,* Vol. 27, No. 2, pp. 163-171.

Kember, D & K. P. Kwan (2000). Lecturers' Approaches to Their Teaching and Their Relationship to Conceptions of Good Teaching. *Instructional Science,* Vol. 28, No. 5-6, pp. 469-490.

Kember, D. & D. Y. P. Leung (2005). The Influence of Active Learning Experiences on the Development of Graduate Capabilities. *Studies in Higher Education,* Vol. 30, No. 2, pp. 155-170.

Kemp, D. (1999). *New Knowledge New Opportunities: A discussion paper on higher education research and research training.* http://www.dest.gov.au/archive/highered/otherpub/greenpaper/index.htm [Accessed 23 June 2009].

Kennedy, D. (2007). *Writing and Using Learning Outcomes: a Practical Guide.* Cork: UCC, Quality Promotion Unit.

Keppell, M. J. (2007). Instructional Designers on the Borderline: Brokering Across Communities of Practice. In M. J. Keppell (ed.) *Instructional Design: Case Studies in Communities of Practice,* Hershey: IGI Global, pp. 68-89.

Kezar, A. & P. D. Eckel (2002). The Effect of Institutional Culture on Change Strategies in Higher Education. *The Journal of Higher Education,* Vol. 73, No. 4, pp. 435-460.

Kift, S. (2002). Harnessing Assessment and Feedback to Assure Quality Outcomes for Graduate Capability Development: A Legal Education Case Study. *Curriculum review for generic competency:* Faculty of Law. http://eprints.qut.edu.au/7474/ [Accessed 15 June 2009].

Killen, R. (2003). Validity in Outcomes–Based Assessment. *Perspectives in Education,* Vol. 21, No. 1, pp. 1-14.

King, P. M. & K. S. Kitchener (1994). *Developing Reflective Judgment: Understanding and Promoting Intellectual Growth and Critical Thinking in Adolescents and Adults.* San Francisco, CA: Jossey–Bass.

Kirschner, P.; J. Sweller & R. Clark (2006). Why Minimal Guidance During Instruction Does Not Work: An Analysis of the Failure of Constructivist, Discovery, Problem–Based, Experiential and Inquiry–Based Teaching. *Educational Psychologist,* Vol. 41, No. 2, pp. 75-86.

Knefelkamp, L. (1999). Introduction. In W. G. Perry (ed.) *Forms of Intellectual and Ethical Development in the College Years: A Scheme.* San Francisco, Jossey–Bass, pp. xi-xxxviii.

Knight W. E.; M. D. Hakel & M. Gromko (2008). The Relationship Between Electronic Portfolio Participation and Student Success. *AIR Professional File,* number 107.

Knight, P. & M. Yorke (2004). *Learning, Curriculum and Employability in Higher Education.* London: Routledge Falmer.

Koballa, T. (2007). *Affective Domain and Key Issues.* Paper presented at the Workshop on Student Motivations and Attitudes: The Role of the Affective Domain in Geoscience Learning.

http://serc.carleton.edu/files/NAGTWorkshops/affective/workshop 07/koballa.ppt [Accessed 25 June 2009].

Kockelmans, J. J. (1979). Why Interdisciplinarity? In J. J. Kockelmans (ed.) *Interdisciplinarity and Higher Education.* University Park, Pennsylvania State University Press, 1979, pp. 123-160.

Kolb, D. A. (1984) Experiential Learning: Experience as the Source of Learning and Development New Jersey: Prentice–Hall.

Kolb. A. Y. & D. A. Kolb (2005). *Learning Styles and Learning Spaces: Enhancing Experiential Learning in Higher Education.* Academy of Management Learning and Education. http://www.learningfromexperience.com/images/uploads/Learning -styles-and-learning-spaces.pdf [Accessed 15 June 2009].

Korey. J. (2002a). The Calculus Trap, *PRIMUS: Problems, Resources and Issues in Mathematics Undergraduate Education*, United States Military Academy West Point, NY, USA, Vol. XII, Issue 3, 2002, pp. 209-218

Korey. J. (2002b). Successful Interdisciplinary Teaching: Making One Plus One Equal One, *Proceedings of the international Conference on the Teaching of Mathematics (at the Undergraduate Level),* Hallett, D. H. & C. Tzanakis, (ed.) Hersonissos, Crete, Greece.

Korthagen, F. & A. Vasalos (2005). Levels in Reflection: Core Reflection as a Means to Enhance Professional Growth. *Teachers and Teaching: Theory and Practice,* Vol. 11, No. 1, pp. 47-71.

Kottke, J. & K. Shultz (1997). Using an Assessment Center as a Developmental Tool for Graduate Students: A Demonstration. *Journal of Social Behavior and Personality*, Vol. 12, No. 5, pp. 289-302.

Krathwohl, D. R.; B. S. Bloom & B. B. Masia (1964). *Taxonomy of educational objectives, Book II. Affective domain.* New York, NY: David McKay Company, Inc.

Krawczyk, D.; K. Holyoak & J. Hummel (2005). The One–to–One Constraint in Analogical Mapping and Inference. *Cognitive Science: A Multidisciplinary Journa*l, Vol. 29, No. 5, pp. 797-806.

Kuh, G. D. (2006). *Student Success in College, Promoting Student Success: What Campus Leaders Can Do.* The 2006 Assessment Institute in Indianapolis. Presented by the Office of Planning and Institutional Improvement at Indiana University Purdue University Indianapolis, October 29-31, 2006.

Kuit, J. A.; G. Reay & R. Freeman (2001). Experiences of Reflective Teaching. *Active Learning in Higher Education,* Vol. 2, No. 2, pp. 128-142.

Kumar, A. (2007). *Personal, Academic and Career Development in Higher Education – SOARing to Success*. London & New York: Routledge Taylor & Francis. Companion website URL http://www.routledge.com/professional/978041542360-1/ [Accessed 12 June 09].

Kumar, A. (2008). *Personal, Academic & Career Development in Higher Education*. London: Routledge.

Kutnick, P.; P. Blatchford & E. Baines (2005). Grouping of Pupils in Secondary School Classrooms: Possible Links between Pedagogy and Learning. *Social Psychology of Education*, Vol. 8, No. 4, pp. 349-374.

Lakoff, G. & M. Johnson (1980) *Metaphors We Live By*. Chicago, Il: University of Chicago Press.

Lampert, M., & Ball, D. (1999). Aligning teacher education with contemporary K–12 reform visions. In L. Darling–Hammond & G. Sykes (eds.), *Teaching as the learning professions: Handbook of policy and practice* (pp. 33-53). San Francisco, CA: Jossey–Bass.

Landy, F. & J. Conte (2007). *Work in the 21st Century: An Introduction to Industrial and Organizational Psychology*. Wiley–Blackwell

Lattuca, L. R. (2001). *Creating Interdisciplinarity: Interdisciplinary Research and Teaching Among College and University Faculty*. Nashville, TN: Vanderbilt University Press.

Lave, J. & E. Wenger (1991). *Situated Learning: Legitimate Peripheral Participation*. Cambridge: Cambridge University Press.

Le Grange, M. J.; E. S. G. Greyling & J. C. Kok (2006). The Training and Development of Lecturers within the Framework of the Relevant Acts on Higher Education. *South African Journal of Higher Education,* Vol. 20, No. 1, pp. 70-86.

Leamnson, R. (2002). *Learning (Your First Job)*. http://users.rowan.edu/~cleary/Freshman/Learning_Your_First_Job.pdf [Accessed 25 June 2008].

Leder, G. C. & J. J. Forgasz (2006). Affect and Mathematics education. In A. Gutierez & P. Boelo (2006). *Handbook of Research in the Psychology of Mathematics Education: Past, Present and Future*. Sense Publishers

Lee, A. & B. Kamler (2008). Bringing Pedagogy to Doctoral Publishing. *Teaching in Higher Education,* Vol. 13, No. 5, pp. 511-523.

Lee, A. (2008). How are Doctoral Students Supervised? Concepts of Doctoral Research Supervision. *Studies in Higher Education,* Vol. 33, No. 3, pp. 267-281.

Lee, A.; B. Green & M. Brennan (2000). Organisational Knowledge, Professional Practice, and the Professional Doctorate at Work. In Garrick, J. & C. Rhodes (eds.) *Research and Knowledge at Work.* London: Routledge.

Leinster, S. (2002), Medical Education and the Changing Face of Healthcare Delivery. *Medical Teacher,* Vol. 24, No. 1, pp. 13-15.

Leitch, S. (2006). *Leitch Review of Skills: prosperity for all in the global economy – world class skills.* Norwich: HMSO.

Lemke, J. (1988). Genres, Semantics and Classroom Education. *Linguistics and Education,* Vol. 1, No. 1, pp. 81-99.

Leonard, D.; R. Becker & K. Coate (2005). To Prove Myself at the Highest Level: The Benefits of Doctoral Study. *Higher Education Research and Development,* Vol. 24, No. 2, pp. 135-149.

Lester, S. (2004). Conceptualizing the Practitioner Doctorate. *Studies in Higher Education,* Vol. 29, No. 6, pp. 757-770.

Levin, B. (2000). Putting Students at the Centre in Education Reform. *Journal of Educational Change,* Vol. 1, No. 2, pp. 155-172.

Levitin, D. J. (2006). *This Is Your Brain on Music: The Science of a Human Obsession.* New York: Dutton.

Lim, M. (2007). *Analogical Learning Process: Sequence and Connection.* New York: Columbia University Teachers College.

Lin, L. & P. Cranton (2005). From Scholarship Student to Responsible Scholar: a Transformative Process. *Teaching in Higher Education,* Vol. 10, No. 4, pp. 447-459.

Lizzio, A. & K. Wilson (2004). Action Learning in Higher Education: an Investigation of its Potential to Develop Professional Capability. *Studies in Higher Education,* Vol. 29, No. 4, pp. 469-488.

Lizzio, A. (2002). University Students' Perceptions of the Learning Environment and Academic Outcomes: Implications for Theory and Practice. *Studies in Higher Education,* Vol. 27, No. 1, pp. 27-52.

Loewenstein, J.; L. Thompson & D. Gentner (2003). Analogical Learning in Negotiation Teams: Comparing Cases Promotes Learning and Transfer. *Academy of Management Learning and Education,* Vol. 2, No. 2, pp. 119-127.

Loughran, J. J. (2002). Effective Reflective Practice: in Search of Meaning in Learning about Teaching. *Journal of Teacher Education*, Vol. 53, No. 1, pp. 33-43.

Lovell, N.; L. Crittenden; D. Stumpf & M. Davis (2003). The Road Less Travelled: A Typical Doctoral Preparation of Leaders in Rural Community Colleges. *Community College Journal of Research and Practice,* Vol. 27, No. 1, pp. 1-14.

Lovitts, B. E. (2005). Being a Good Course–Taker is not Enough: a Theoretical Perspective on the Transition to Independent Research. *Studies in Higher Education,* Vol. 30, No. 2, pp. 137-154.

Lovitts, B. E. (2007). *Making the Implicit Explicit. Creating Performance Expectations for the Dissertation.* Sterling: Stylus.

Lovitts, B. E. (2008). The Transition to Independent Research: Who Makes, Who doesn't and Why. *The Journal of Higher Education,* Vol. 79, No. 3, pp. 296-325.

Lowe, H. & A. Cook (2003). Mind the Gap: are Students Prepared for Higher Education? *Journal of Further and Higher Education*, Vol. 27, No. 1, pp. 53-76.

Lucas, U. & Meyer, J. H. F. (2003a). *Understanding Students' Conceptions of Learning and Subject in 'Introductory' Courses: the Case of Introductory Accounting.* Study presented at the Symposium Meta learning in higher education: taking account of the student perspective (Padova, August: European Association for Research on Learning and instruction, 10th Biennial Conference).

Lucas, U. (2000). Worlds Apart: Students' Experiences of Learning Introductory Accounting. *Critical Perspectives on Accounting,* Vol. 11, No. 4, pp. 479-504.

Lugg, A. (2006). *Sustainability Education in Higher Education Curricula: Possibilities and Issues for Outdoor Experiential Pedagogy.* Proceedings of the 3rd International Educational Research Conference. UCLAN, Penrith, 4-7 July 2006.

Lugg, A. (2007). Developing Sustainability–Literate Citizens through Outdoor Learning: Possibilities for Outdoor Education in Higher Education. *Journal of Adventure Education and Outdoor Learning,* Vol. 2, No. 2, pp. 97-112.

Madill, G. & S. F. de Azevedo (2008). Final Report and Recommendations of the Bologna Seminar on 'Development of a Common Understanding of Learning Outcomes and ECTS' Porto, Portugal.
http://portobologna.up.pt/documents/BS_P_Report_20080915_FI NAL.pdf [Accessed 23 June 2009].

Magee, B. (1998). *The Story of Philosophy*. London: Dorling Kindersley.

Maher, A. (2004). Learning Outcomes in Higher Education: Implications for Curriculum Design and Student Learning. *Journal of Hospitality, Sport and Tourism Education*, Vol. 3, No. 2, pp. 46-54.

Maher, D.; L. Seaton; C. McMullen; T. Fitzgerald; E. Otsuji & A. Lee (2008). Becoming and Being Writers: the Experiences of Doctoral Students in Writing Groups. *Studies in Continuing Education,* Vol. 30, No. 3, pp. 263-275.

Maheu, L. (2008). Doctoral Education and the Workings of Canadian Graduate Schools: a Differentiated Tier within Canadian Universities Facing the Challenges of Tension–Driven Functions. *Higher Education in Europe,* Vol. 33, No. 1, pp. 93-110.

Manathunga, C.; P. Lant & G. Mellick (2006). Imagining an Interdisciplinary Doctoral Pedagogy. *Teaching in Higher Education*, Vol. 11, No. 3, pp. 365-379.

Markman, A. & D. Gentner (1997). The Effects of Alignability on Memory. *Psychological Science*, Vol. 8, No. 5, pp. 363-367.

Markman, A. & D. Gentner (2000). Structure Mapping in the Comparison Process. *The American Journal of Psychology*, Vol. 113, No. 4, pp. 501-538.

Markman, A. (1997). Constraints on Analogical Inference. *Cognitive Science*, Vol. 21, No. 4, pp. 373-418.

Marsh, C.; K. Richards & P. Smith (2001). Autonomous Learners and the Learning Society: Systematic Perspectives on the Practice of Teaching in Higher Education. *Educational Philosophy and Theory,* Vol. 33, No. 3-4, pp. 381-395.

Martin, B. L. & C. M. Reigeluth (1999). Affective Education and the Affective Domain: Implications for Instructional–Design Theories and Models. In C. M. Reigeluth (ed.) *Instructional–design theories and models: A new paradigm of instructional theory. Volume II.* London: Lawrence Erlbaum Associates, pp. 485-509.

Martin, E.; M. Prosser; K. Trigwell; P. Ramsden & J. Benjamin, (2000). What University Teachers Teach and How They Teach it. *Instructional Science*, Vol. 28, No. 5, pp. 387-412.

Martin, M. (2006). The Cognitive and Affective Outcomes of a Cultural Diversity in Business Course in Higher Education. Unpublished Dissertation, University of Missouri–Columbia.

Martocchio, J. J. & E. J. Hertentein (2003). Learning Orientation and Goal Orientation Context: Relationships with Cognitive and

Affective Learning Outcomes. *Human Resource Development Quarterly*, Vol. 14. No. 4, pp. 413-434.

Marton, F. & R. Säljö (1976a). On Qualitative Differences in Learning I: Outcome and Process. *British Journal of Educational Psychology,* Vol. 46, No. 1, pp. 4-11.

Marton, F. & R. Säljö (1976b). On Qualitative Differences in Learning II: Outcome as a Function of the Learner's Conception of the Task. *British Journal of Educational Psychology*, Vol. 46, No. 1, pp. 115-127.

Marton, F. & R. Säljö (1984). Approaches to Learning. In F. Marton; D. Hounsell & N. Entwistle (eds.) *The Experience of Learning: Implications for Teaching and Studying in Higher Education.* Edinburgh: University of Edinburgh, Centre for Teaching, Learning and Assessment, pp. 36-55.

Marton, F. & R. Säljö (1997). Approaches to Learning. In F. Marton; D. J. Hounsell & N. J. Entwistle (eds.) *The Experience of Learning.* Edinburgh: Scottish Academic Press , 2nd edition, pp. 39-58.

Marton, F. & Ramsden, P. (1988) What Does it Take to Improve Learning? In F. Marton, D. Hounsell, & N. Entwistle (eds.) *The Experience of Learning: Implications for Teaching and Studying in Higher Education.* Edinburgh: University of Edinburgh, Centre for Teaching, Learning and Assessment.

Marton, F. & S. Booth (1997). *Learning and Awareness.* Mahwah, NJ: Lawrence Erlbaum.

Marton, F.; G. Dall'Alba & E. Beaty. (1993). Conceptions of Learning. *International Journal of Educational Research,* Vol. 19, No. 3, pp. 277-300.

Mauffette–Leenders, L. A.; J. A. Erskine; M. R. Leenders (1997). *Learning with cases.* Ivey: Richard Ivey School of Business.

Max–Neef, M. A. (2005). Foundations of Transdisciplinarity. *Ecological Economics,* Vol. 53, No. 1, pp. 5-16.

McAlpine, L. & C. Weston (2000). Reflection: Issues Related to Improving Professors' Teaching and Students' Learning. *Instructional Science*, Vol. 28, No. 5-6, pp. 363-385.

McAlpine, L. & J. Norton (2006). Reframing our Approach to Doctoral Programs: an Integrative Framework for Action and Research. *Higher Education Research and Development,* Vol. 25, No. 1, pp. 3-17.

McCarthy, M. (2009). Teaching for Understanding: What has it to Offer in the Context of SoTL? *EDIN Symposium*, University of Limerick February 2009.

McClenney, K. (2003). The Learning–Centered Institution: Key Characteristics. *Inquiry & Action*, Spring 2003, No. 1, American Association for Higher Education: Washington, DC., pp. 5-6.

McClintock, R. (2007). Educational Research. *Teachers College Record Online*, March 28, 2007. http://studyplace.ccnmtl.columbia.edu/files/McClintock/2007-Educational-Research-McClintock.pdf [Accessed 20 June 2009].

McCormack, C. (2004). Tensions Between Student and Institutional Conceptions of Postgraduate Research. *Studies in Higher Education,* Vol. 29, No. 3, pp. 320-334.

McMahon, M. & C. Ojeda (2008). A Model of Immersion to Guide the Design of Serious Games. In G. Richards (ed.) *Proceedings of World Conference on E–Learning in Corporate, Government, Healthcare, and Higher Education 2008*. Chesapeake, VA: AACE, pp. 1833-1842.

McMahon, M.; W. Patton & P. Tatham (2003). *Managing Life, Learning and Work in the 21st Century*. Perth: Miles Morgan Australia.

Meier, F. & C. Nygaard (2008). Problem Oriented Project Work in Higher Education. In C. Nygaard & C. Holtham (eds.) *Understanding Learnimg–Centred Higher Education*. Frederiksberg: CBS Press, pp. 131-144.

Mercer. N. & K. Litteton (2007). *Dialogue and the Development of Children's Thinking*. London: Routledge.

Meyer, J. & R. Land (2005). Threshold Concepts and Troublesome Knowledge (2): Epistemological Considerations and a Conceptual Framework for Teaching and Learning. *Higher Education,* Vol. 49, No. 3, pp. 373-388.

Meyer, J. H. F. & M. W. Muller (1990). Evaluating the Quality of Student Learning. I – An Unfolding Analysis of the Association between Perceptions of Learning Context and Approaches to Studying at an Individual level. *Studies in Higher Education*, Vol. 15, No. 2, pp. 131-154.

Meyer, J. H. F. & R. Land (2003). Threshold Concepts and Troublesome Knowledge: Linkages to Ways of Thinking and Practicing within the Disciplines. In C. Rust (ed.) *Improving Student Learning Theory – Ten Years On*. Oxford: OCSLD, pp. 412-424.

Mezirow, J. (1997). Transformative Learning: from Theory to Practice. *New directions for Adult and Continuing Education*, No. 74, pp. 5-12.

Miclea, M. (2008). Doctoral Studies in Romania: Admission Procedures, Social, and Legal Aspects of Doctoral Training. *Higher Education in Europe*, Vol. 33, No. 1, pp. 89-92.

Mintzberg, H. (2004). *Managers Not MBAs A Hard Look at the Soft Practice of Managing and Management Development*. San Francisco: Barrett–Koehler Publishers, Inc.

Mishra, P. & M. J. Koehler (2006). Technological Pedagogical Content Knowledge: A Framework for Teacher Knowledge. *Teachers College Record*, Vol. 108, No. 6, pp. 1017-1054.

Mooney, L. & B. Edwards (2001). Experiential Learning in Sociology: Service Learning and Other Community–Based Learning Initiatives. *Teaching Sociology*, Vol. 29, No. 2, pp. 181-194.

Moore, W. S. (1989). The "Learning Environment Preferences": Exploring the Construct Validity of an Objective Measure of the Perry Scheme of Intellectual Development. *Journal of College Student Development*, Vol. 30, pp. 504-514.

Moore, W. S. (1991). *The Perry Scheme of Intellectual and Ethical Development: An Introduction to the Model and Major Assessment Approaches*. Paper presented at The American Educational Research Association, Chicago, Il.

Morgan, A.; E. Taylor & G. Gibbs (1980). *Students' Approaches to Studying the Social Science and Technology Foundation Courses: Preliminary studies*. Study Methods Group Report No. 4). Milton Keynes: Open University.

Mullin, A. J. (1998). Portfolios: Purposeful Collections of Student Collections of Student Work. *New Directions for Teaching and Learning*, Vol. 74, Summer, pp. 79-87.

National College for School Leadership (2003). *Distributed Leadership. Full Report.* http://www.ncsl.org.uk/mediastore/image2/bennett-distributed-leadership-full.pdf [Accessed 25 June 2009].

National Science Foundation (1996). *Shaping the Future:New Expectation for Undergraduate Education in Science, Mathematics, Engineering, and Technology*. Arlington, VA: NSF (NSF96-139).

Nelson, P. & P. Holdren (1995). *Promoting Democracy and Inclusion through Outcome–Based Teacher Education*. Paper presented at the Annual Meeting of the Association of Independent Liberal Arts Colleges for Teacher Education, Washington, DC, February 1995.

Neumann, R. (2005). Doctoral Differences: Professional Doctorates and PhDs Compared. *Journal of Higher Education Policy and Management,* Vol. 27, No. 2, pp. 173-188.

New Zealand Qualifications Authority (2001). *National Qualifications Framework.* Wellington, New Zealand Qualifications Authority.

Newble, D. J. & N. J. Entwistle (1986). Learning Analysis and Approaches: Implications for Medical Education. *Medical Education,* No 20, pp. 162-175.

Nicol, D. & D. Macfarlane–Dick (2006). Formative Assessment and Self–Regulated Learning: a Model and Seven Principles of Good Feedback Practice. *Studies in Higher Education,* Vol. 31, No. 2, pp. 199-218.

Nicol, R. (2004). Creating Sustainable Communities through Education. *Report of the International Forum of Experiential Environmental Educators.* Based on activities of the World School Network, Japan, Ecoplus, pp. 14-22.

Nissani, M. (1997). Ten Cheers for Interdisciplinarity: The Case for Interdisciplinary Knowledge and Research, *Social Science Journal,* Vol. 34, No. 2, pp. 201-216.

Noddings, N. (2007). *Philosophy of Education.* Westview Press.

NSF (National Science Foundation) (1995). *http://www.nsf.gov/pubs/stis1995/nsf9610/nsf9610.txt* [Accessed 23 June 2009].

Nygaard, C & P. Bramming (2008). Learning–Centred Public Management Education. *International Journal of Strategic Public Management,* Vol. 21, No. 4, pp. 400-417.

Nygaard, C. & C. Holtham (2008). The Need for Learning–Centred Higher Education. In C. Nygaard (*et al.*) (eds.). *Understanding Learning Centred Higher Education.* Frederiksberg, CBS Press, pp. 11-29.

Nygaard, C. & I. Andersen (2005). Contextual Learning in Higher Education. In Milter, R. (eds.) *Educational Innovation in Economics and Business IX. Breaking Boundaries for Global Learning.* Springer Verlag.

Nygaard, C.; T. Højlt & M. Hermansen (2008): Learning–Based Curriculum Development. *Higher Education,* Vol. 55, No. 1, pp. 33-50.

Nygaard, Claus & C. Holtham (eds.) (2008). *Understanding Learning–Centred Higher Education.* Frederiksberg: CBS Press.

Oliveira J. M. (2006). Project Based Learning in Engineering: The Águeda Experience. In Graaff, E. & A. Kolmos (eds.) *Management of Change – Implementation of Problem–Based and Project–Based Learning in Engineering,* Rotterdam/Taipei, Sense Publishers, pp. 169-180.

Olsen, P. B. & K. Pedersen (2003). *Problemorienteret projektarbejde – en værktøjsbog.* Frederiksberg: Roskilde Universitetsforlag.

Orgill, M. & M. Thomas (2007). Analogies and the 5E Model. *The Science Teacher,* Vol. 74, No. 1, pp. 40-45.

Palomba, C. A. (2002). Scholarly Assessment of Student Learning in the Major and General Education. In T. W. Banta & Associates (eds.), *Building a Scholarship of Assessment.* San Francisco, CA: Jossey–Bass, pp. 201-222.

Paris, N. & S. Glynn (2004). Elaborate Analogies in Science Text: Tools for Enhancing Preservice Teachers' Knowledge and Attitudes. *Contemporary Educational Psychology,* Vol. 29, No. 3, pp. 230-247.

Park, C. (2007). *Redefining the Doctorate.* Heslington: The Higher Education Academy.

Parker, S. (1997). *Reflective Teaching in the Postmodern World: a Manifesto for Education in Postmodernity.* Buckingham: Open University Press.

Paul, J. L. & K. Marfo (2001). Preparation of Educational Researchers in Philosophical Foundations of Inquiry. *Review of Educational Research,* Vol. 71, No. 4, pp. 525-547.

Paxton, T. D. (1996). Modes of Interaction between Disciplines. *The Journal of Education,* Vol. 45, No. 2, pp. 79-86.

Perkins, D. (1998). What is understanding? In M. S. Wiske (ed.) *Teaching for Understanding: Linking Research with Practice.* San Francisco, CA: Jossey–Bass.

Perkins, D. N. & G. Salomon (1989). Are Cognitive Skills Context–Bound? *Educational Researcher,* Vol. 18, No. 1, pp. 16-25.

Perlas, N. (1999). *Shaping Globalization: Civil Society, Cultural Power, and Threefolding.* Quezon City, Philippines: Center for Alternative Development Initiatives.

Perry, W. G. (1970). *Forms of Intellectual and Ethical Development in the College Years.* New York: Holt, Reinhart and Winston.

Perry, W. G. (1981). Cognitive and Ethical Growth: The Making of Meaning. In A. W. Chickering (ed.) *The Modern American College.* San Francisco, CA: Jossey–Bass, pp. 76-116.

Peterson, M. W. & D. S. Vaughan (2002). Promoting Academic Improvement: Organizational and Administrative Dynamics that Support Student Assessment. In T. W. Banta (ed.) *Buidling a Scholarship of Assessment,* San Francisco, CA: Jossey–Bass.

Petocz, P. & A. Reid (2001) Students' Experience of Learning in Statistics, *Quaestiones Mathematicae,* Supplement 1, pp. 37-45.

Petocz, P. & A. Reid (2006). *The Contribution of Mathematics to Graduates' Professional Working Life.* Australian Association for Research in Education 2005 Conference Papers. AARE, Melbourne.

Pfundt, H. & R. Duit (1991). *Bibliography of Students' Alternative Conceptions and Science Education.* Kiel: IPN.

Phelps, R., K. Fisher & A. Ellis (2006). Organisational and Technological Skills: The Overlooked Dimension of Research Training. *Australasian Journal of Educational Technology,* Vol. 22, No. 2, pp. 145-165.

Piaget, J. (1953). *The Origin of Intelligence in the Child.* London: Routledge & Kegan.

Piaget, J. (1977). *Equilibration of Cognitive Structures.* New York: Viking.

Picard, R.W.; S. Papert; W. Bender; B. Blumberg; C. Breazel; D. Cavallo; T. Machover; M. Resnick; D. Roy & C. Strohecker (2004). Affective learning – A manifesto. *BT Technology Journal,* Vol. 22, No. 4, pp. 253-269.

Pillay, H. & G. Boulton–Lewis (2000). Variations in Conceptions of Learning in Construction Technology: Implications for Learning. *Journal of Education and Work,* Vol. 13, No. 2, pp. 163-181.

Pillay, H.; J. Brownlee & A. McCrindle (1998). The Influence of Individuals' Beliefs about Learning and Nature of Knowledge on Educating a Competent Workforce. *British Journal of Education and Work,* Vol. 11, No. 3, pp. 239-254.

Polya, G. (1957). *How to Solve It: A New Aspect of Mathematical Method.* Garden City, NY: Doubleday.

Pratt, D. D. (1992). Conceptions of Teaching. *Adult Education Quarterly,* Vol. 42, No. 4, pp. 203-220.

Pressley, M.; B. L. Snyder & T. Cariglia–Bull (1987). How can Good Strategy use be Taught to Children? Evaluation of Six Alternative Approaches. In S. M. Cormier & J. D. Hagman (eds.) *Transfer of Learning.* New York: Academic, pp. 81-120.

Prosser, M. & K. Trigwell (1999). *Understanding Learning and Teaching.* Buckingham: SRHE and Open University Press.

Prosser, M. & R. Millar (1989). The "how" and "why" of Learning Physics. *European Journal of Psychology of Education*, Vol. 4, No. 4, pp. 513-528.

Purdie, N.; J. Hattie & G. Douglas (1996). Student Conceptions of Learning and Their use of Self–Regulated Learning Strategies: A Cross–Cultural Comparison. *Journal of Educational Psychology*, Vol. 88, No. 1, pp. 87-100.

QAA. (2008). *Subject Benchmark Statements.* http://www.qaa.ac.uk/academicinfrastructure/benchmark/default.as p [Accessed 22 June 2009].

Ramos, F.; N. Costa; J. Tavares & I. Huet (2006). A Staff Development Program for Promoting Change in Higher Education Teaching and Learning Practices. Paper presented at: *19th IFIP World Computer Congress*, Chile, pp. 405-409.

Ramsden, P. (1987). Improving Teaching and Learning in Higher Education: the Case for a Relational Perspective. *Studies in Higher Education*, Vol. 12, No. 3, pp. 275-286.

Ramsden, P. (1992). *Learning to Teach in Higher Education.* London and New York: Routledge.

Ramsden, P. (2003). *Learning to Teach in Higher Education.* New York: Routledge, 2nd edition.

Ramsden, P.; D. Beswick & J. Bowden (1986). Effects of Learning Skills Interventions on First Year University Students' Learning, *Human Learning*, Vol. 5, No. 3, pp. 151-164.

Ramsden, P.; G. Masters; A. *Stephanou; E. Walsh; E. Martin;* D. *Laurillard* & F. *Marton* (1993). Phenomenographic Research and the Measurement of Understanding: an Investigation of Students' Conceptions of Speed, Distance, and Time. *International Journal of Educational Research and Development in Higher Education,* Vol. 19. No. 3, pp. 301-316.

Rassow, L. C. (1998). Assessing the Under Graduate International Business Major. *Journal of Studies in International Education*, Vol. 2, No. 1, 59-80

Rawson, M. & T. Richter (2000). *The Educational Tasks and Content of the Steiner Waldorf Curriculum.* Forest Row: Steiner Waldorf Schools Fellowship.

Reed, S.; G. Ernst & R. Banerjee (1974). The Role of Analogy in Transfer Between Similar Problem States. *Cognitive Psychology*, Vol. 6, pp. 466-450.

Reid, A. & A. Davies (2003). Teachers' and Students' Conceptions of the Professional World. In C. Rust (ed.) *Improving Student*

Learning Theory and Practice – 10 years on. Oxford Brookes, pp. 88-98.

Reid, A. & P. Petocz (2002). Students' Conceptions of Statistics: a Phenomenographic Study. *Journal of Statistics Education*, Vol. 10, No. 2.

Reid, A. (1997). The Meaning of Music and the Understanding of Teaching and Learning in the Instrumental Lesson. In A. Gabrielsson (ed.) *Proceedings of the Third Triennial ESCOM Conference*, Uppsala University, pp. 200-205.

Reid, A. (2000). Self and Peer Assessment in a Course on Instrumental Pedagogy. In D. Hunter & M. Russ (eds.) *Peer Learning in Music*, 56-62, University of Ulster, Belfast.

Reid, A. (2001). Variation in the Ways that Instrumental and Vocal Students Experience Learning in Music. *Music Education Research*, Vol. 3, No. 1, pp. 25-40.

Reid, A.; G. H. Smith; L. N. Wood & P. Petocz (2005). Intention, Approach and Outcome: University Mathematics Students' Conceptions of Learning Mathematics. *International Journal of Science and Mathematics Education*, Vol. 4, pp. 567-586.

Reid, A.; P. Petocz; G. H. Smith; L. Wood & E. Dortins (2003). Maths Students' Conceptions of Mathematics. *New Zealand Journal of Mathematics*, Vol. 32, Supplementary Issue, pp. 163-172.

Reid, A.; V. Nagarajan & E. Dortins (2006). The Experience of Becoming a Legal Professional. *Higher Education Research and Development*, Vol. 25, No. 1, pp. 85-99.

Renkl, A.; H. Mandl & H. Gruber (1996). Inert Knowledge: Analyses and Remedies, *Educational Psychologist,* Vol. 31 No. 2, pp. 115-121.

Richardson, J. T. E. (1994). Cultural Specificity of Approaches to Studying in Higher Education: A Literature Survey. *Higher Education*, Vol. 27, No. 4, pp. 449-468.

Rickinson, M.; J. Dillon; K. Teamey; M. Morris; M. Choi; D. Sanders & P. Benefield (2004). *A Review of Research on Outdoor Learning.* Shrewsbury, Field Studies Council.

Rigney, J. & K. Lutz (1976). Effect of Graphic Analogies of Concepts in Chemistry Learning and Attitude. *Journal of Educational Psychology*, Vol. 68, No. 3, pp. 305-311.

Ritzer, G. (2008). *The McDonaldization of Society 5,* University of Maryland: Pine Forge Press

Roberts, C.; M. Lawson; D. Newble; A. Self & P. Chan (2005). The Introduction of Large Class Problem–Based Learning into an

Undergraduate Medical Curriculum: an Evaluation. *Medical Teacher*, Vol. 27, No. 6, pp. 527-533.

Rogers, C. R. (1969). *Freedom to Learn*. Columbus, OH: Merrill.

Rogoff, B. (1990). *Apprenticeship in Thinking. Cognitive Development in Social Contexts*. New York: Oxford University Press.

Root–Bernstein, R. (1989). *Discovering: Finding and Solving Problems at the Frontiers of Science*. Boston: Harvard University Press

Rose, J. (2008). *The Independent Review of the Primary Curriculum*. http://publications.teachernet.gov.uk/eOrderingDownload/Primary _curriculum-report.pdf [Accessed 15 June 2009].

Ross, B. & M. Kilbane (1997). Effects of Principle Explanation and Superficial Similarity on Analogical Mapping in Problem Solving. *Journal of Experimental Psychology: Learning, Memory and Cognition*, Vol. 23, No. 2, pp. 427-440.

Royer, J. & G. Cable (1975). Facilitative Transfer in Prose Learning. *Journal of Educational Psychology*, Vol. 68, No. 2, pp. 116-123.

Royer, J. & G. Cable (1976). Illustrations, Analogies and Facilitative Transfer in Prose Learning. *Journal of Educational Psychology*, Vol. 68, No. 2, pp. 205-209.

RSA (Republic of South Africa) (1995). South African Qualifications Authority Act, *Government Gazette*, Vol. 364, No. 16725. Cape Town: Office of the President.

Rumelhart, D. & D. Normann (1981). Analogical Processes in Learning. In J. Anderson (ed.) *Cognitive Skills and their Acquisition*. Hillsdale, NJ: Lawrence Erlbaum Associates, pp. 335-359.

Ruppert, S. S. (2006). *Critical Evidence: How the ARTS Benefit Students Achievement*. National Assembly of State Arts Agencies.

Ryan, M. P. (1984). Conceptions of Prose Coherence: Individual Differences in Epistemological Standards. *Journal Educational Psychology*, Vol. 76, No. 6, pp. 1226-1238.

Säljö, R. (1979). Learning in the Learner's Perspective: Some Common–Sense Conceptions. *Reports from the Department of Education, University of Goteborg*, No. 76.

Salomon, G. & D. N. Perkins (1989). Rocky Roads to Transfer: Rethinking Mechanisms of a Neglected Phenomenon, *Educational Psychologist,* Vol. 24, No. 2, pp. 113-142.

SAQA (South African Qualifications Authority) (2001). *Criteria and Guidelines for Assessment of NQF Registered Unit Standards and Qualifications*.

http://www.saqa.org.za/docs/critguide/assessment/assessment.pdf
[Accessed 21 June 2009].

Schmuck, R. A. (2008). *Practical Action Research: A Collection of Articles.* Corwin Press.

Schommer, M. (1990). Effects of Beliefs About the Nature of Knowledge on Comprehension. *Journal of Educational Psychology*, Vol. 82, No. 3, pp. 498-504.

Schommer, M. (1998). The Influence of Age and Education on Epistemological Beliefs. *British Journal of Educational Psychology,* Vol. 68, No. 4, pp. 551-562.

Schön, D. A. (1990). *Educating the Reflective Practitioner.* San Francisco, CA: Jossey–Bass.

Schön, D.A. (1983). *The Reflective Practitioner.* New York: Basic Books.

Schreiterer, U. (2008). Concluding Summary. Form Follows Function: Research, the Knowledge Economy, and the Features of Doctoral Education. *Higher Education in Europe,* Vol. 33, No. 1, pp. 149-157.

Schwandt, T. (1997). *Qualitative Inquiry: A Dictionary of Terms.* Thousand Oaks, USA: Sage Publications.

Schwier, R. A.; K. Campbell & R. F. Kenny (2007). Instructional Designers' Perceptions of Their Agency: Tales of Change. In M. J. Keppell (ed.) *Instructional Design: Case Studies in Communities of Practice.* Information Science Publishing.

Scott, D. (2008). Critical Essays on Major Curriculum Theorists. London: Routledge.

SEER (State Education and Environment Roundtable) (2000). *The effects of environment–based education on student achievement.* Available online at: http://www.seer.org/pages/csap.pdf [accessed 15 June 2009].

Seifert, K. (2002). Sociable Thinking: Cognitive Development in Early Childhood Education. In O. Saracho & B. Spodek (eds.) *Contemporary Perspectives on Early Childhood Curriculum.* Information Age Publishing, pp. 15-40.

Shapiro, M. (1985). *Analogies, Visualization and Mental Processing of Science Stories.* Paper presented to the Information Systems Division of the International Communication Association.

Sharma, D. (1997). Accounting Students' Learning Conceptions Approaches to Learning, and the Influence of the Learning–Teaching Context on Approaches to Learning. *Accounting Education: an international journal*, Vol. 6, No. 2, pp. 125-146.

Shephard, K. (2008). Higher Education for Sustainability: Seeking Affective Learning Outcomes. *International Journal of Sustainability in Higher Education*, Vol. 9, No. 1, pp. 87-98.

Shuell, T. J. (1986). Cognitive Conceptions of Learning. *Review of Educational Research,* Vol. 56, No. 4, pp. 411-436.

Simonson, M. & N. Maushak (2001). Instructional Technology and Attitude Change. In D. Jonassen (ed.) *Handbook of Research for Educational Communications and Technology,* Mahwah, NJ: Lawrence Erlbaum Associates, pp. 984-1016.

Skemp, R. R. (1987). *The Psychology of Learning Mathematics,* Hillsdale, NJ: Lawrence Erlbaum Associates.

Skinner, B. F. (1974). *About Behaviorism.* New York: Vintage.

Smith, P. & T. J. Ragan (1999). *Instructional Design.* New York: John Wiley & Sons.

Sorbonne Joint Declaration (1998). *Joint Declaration on Harmonisation of the Architecture of the European Higher Education System.* http://www.bologna-berlin2003.de/pdf/Sorbonne_declaration.pdf [Accessed 23 June 2009].

Sorcinelli, M. D. (2002). New Conceptions of Scholarship for a New Generation of Faculty Members. *New Directions for Teaching and Learning,* Vol. 90, Summer, pp. 41-48.

Speck, W. B. (1998). Unveiling Some of the Mystery of Professional Judgment in Classroom Assessment. *New Directions for Teaching and Learning*, Vol. 74, Summer, pp. 17-31.

Spiro, R.; P. Feltovich; R. Coulson & D. Anderson (1989). Multiple Analogies for Complex Concepts: Antidotes for Analogy–Induced Misconceptions in Advanced Knowledge Acquisition. In S. Vosniadou & A. Ortony (eds.) *Similarity and Analogical Reasoning.* Cambridge: Cambridge University Press, pp. 498-531.

Sporn, B. (1996). Managing University Culture: an Analysis of the Relationship between Institutional Culture and Management Approaches. *Higher Education,* Vol. 32, No. 1, pp. 41-61.

Springer, S. & G. Deutsch (1981). *Left Brain, Right Brain.* New York: W. H. Freeman & Co.

Steinert, Y. & L. S. Snell (1999). Interactive Lecturing: Strategies for Increasing Participation in Large Group Presentations. *Medical Teacher,* Vol. 21, No. 1, pp. 37-42.

Stember, M. (1991). Advancing the Social Sciences: Through the Interdisciplinary Enterprise, *The Social Science Journal,* Vol. 28 No. 1, pp. 1-14.

Stephani, L.; R. Mason & C. Pegler (2007). *The Educational Potential of e–Portfolios: Supporting personal development and reflective writing.* London and New York: Routledge.

Sterling, S. (2001). *Sustainable Education: Re–Visioning Learning and Change.* Bristol: Schumacher UK.

Sternberg, R. J. (1997). *Successful Intelligence: how Practice and Creative Intelligence Determine Success in Life.* New York: Plume.

Sutherland, L. & G. Peckham (1998). A Re–appraisal of Assessment Practices in the Light of the South African Qualifications Authority (SAQA) Act. *South African Journal of Higher Education,* Vol. 12, No. 2, pp. 98-103.

Svensson, L. (1977). On Qualitative Differences in Learning: III – Study Skill and Learning. *British Journal of Educational Psychology*, Vol. 47, No. 3, pp. 233-243.

Swain, H. (2007). The Changing Face of the Doctorate. *The London Independent,* January 18, 2007. http://www.independent.co.uk/student/postgraduate/the-changing-face-of-the-doctorate-432504.html [Accessed 23 June 2009].

Tenney, Y. & D. Gentner (1985). What Makes Analogies Accessible: Experiments on the Water-Flow Analogy for Electricity. In R. Duit & C. von Rhöneck (eds.) *Aspects of Understanding Electricity.* Kiel: IPN, pp. 311-318.

The Higher Education Academy (2006.) *Sustainable Development in Higher Education: Current Practice and Future Developments. A Progress Report for Senior Managers in Higher Education.* http://www.heacademy.ac.uk/assets/York/documents/resources/res ourcedatabase/id587_sustainable_development_managers_report.p df [Accessed 15 June 2009].

Thomas, P. R. & J. D. Bain (1984). Contextual Dependence of Learning Approaches: the Effects of Assessments. *Human Learning*, Vol.3, pp. 227-240.

Thorndike, E. L. (1966) *Human Learning.* New York, NY: Johnson Reprint Corporation, reissue of 1929 publication.

Tierney, D. (1988). *How Teachers Explain Things: Metaphoric Representation of Social Studies Concepts.* Paper presented at the Annual Meeting of the American Educational Research Association.

Torrance, H. & J. Pryor (2002). *Investigating Formative Assessment.* Philadelphia: Open University Press.

Treagust, D.; R. Duit; P. Joslin & I. Lindauer (1990). *A Naturalistic Study of Science Teachers' Use of Analogies as Part of Their Regular Teaching.* Paper presented at the Annual Meeting of the American Educational Research Association.

Trigwell, K. & M. Prosser (1991a). Improving the Quality of Student Learning: the Influence of Learning Context and Student Approaches to Learning on Learning Outcomes. *Higher Education,* Vol. 22, No. 3, pp. 251-266.

Trigwell, K. & P. Ashwin (2006). An Exploratory Study of Situated Conceptions of Learning and Learning Environments. *Higher Education,* Vol. 51, No. 2, pp. 243-258.

Trigwell, K. (1995). Increasing Faculty Understanding of Teaching. In W. A. Wright (ed.) *Teaching Improvement Practices: Successful Faculty Development Strategies.* Bolton, MA: Anker Publishing Co., pp. 76-100.

Trigwell, K.; M. Prosser & F. Waterhouse (1999). Relations between Teachers' Approaches to Teaching and Students' Approaches to Learning. *Higher Education,* Vol. 37, pp. 57-70.

Tripp, D. (1990). Socially Critical Action Research. *Theory into Practice,* Vol. 24, No. 3, pp. 158-166.

Tripp, D. (2003). *Action Inquiry, Action Research e–Reports http://www2.fhs.usyd.edu.au/arow/arer/017.htm* [Accessed 23 June 2009].

Trowler, P. & R. Bamber (2005). Compulsory Higher Education Teacher Training: Joined–up Policies, Institutional Architectures and Enhancement Cultures. *International Journal for Academic Development,* Vol. 10, No. 2, pp. 79-93.

Tversky, A (1977). Features of Similarity. *Psychological Review,* Vol. 84, No. 4, pp. 327-352.

UKCES (UK Commission for Employment and Skills) (2009). *The Employability Challenge.* London: UKCES.

United Kingdom Quality Assurance Agency for Higher Education (2001). *The Framework for Higher Education Qualifications in England, Wales and Northern Ireland.* Gloucester, Quality Assurance Agency.

United Kingdom Research Council (2001). *Joint Statement of Skills Training Requirements of Research Postgraduates.* http://www.grad.ac.uk/jss/ [Accessed 25 June 2009].

United States of America Council of Graduate Schools (1995). *Research Student and Supervisor: An Approach to Good Supervisory Practice.* CGS, Washington D.C.

Usher, R. & N. Solomon (1999). Experiential Learning and the Shaping of Subjectivity in the Workplace. *Studies in the Education of Adults*, Vol. 31, No. 2, pp. 155-163.

Van Manen, M. (1977). Linking Ways of Knowing to Ways of Being Practical. *Curriculum Inquiry,* Vol. 6, No. 3, pp. 205-228.

Van Manen, M. (1995). On the Epistemology of Reflective Practice. *Teachers and Teaching: theory and practice,* Vol. 1, No. 1, pp. 33-50.

Van Rossum, E. J. & I. P. Taylor (1987). *The Relationship between Conceptions of Learning and Good Teaching: a Scheme of Cognitive Development.* Paper presented at the AERA Annual Meeting, Washington, 1987.

Van Rossum, E. J. & S. M. Schenk (1984). The Relationship between Learning Conception, Study Strategy and Learning Outcome. *British Journal of Educational Psychology*, Vol. 54, No. 1, pp. 73-83.

Van Rossum, E. J.; R. Deikers & R. Hamer (1985). Students' Learning Conceptions and their Interpretation of Significant Educational Concepts. *Higher Education,* Vol. 14, No. 6, pp. 617-641.

Varnava–Marouchou, D. (2007). *Teaching and Learning in an Undergraduate Business Context: An Inquiry into Lecturers' Conceptions of Teaching and their Students' Conceptions of Learning.* PhD Thesis, University of Nottingham.

von Glasersfeld, E. (1995). *Radical Constructivism: A Way of Knowing and Learning.* London & Washington: The Falmer Press.

Vygotsky, L. S. (1962). *Thought and Language.* Cambridge, MA: The MIT Press.

Vygotsky, L. S. (1978). *Mind in Society: Development of Higher Psychological Processes.* Cambridge, MA: Harvard University Press.

Vygotsky, L. S. (1986). *Thought and Language.* Cambridge, MA: The MIT Press, 2nd edition.

Waite, S. & B. Davis (2006a). Developing Undergraduate Research Skills in a Faculty of Education: Motivation Through Collaboration. *Higher Education Research and Development,* Vol. 25, No. 4, pp. 403-419.

Waite, S. & B. Davis (2006b). Collaboration as a Catalyst for Critical Thinking in Undergraduate Research. *Journal of Further and Higher Education,* Vol. 30, No. 4, pp. 405-419.

Waite, S. (2007). "Memories are Made of This": Some Reflections on Outdoor Learning and Recall. *Education 3–13*, Vol. 35, No. 4, pp. 333-347.

Walker, G. E.; C. M. Golde; L. Jones; A. C. Bueschel & P. Hutchings (2008). *The Formation of Scholars. Rethinking Doctoral Education for the Twenty–first Century.* The Carnegie Foundation for the Advancement of Teaching. San Francisco, CA: Jossey–Bass.

Wals, A. E. J. & B. Jickling (2002). "Sustainability" in Higher Education: From Doublethink and Newspeak to Critical Thinking and Meaningful Learning. *Higher Education Policy*, Vol. 15, No. 2, pp. 121-131.

Watkins, D. & Hattie, J. (1981). The Learning Processes of Australian University Students: Investigations of Contextual and Personalogical Factors. *British Journal of Educational Psychology*, Vol. 51, No. 3, pp. 384-393.

Watkins, D. (1996). *Learning Theories and Approaches to Research: a Cross–Cultural Perspective.* In D. A. Watkins & J. B. Biggs (eds) *The Chinese Learner: Cultural, psychological and contextual influences.* HK: CERC and ACER, pp. 3-24.

Watts, A.; B. Law; J. Killeen; J. Kidd & R. Hawthorn (1996). *Rethinking Careers Education and Guidance: Theory, Policy and Practice.* London and New York: Routledge.

Webster, J. (2009). Classrooms as Laboratories in the R-1 University: Cracking the Problem of How Best to Value Teaching. *Pedagogy*, Vol. 9, No. 1, pp. 185-189.

Wells, G., & T. Ball (2008). Understanding – The Purpose of Learning. In C. Nygaard, & C. Holtham (eds.) *Understanding Learning–Centred Higher Education.* Frederiksberg: CBS Press.

Wenger, E. (1998). *Communities of Practice: Learning, Meaning and Identity.* Cambridge: Cambridge University Press.

Wenger, E. (2000). *Communities of Practice: Learning, Meaning and Identity.* Cambridge: Cambridge University Press, 2nd edition.

Wertsch, J. V. (1991). *Voices of the Mind: A Sociocultural Approach to Mediated Action.* Cambridge, MA: Harvard University Press.

Wertsch, J. V. (1998). *Mind as Action.* New York: Cambridge University Press.

White, C. & E. Caropreso (1989). Training in Analogical Reasoning Processes: Effects on Low Socioeconomic Status Preschool Children. *Journal of Education Research*, Vol. 83, No. 2, pp. 112-118.

Wiener, P. (1973). *The Dictionary of the History of Ideas: Studies of Selected Pivotal Ideas.* New York: Charles Scribner's Sons.

Wigen, K.; A. Holen & Ø Ellingsen (2003). Predicting Academic Auccess by Group Behaviour in PBL. *Medical Teacher,* Vol. 25, No. 1, pp. 32-37.

Wilson, K. & J. Fowler (2005). Assessing the Impact of Learning Environments on Students' Approaches to Learning: Comparing Conventional and Action Learning Designs. *Assessment and Evaluation in Higher Education*, Vol. 30, No. 1, pp. 87-101.

Wiske, M. S. (ed.) (1998). *Teaching for Understanding.* San Francisco, Jossey–Bass.

WSAC (2003). *Stimulating the Brain and Senses through Art.* Newsletter of the Washington State Arts Commission, Winter. http://www.arts.wa.gov/resources/documents/WSAC-Winter-2003-Newsletter.pdf [Accessed 25 June 2009].

Yeats W. B. (1865-1939). *Famous Quotes.* http://www.yuni.com/quotes/yeats.html [Accessed 10 June 2009].

Yorke, M. & P. Knight (2006). *Embedding Employability into the Curriculum.* York: ESECT & The Higher Education Academy.

Zeitoun, H. (1984). Teaching Scientific Analogies: A Proposed Model. *Research in Science and Technology Education*, Vol. 2, No. 2, pp. 107-125.

Zuber–Skerritt, O. (2001). Action Learning and Action Research: Paradigm, Praxis and Programs. In S. Sankaran; B. Dick; R. Passfield & P. Swepson (eds.) *Effective Change Management Using Action Research and Action Learning: Concepts, Frameworks, Processes and Applications.* Lismore, Australia: Southern Cross University Press.